Turkeys: Their Care and Management
How To Raise Turkeys Book 2

by American Poultry Assoc.

with an introduction by Jackson Chambers

Introduction

I am pleased to present this second title in the "How To Raise Turkeys" series.

This volume is entitled "Turkeys: Their Care and Management" and was authored by various authorities in 1909.

The work is in the Public Domain and is re-printed here in accordance with Federal Laws.

Though this work is a century old, "Turkeys: Their Care and Management" contains much information on raising turkeys that is still pertinent today.

Jackson Chambers
Josephine County, Oregon

1

INTRODUCTORY

IF THE American people have one fowl of which they are especially proud, it is the turkey.

One of our correspondents writes: "A Christmas without a Christmas tree, a Fourth of July without firecrackers, would be on a par with a Thanksgiving without a turkey."

On November 21, 1620, the Mayflower with one hundred and two Pilgrims cast anchor off Cape Cod. The first six months of their first year which was spent on the ocean edge of the wilderness, were full of hardships and dangers, many deaths occurred and the small company was greatly reduced. Luckily the Indians proved to be friendly and taught them how to plant maize, which they planted well, and in spite of the hardships of the first six months they considered the year comparatively successful. William Bradford, their second Governor, on account of this success proclaimed a season of Thanksgiving. It is supposed that this idea was taken from the old English custom of observing the harvest festival. The records show that the Governor sent four men out fowling and they brought in wild turkeys and partridges in abundance. From that day to the present time this holiday has been observed each autumn and the turkey has been the bird that graced the feast.

Although the turkey is classed with the domesticated fowls, it retains to a certain extent, the instincts of its wild ancestors and persons who are going to raise turkeys should bear this in mind.

Ever since their discovery in this country they seem to have been kept in a sort of a domesticated state. The Cortez expedition into Mexico in 1518 or 1519, found them in a state of domestication. The Pilgrims reported that some of the Indians had them partly domesticated, yet after all these years the bronze variety especially, retains to a certain extent its wild instincts and will do much better if allowed to roam. They may be kept enclosed during a certain period, say during the breeding season, but they will not do as well if kept continually confined.

The farm is the natural home for the turkey, and one that has a woodland on it is all the better, as it gives the turkeys a chance to indulge in some of their wild traits; it forms a natural breeding spot and furnishes food that is particularly palatable to their taste.

BREEDING TURKEYS

Turkey breeders, as a class, have not given the study to turkey culture that breeders have to other branches of poultry culture, but they will almost without exception, tell you, "Do not in-breed." In-breeding or line-breeding should not be undertaken except by the breeders who have the time and inclination to do a lot of hard work, for the love of it.

Turkeys in their wild state generally mated in pairs and during the breeding season it was a case of the "survival of the fittest." The survivor had his choice of the flock and proudly walked away with his mate. Cases have been recorded where a large, wild tom would fight and kill another tom and take unto him the new mate, while his first mate was sitting. It is owing to this rule that we have such a fine bird today. When man tries to confine and in-breed this great bird of the forest, nature steps in and says, "no."

Breeders have had this pretty well drilled into their minds, many of them to their sorrow, consequently it is by continual outcrossing or the adding of new blood, that the vigor, health and size of the flock are preserved. Many prominent breeders line-breed to a certain extent; that is, they keep within one particular strain as much as possible, but they have to introduce outside blood every few years.

In mating domestic flocks one male can be given as many as eighteen or twenty females, but generally eight to twelve is the limit. Many breeders are glad to introduce wild blood into their flock in order to get increased size and vigor. The bronze turkeys especially, have been bred so long and are so similar to the wild, that they breed very true to type and color, consequently do not need to be in-bred or line-bred as do some of our manufactured or artificial breeds of poultry. They were already made when we first got them and man has been unable to improve upon nature; they are in fact the real descendants of the wild turkey.

Wild turkeys are becoming very scarce and domestic turkeys are becoming tamer and less inclined to roam, because of the fact that wild turkey blood is harder to get and is not so generally introduced as it was a few years ago. The wild spots in our country are becoming smaller every year; even the cattle of the western ranges have been deprived of their unlimited range which has been cut up into farms.

"Necessity is the mother of invention," still as the wild turkey blood becomes extinct, the domesticated ones will become more and more contented to stay within the boundaries of the home farm, and with the progress that is being made at the Agricultural Colleges in studying turkey diseases, we shall no doubt in a few years be able to raise turkeys in the little orchard back of the farm house. The old tom whose ancestors used to roam for miles and miles in search of conquest, will be content to settle down with his flock and the old hen will be induced to sit in the hen house or box as contented as any old biddy.

THE CARE OF TURKEYS

As long as there is any wild instinct left in them we believe that the turkey industry will be benefitted by cultivating that trait as long as possible. It is natural for turkeys to roost outside. Let them do it. At one time we built a large turkey shed with good high roosts, etc. We fed them inside at night and shut them in, but the first time the door was open, up in the big oak tree they would fly, face the storm, draw their heads in like turtles and sleep all night, happy and contented no matter how cold and stormy it was.

They tell us that young poults should be kept confined until the dew is off the grass, and it is good advice. They will not stand dampness and no doubt many young poults were lost from this cause when in their wild state. Timbered lands where there is not much underbrush, make an ideal place for raising young poults. The turkey hen has a good chance to keep them dry and there is no wet grass to wet and chill them. Then, too, there is plenty and a variety of nature's food for them and they are not as subject to bowel trouble as where they are kept confined and liable to be over-fed. Lice will not bother them as much, for they have plenty of chance to dust themselves in the cool earth of the woodlands, neither will lice multiply as fast in the open as where the birds are kept confined.

It seems to be the general opinion that turkeys are hard to raise and perhaps they are, but if we will study nature and be benefitted by the lessons she teaches and accept the advice of others who have learned their lesson well, we ought to succeed. We used to think that artificial incubation was a failure and it was, to a certain extent, until we studied the old hen and her methods and profited by what we observed, so today we can hatch and raise chickens just as well, if not better, by artificial means as by nature's methods.

Keep a hen and her brood in a coop for a week or two and when released she seems to have accepted that as her permanent abode and will not go far away. Not so with the turkey. Confine her and then let her out with her brood and she will try to see how far away she can get.

Young poults seem very weak and it is well to keep them confined at night and until the grass is dry in the morning, as is advised in several of the following articles. The place to raise them in preference to all others is a woodland or some pasture where the grass is short and insects are plenty.

The breeding turkeys should not be too fat but should be put in good condition by being given free range all day and being fed their evening meal at home, which will induce them to come in at night. Some breeders at this time confine them in a large enclosure and keep them there until the hens have laid the next morning. These matters are all covered in the many articles throughout this book so we need not go into details. Turkey meat is the cheapest that can be raised on the farm and every farm should have its flock of turkeys.

In addition to being a cheap thing to raise, think of the many insects they destroy and turn into cash. Many a farmer's wife buys her fall and winter outfits, from bonnet to boots, with the money she gets for the small flock of turkeys she gave a start and then let raise themselves.

THE BRONZE TURKEY

The bronze variety is without doubt the most popular variety we have. They were recognized in our first Standard, known as the "Lockwood" Standard, which was published in 1871. The wording of the different Standards as they were revised from time to time, has been changed to keep the requirements abreast of the improvements made in breeding them. As has been said before, they are direct descendants from the wild birds and are frequently crossed with the wild in order to get more size and vigor. They are also the largest variety we have. We have handled or rather tried to handle one that weighed 62 pounds. He was the largest one we ever saw, but it is no uncommon thing to see specimens in our winter shows weighing 40 to 50 pounds.

In spite of the fact that exhibition specimens are very large and fine to look at, they sometimes get so large that they are useless as breeders and markets do not want such a large bird. The weights prescribed by the American Poultry Association in their Standard of Perfection, are believed to be the best for all-round purposes and it is well to stay pretty close to these weights for best results.

STANDARD VARIETIES

There are seven varieties of turkeys, that is seven varieties that are recognized by the American Poultry Association, as follows:—The Bronze, Narragansett, Buff, White Holland, Black, Slate and Bourbon Red.

The Bronze variety is described at length in the article on "Judging and Mating." Their principal defects

are explained, also how much they should be cut in scoring.

The Blacks, Buffs, Slates and Narragansetts were admitted to the Standard in 1874 and are described in Mr. McClave's article, "Turkeys and Their Management." The White Holland variety was admitted to the Standard in 1878 and is also described in Mr. McClave's article.

The Bourbon Reds, the new Standard variety just admitted to the Standard, originated, according to the most reliable authority, in Bourbon County, Kentucky, and are brought up from what in the early days was called the wild Yellow Turkey. We have heard tourists of today, tell of seeing a yellow turkey in a wild state in Yellowstone Park. Standard weights for the Bourbons are as follows:—

Cock	30 lbs.	Hen	18 lbs.
Cockerel	22 lbs.	Pullet	14 lbs.

The neck and back color should be brownish red; the tail, white; the wingbows, deep, brownish red and the primaries and secondaries should be white. The breast and body should be deep, brownish red and the fluff, brownish red. The thighs are the same as the fluff, and the shanks and toes should be reddish pink.

THE WHITE HOLLANDS

Next to the Bronze, in popularity, come the White Holland. For many years it was difficult to get the Whites up to Standard weight, but of late years breeders have been making some great improvements, and today we see specimens in our show-rooms that will weigh 40 pounds. There is some complaint heard these days about getting the weight of this variety too high and it seems to be well founded. The Whites have won public favor by being a medium weight fowl and that is what the marketmen demand. We should dislike very much to see the Whites get too large and lose the prestige they have been gaining.

THE NARRAGANSETTS

Probably the Narragansett closely follows the White, as far as public favor is concerned. They have made some rapid strides toward the front, during the past few years, especially in parts of the New England States.

CONCLUSION

Our export trade has grown to such proportions that the home markets have felt it and the past two or three years have caused breeders to notice that the turkey crop was getting shorter each year.

Missouri, Kentucky and Texas are probably the greatest turkey producing states. Eastern Canada also raises many turkeys, but we need more of them.

Rhode Island and the adjacent territory used to be one of the greatest turkey raising sections of this country. The dread disease known as blackhead, has practically wiped out the industry in that section, in spite of the great efforts that have been made to stop the disease. The State Agricultural College at Kingston, R. I., has been making exhaustive experiments in combating blackhead and other turkey diseases and their bulletins can be had upon application.

We trust as you read the following pages written by well-known and successful breeders and study the charts drawn by Mr. Franklane L. Sewell (the best thing of their kind ever drawn) that you will gain confidence and feel capable of making a success of raising the king of fowls. the bird that is so near to nature, that is liked by everybody and whose destiny is a Thanksgiving feast.

HOW THE TURKEY GOT ITS NAME

Our Domestic Varieties of Turkeys are Descended from the Wild Turkey of North America—Three Varieties of Wild Turkeys—
Growth of the Word Turkey—The Introduction of Turkey into Europe—First Sent to the Old World by Cortez

D. E. HALE

UMEROUS writers in the past have endeavored to trace the origin of our national bird and to learn the derivation of its name. They have agreed on many points and differed on many.

For the historic information contained in the following article, we are pleased to give credit to the gentlemen who have charge of the Reference Department in the Buffalo, N. Y., Public Library, who very courteously assisted the writer in his search for authentic information in regard to turkeys.

There is little doubt that our domestic varieties of turkeys are all descended from the wild turkey of North America. How and when they were developed forms an interesting study.

Lewis Wright, the great English writer and authority, in his book "The New Book of Poultry," says in speaking of their originating in America: "This is no question now; and the obstinate incredulity of some naturalists respecting the fact is one of the most curious phenomena in the history of Science."

Americans generally believe our grand bronze turkey is the lineal descendant of the northern wild turkey. Why

Canada were known as "Meleagris Americana." These latter were darker and more bronze in color.

Some naturalists think that the brighter plumage of the southern birds was caused by the warmer climate where a larger assortment of food was to be had, owing to climatic conditions.

The northern wild turkey being more bronze in color and also more robust, owing to climatic and food condi-

A reproduction of the female wild turkey as shown in "Burnham's New Poultry Book," published in 1877

A reproduction of the male wild turkey as shown in "Burnham's New Poultry Book," published in 1877. This picture certainly resembles the peacock to a great extent, and it is not surprising that the Spaniards of the Cortez expedition called them peacocks.

northern? In order to make it clear let us explain that there are, or were, three varieties of wild turkeys. Those found in Honduras and Central America were known as "M. Ocellata," and were distinguished by the absence of the breast-tuft. They also had a different carunculation and a much brighter plumage. Those found in the southern states and Mexico were known to the naturalists as "M. Mexicana," while those of the northern states and

tions, it is quite reasonable to presume that it is from this variety that we have our elegant bronze turkey of today.

It is hard to say when turkeys were first domesticated. The first settlers who landed on our shores found that some of the Indians had them in a sort of domesticated condition. We will go back farther than that, although these same domesticated turkeys may have been the progenitors of our bronze turkey.

THEIR INTRODUCTION INTO EUROPE

Let us see whence the name came and in doing so we will be able to tell of their introduction into Europe.

Mr. Wright in his book mentioned above, says: "As no one ever supposed that these birds came from Turkey, or anywhere except North America, not one single old writer can be quoted for any such mistake. The origin of the name is a very curious question. Some have suggested that it came from a supposed resemblance of the red carunculations to the old Turkish costume of a red fez coming down to the ears, with a dark flowing robe beneath. Another guess is that the word is corrupted from turquoise, supposed to be applied to that bluish carunculation about the head. Others point out that the name of 'A Turk' is often applied in popular language to any one remarkable for domineering and pompous disposition or appearance and thus it became attached to the turkey cock, and gradually modified."

We personally are inclined to agree with Mr. E. Richardson who in the book entitled, "Turkeys and How to Grow Them" says that the name was derived from the Hebrew word "Tukki," meaning peacock.

Prescott in his "Conquest of Mexico," explains how Cortez was sent on his voyage of discovery and conquest, and that he was to send to his emperor one-fifth of all the spoils taken, etc. We quote Mr. Richardson as follows:

"The introduction of the bird into Europe naturally followed, and not long after, for in July, 1519, Cortez dis-

Mammoth Bronze Turkey, reproduced from "Burnham's New Poultry Book," published in 1877. This shows the type of turkey that has been crossed with the wild turkey, which cross has been very instrumental in producing the splendid Bronze Turkey of today.

patched 'his first letter' to his emperor, Charles the Fifth, with a collection of fabrics, minerals and other products of the new world, and it is not to be supposed that the turkey was omitted, especially as it was so easily obtained. History tells us that the turkey was first brought to England in 1524, five years after Cortez sent specimens to Spain.

(Note:—This introduction into England is 17 years earlier than is claimed by Mr. McGrew in "Bailey's Cyclopedia of Agriculture," which gives 1541 as the date.—D. E. H.)

"At first it was only in the hands of the rich, as naturally would be the case, but in course of time became accessible to the poor as well. So much then as to the origin of the bird itself, in which is shown how it is a native of Mexico, and was introduced into Europe by the expedition of Cortez to the new world, and called by his followers the 'American' or 'Mexican' peacock from its habit of strutting.

"Strange, then, how the bird came to be called turkey, a word in no way similar to the Anglo-Saxon pawa,

the German pfau, the French paon or the Latin pavo, all names similar to one another and derived from the Latin, the bird (peacock) having been brought from the east by the Romans. The mystery then is how, in view of all these facts, the name 'turkey' came to be applied to this bird. It is obvious that we must look to some other language for a solution to the problem. Going to the far off home of the peacock, we find in the Tamil language of India, a word 'toka'—peacock, the primitive meaning of which refers to a train or trailing skirt. This word adopted into the Hebrew language becomes 'tukki' and by a slight change of the genius of the English language becomes what we are looking for, 'turkey.'

"But it is asked, 'How came it through the Hebrew?' Let it be said, then, that at the time of the expedition of Cortez to Mexico the despised and persecuted Jews were very numerous in Spain and engaged, as they usually are, by their natural adaptability for gain, in merchandising. Their acuteness led them to deal in foreign birds, curiosities and rarities, by which they reaped large profits, as these things were only purchased by the rich. Naturally, then, they saw in this new importation an opportunity for gain, which they seized, and as they used their own language as much as possible, it was not long before the Hebrew name for peacock became well known. Doubtless they designated it as the 'American' peacock, for it was well known whence it came.

"Thus it would be constantly heard in the market places, while the more scientific name of 'pavo' would only be heard among the educated few, and so by force of numbers the name was used and anglicized into turkey.

"Furthermore, the name was formerly spelled 'turky,' as when Corbet, Bishop of Oxford, writes to Buckingham:

"'Like very poore or counterfeit poore man, who, to preserve their turky or their hen, do offer up themselves.'

In tracing the word to the Hebrew, the rules governing etymologies have been complied with, since here we have preserved the radicals T and K, which fact only tends to prove the origin of the word, according to the views herein set forth."

After investigating the authorities available, we are inclined to believe that Mr. Richardson is right in regard to the origin of the word and also about the introduction of the turkey into Europe.

It is quite reasonable to presume that the Mexican or southern turkey was the first introduced throughout Europe. Later, when the pilgrims settled here and found that the Indians were domesticating them and that they were numerous in the woods, they were no doubt used as a bird of feast, owing to their size and numbers.

"Holy Days and Holidays" by Deems, says in regard to Thanksgiving:

"When after the ingathering of the first harvest in a new world, Gov. Bradford sent four men out to shoot wild fowl that the infant colony 'might after a more special manner rejoice together,' he little dreamed to what that pious act would grow."

It was not until the Revolutionary War that the feast became national and after 1784 it was only occasionally observed, except in New England.

Henry Austin in "Holy Days and Holidays" writes, in speaking of the four hunters mentioned: "They killed many wild turkeys which the women in dressing probably stuffed with beechnuts, and they brought home wood-pigeons and partridges in abundance."

As the climatic conditions of the north gave the wild turkeys of that section their bronzy color and hardy constitution and as it is a fact that the Indians were domesticating these turkeys when the country was discovered and that our ancestors were progressive, we believe it is safe to conclude that our bronze turkey of today is descended from the "Meleagris Americana."

TURKEYS AND THEIR MANAGEMENT

Origin—Description of All Standard Varieties—Breeding—Feeding—When to Market—Turkeys Pay the Greatest Profit

CHAS. McCLAVE, 1909, AMERICA'S PREMIER TURKEY JUDGE

THE origin of the domestic turkey is in a sense almost unknown. Turkeys have been bred as a domestic fowl for hundreds of years in the United States and Europe. Turkeys as a fowl or bird may be divided into four classes, as follows: The Wild American turkey of the United States and Canada; the Mexican turkey of Mexico, Central America, and the northern portion of South America; the Ocellata variety of Honduras, and the last but not least, our Standard varieties of domestic turkeys.

STANDARD VARIETIES

The American Standard of Perfection recognizes seven pure or Standard varieties as follows:—The Bronze, Black, White Holland, Narragansett, Buff, Bourbon Red and Slate. Bronze are the largest and most numerous of all our domestic varieties and are purely American, having been a cross of the American Wild and the common domestic turkey brought from Europe.

THE BRONZE TURKEY

The cross has produced the largest and hardiest turkey known. The well bred Bronze of today rivals the famous American Wild Turkey in brilliant color of plumage and beauty. The Standard weights of Bronze are as follows:—adult gobblers 36 pounds, adult hens 20 pounds, young gobblers 25 pounds, pullets 16 pounds; however, these weights are far exceeded by some specimens found in our large poultry shows.

At the last New York show held in Madison Square Garden last December the writer found several adult males weighing over 40 pounds each, and hens as high as 30 pounds, making a single pair, weighing above 70 pounds. These are extra weights and are valuable for show purposes, but as a rule do not make the best breeders. For general purposes and in the breeding flock I prefer a medium sized Bronze. A young gobbler weighing in breeding condition 25 pounds and pullets 15 to 17 pounds, or hens 17 to 20 pounds, make the best breeders.

It is desirable always to mate not akin if possible, which insures a much stronger chick or poult. The gobbler whether old or young should be large in bone and frame, deep in body, with deep, round, full breast, head of good size, and eye alert, with bold expression.

The leg and shank should be large and straight, with outlines of all sections in perfect harmony. The hen should in every way conform in outlines to that of the male, except in size.

In color the entire plumage of the male should be a rich, brilliant, golden bronze, for neck, back, breast and surface of wings. Wing flights when spread are black with white barring across each feather, the more regular the better.

The tail is black, evenly marked, transversely, with parallel lines of brown, and each feather ending with wide edging of white. Red or rusty tips are very objectionable.

The color of the hen is similar to the male, except an edging of white or gray on each feather of the breast, body, wings and back.

As layers the Bronze surpasses all other varieties, and if not allowed to sit, will lay from three to four clutches of eggs of from 13 to 18 in a clutch.

THE BLACK TURKEY

One of the most promising varieties, the Blacks, are being bred in large numbers in some sections at the

Bronze Turkeys on the Farm of Mr. Chas. McClave.

present time. The modern Black turkey is nearly equal to the Bronze in size. The old style Blacks were not only inferior in size, but poor in quality; however, by careful breeding and handling and with an infusion of new blood, they have been greatly improved in size and

appear at maturity. Good strains of Blacks are strictly hardy, their eggs hatch well, and they are fully as good layers as the Bronze or White. They are very docile in their habits and are not inclined to ramble as much as other varieties. The young grow rapidly from the start, and at selling time always command the top of the market.

The head and beak should be long and broad and of good shape; eyes bright hazel; neck of medium length and well curved; back broad, of good length and highest in the center and curved the shape of an egg. The breast should be broad, deep and full; body of good length and round in outline; wings of good length and snugly folded against the sides; tail of medium length and when folded comparatively small. Thighs, shanks and toes should be of good length with strong bone and perfectly straight.

The Black Turkeys are also an American production; however, the Norfolk or Black Turkey has been bred in England for more than two centuries. Thirty years ago the Blacks were, as a class, small in size but by the judicious infusion of Bronze blood they have greatly improved in size and nearly rival the Bronze in this respect.

When the good qualities of the Black Turkey become better known we predict that they will rival their Bronze and White cousins in popularity.

WHITE HOLLAND TURKEYS

The White Holland is also a native of America. They are a sport of the Bronze or dark varieties and were also rated as a small turkey until within the past twenty years.

By careful breeding and the introduction of new blood from larger varieties, they have been greatly improved in size. They are the most domestic in their habits of any variety and not inclined to roam; are the best of layers; a fine table fowl, and in the past few years a great demand has developed for their feathers. Market turkey buyers and dressers all over the country are urging farmers and growers to breed White Holland turkeys on this account.

A Fine Specimen of the Mammoth Bronze Turkey

general make up. To attain their present weights and general characteristics there is no question whatever but more or less Bronze blood has been judiciously used.

From a market standpoint there is no question but the Blacks will dress yellower and even plumper than any other Standard variety. The Standard weights of Black turkeys are: Cocks, twenty-seven pounds; hens, eighteen pounds; cockerels, eighteen pounds and pullets, twelve pounds. At the present time these weights are entirely too low except on hens. We have no trouble at Christmas time in having pullets from fourteen to fifteen pounds, cockerels twenty to twenty-four pounds and cock birds thirty or over. The Standard requires males and females to be lustrous black throughout, but it is a difficult matter to secure young birds with solid colored plumage, as more or less feathers in wings will invariably be tipped with white. This will usually dis-

THE NARRAGANSETT TURKEY

The Narragansett turkeys are a large variety nearly rivaling the Bronze in size, and are a native of New England, having derived their name from the Indian tribe, also Narragansett Bay on the east coast of Rhode Island.

They are bred largely throughout New England and the Atlantic coast and are becoming more popular in the west. As a market variety they rank well with the other large kinds.

In color they are different than any other kind, the ground color being black, each feather ending with steel gray, edged with black, giving the entire plumage a grayish effect. See illustration page 9. The male and female are the same in color except the female is a shade the lighter.

THE BUFFS

Buff turkeys are one of the older varieties; however, they have never been popular and in some localities are practically unknown; are of medium size and rarely ever attain Standard weights. Very few specimens have ever been produced that are really buff in color, as they usually are of a chestnut or reddish shade of color with white flights. They are fairly good layers and good specimens mature early.

THE SLATE VARIETY

Slate turkeys are a medium size turkey and sports from other Standard varieties, are slate or blue in color and many times will produce black and white specimens from the same flock. They are only bred in small numbers, therefore have never been popular. Some very good ones were shown at the New York show last December, especially the first old cock bird. They are fairly good layers, and should receive more attention from turkey growers.

THE BREEDING STOCK

In selecting the breeding stock, no matter what variety, they should be well matured, strong, vigorous, and healthy. Yearling and two year old hens will lay larger eggs and produce stronger poults than eggs laid by pullets.

Always use a gobbler not akin to the hens, which insures strong poults. Avoid large or overgrown specimens as breeders. It is not necessary to have more than one male to six to ten hens under ordinary conditions. If more than one male is used with the flock, keep one yarded, changing them from two to five times a week.

During the laying season if two or more males run with the flock they are constantly fighting and destroying each other's work. Past experience has taught that the breeding stock thrive better with free range of the farm; however, if provided with a large yard or orchard, they can be kept confined during laying time.

In most localities this is almost a necessity on account of crows robbing the turkey nest.

WHAT TO FEED

To insure good health, the breeding stock must be provided with a variety of grain, grit and charcoal. As a conditioner and health preserver, charcoal has no equal for the turkey family. When turkeys have free access to charcoal very few will become sick or ailing.

The writer has found oats to be the best all around grain for turkeys, especially during breeding time. A small amount of corn and wheat can also be fed to good advantage. Over-fat specimens are as a rule very poor breeders. Turkeys require a considerable amount of water and should always have a liberal supply.

Where the breeders have the range of the farm they require very little grain food after they commence to lay. Many farmers hatch the first laying of turkey eggs under chicken hens and the turkeys sit and hatch the second clutch.

While some make a success by this method, many more make a failure, as young poults do not thrive with chicken hens, for two principal reasons, namely, proper food, and lice. In their natural state the young poults

live almost entirely on insect food, which is not and cannot be provided where brooded with the chicken hen, therefore we are feebly trying to make them thrive on food entirely foreign to nature.

One of Chas. McClave's Narragansett Turkeys, winner of first prize at the St. Louis World's Fair.

Every chicken hen will transmit enough lice to the young poults to injure them to a greater or less extent. The writer strongly recommends the hatching of all turkey eggs by the turkey hen, which is the only natural mother. If you must hatch with chicken hens, use plenty of insect powder before the eggs hatch.

After the poults hatch, isolate them from the flock of chickens to a dry sunny place and after thirty hours old give a ration of hard boiled eggs and bread crumbs. When a few days old add cracked corn and wheat, cottage cheese, and in fact a little of everything they will eat.

Animal matter should be supplied for young poults, which can be provided in the form of ground meat scraps, beef liver cooked and chopped fine. This must be fed at least every other day and in a small quantity at a time. Keep a liberal supply of fresh water and granulated charcoal before them at all times. Never allow their coops or runs to become wet or filthy. If possible move the run every two days to a fresh ground.

as in a natural state they rarely ever remain in the same place more than one night.

After they are four weeks old, turn them loose to range over the farm, and still supply them with wheat and corn until grasshoppers become plentiful. I believe a flock of 25 to 50 turkeys ranging over a farm are a benefit to any farmer because of the thousands of insects and worms which they devour daily. All these insects and worms destroy a large amount of grain and grass every year, on every farm. On our own farm turkeys have been kept for near 30 years and in numbers from seven to four hundred and fifty head, and during

Buff Turkey Cock
A specimen of this rare variety of the turkey family which won first prize at many State Fairs in the hands of its owner, Mr. A. J. Ziemer.

that time they have rarely ever destroyed wheat, oats or corn when in the shock. This cannot be said of other poultry, as chickens, geese and ducks will destroy growing and shocked grain should they have access to the same.

WHEN TO MARKET

Past experience has taught that to keep your turkeys healthy, keep them busy and on the move. The busy turkey is the healthy turkey. Always encourage them to come near the buildings to roost, by a liberal supply of grain at night. During October increase their grain rations and by November give them all they will eat. Oats and corn equal parts are the best for this purpose. Many farmers get excited and rush their turkeys off for the Thanksgiving market regardless of flesh, and it is safe to say that fully 90 per cent of the turkeys marketed for Thanksgiving are thin in flesh and not fit to go, while on the other hand if fed until Christ-

mas they command the same price per pound and gain in weight from 20 to 25 per cent.

I have heard farmers with a flock of 30 or 40 head of turkeys say they could not afford to feed them longer than November 15th or 20th, when they were offered 15 cents per pound, live weight, while at the same time they were feeding a bunch of hogs at four cents per pound and really making themselves believe the hogs were making them money. After feeding both for many years I firmly believe that a pound of turkey meat can be made during October and November just as cheap as a pound of pork, and there is a noticeable difference between four cents a pound for one and fifteen cents per pound for the other. In proof of this statement I have not owned or fed a hog on my home farm for three years, but have fed as many as 400 turkeys at one time.

One day recently Cleveland market quoted hogs at $6.50 per hundred and turkeys at $20 per hundred. These comparisons are made simply to show the difference in value of the two farm commodities; however they are not made to discourage the grower of hogs on the farm. I am safe in saying that not more than one farmer in ten the state over, grows any turkeys, therefore it can easily be seen that fully five times as many turkeys could be grown and marketed as are produced at the present time.

Fully 90 per cent of the farmers in Ohio who do raise turkeys, sell too close and retain too few for breeders for the coming year. Many will only reserve a gobbler and two small hens, when four or eight would prove large money for them.

TURKEYS THE BEST PROFIT PAYERS

As an illustration of what can be and has been done with a few turkeys, will state, that one of my neighbors a few years ago purchased a trio of young Bronze Turkeys for $9.00, and with the use of some chicken hens to hatch the first eggs, he raised 63 head of young turkeys, and in November he sold the entire lot to a buyer at market rates for an even $100, and the purchaser took them at the farm with no time or expense lost for the grower. in delivering. These same turkeys were later retailed out for breeders for more than double the $100.00.

At this date (March 4th) good breeding turkeys can hardly be found at any price. On February 25th to test this matter I sent letters to thirteen Bronze turkey breeders and all were advertisers at this writing in leading agricultural journals. When replies were received, only six of the thirteen had a turkey left to sell, the others were sold out. The six that had a few to sell, which were mostly late hatched, were quoted from $5.00 to $20.00 each, with the positive injunction to order at once, for they could not guarantee to hold even five days. This shows conclusively that the demand far exceeds the supply in Bronze Turkeys, or in fact any other variety for breeders.

I believe no branch of the poultry business on the farm offers so much opportunity, considering the investment, to make a few dollars as the breeding of turkeys. No housing in winter is necessary as they prefer to roost in the trees about the place, or on the ridge of some building on the farm.

STANDARD-BRED BRONZE TURKEYS

An Illustrated, Detailed Description of What The Standard of Perfection Requires in Bronze Turkeys, Male and Female—Instructions on Judging by Score Card

D. E. HALE, WITH SPECIAL CHARTS BY MR. FRANKLANE L. SEWELL

UR national experimental stations have done some good work in investigating several of the very troublesome and fatal turkey diseases and many excellent articles are written each season by our most prominent breeders, on breeding, care and management of turkeys, so that turkey culture today is not such a hazardous undertaking as it was a few years ago. The turkey is also becoming more popular as an exhibition fowl and many fine exhibits are seen at our annual poultry shows throughout the country. While there are presented in this book many excellent articles relating to turkeys and turkey culture, we realize that many of our readers will wish to exhibit some of their choice specimens and for that reason this article has been prepared. We shall try to show how a turkey is scored and why the cuts are made. By the word "cut" we mean the amount deducted from the number of points allotted each perfect section.

For the benefit of those who are just starting to raise turkeys and who perhaps have never exhibited poultry of any kind, we will say that in scoring a turkey we work on the basis that a perfect specimen is valued at 100 points, a certain number being allowed to each section, so many for shape and so many for color. The judge examines each section, first for shape, then for color, and deducts whatever amount he thinks is lacking from perfection.

Pictures usually speak plainer than words, hence in order to give a clearer idea of the correct markings of each section, we have had the charts which appear in connection with this article, prepared by Artist Sewell. These charts showing the feathers as they appear in the different sections of the fowl, we believe will give the amateur a clear understanding of the plumage and a feeling of confidence in selecting his show specimens and breeders that he could obtain in no other way unless he visited shows and studied the living birds under the directions of a competent judge or breeder, or visited a successful breeder's yards, either course being frequently out of the question. We present a chart of a male and female Bronze turkey which will be referred to as Figs. 1 and 3 in our description.

There is always something to be learned so we trust that every reader, both the experienced turkey exhibitor and the amateur, will derive some benefit from it.

Of course, we must take as our guide, the Standard of Perfection. We shall try to give in a clear, concise manner our interpretation of its meaning as applied to Bronze turkeys.

SYMMETRY

Symmetry is the first section that appears under the Scale of Points. There is probably no section that has been so much abused, or so little understood as this one. It is no wonder that it was reduced to four points when it had heretofore been valued at eight points. Judges pay too little attention to this important section and do not study it enough to get a clear understanding of its true meaning. The Standard defines it as, "Perfection of pro-portion; the harmony of all the parts or sections of a fowl, viewed as a whole, with regard to the standard type of the breed it represents."

The latter part of that definition is what should be kept in mind at all times; i.e., "viewed as a whole, with regard to the standard type of the breed it represents." It has been described as "Typical Carriage" which caused more or less disputing. The following illustration may help our readers to an understanding of the term. Notice a company of picked soldiers coming down the street, they march in perfect time, with shoulders back, chests out and heads erect, the symmetry of each one and of the whole body is unquestioned. But notice the same men in quarters. They are the same men with the same clothes but they are relaxed, they lounge about with shoulders drooped—symmetry is lacking.

In order to present your turkeys to best advantage to both the judge and the public, each one should be cooped separately, and the coop should be large enough so that it can turn around and stand naturally without having the tail broken and twisted and the head forced into an unnatural, uncomfortable position. Insist that your turkeys be cooped singly.

THE MALE TURKEY

Now let us study the symmetry of the male for a moment. He should be large in frame and deep in body, with a broad, full, well rounded breast, which varies in prominence according to the variety and which gives the fowl a stately, majestic appearance. The head should be of good size, long, broad and carunculated, while the eye should have an alert, bold expression; the legs and shanks should be large, strong and straight and the different sections should harmonize one with the other.

We must remember that we are scoring these turkeys according to the latest Standard of Perfection which goes into effect July first, 1910.

Symmetry is now worth but four points; it was formerly worth eight. In looking at Fig. 1 we see a perfect specimen or one as near perfect as can be depicted by the greatest poultry artist. We find each part harmonizing with the other and each part or section perfect in itself. Were we judging a living specimen that showed the perfection of every part or section and all parts harmonizing as they do in Fig. 1, we could not cut anything for symmetry. But, were the tail too long and carried too high, we should cut one-half point, if the breast were immature or flat and the neck apparently too long, giving the fowl a lanky, ungainly appearance, we should cut a half point, if the bird were too narrow across the breast and back when viewed from in front and above, we should cut one-half point. An outline drawing does not give the true idea of symmetry because breadth and thickness are to be considered as much as the profile or outline. In 1888 the American Poultry Association voted to have the Standard of Perfection illustrated by profile or outline drawings. An attempt was made at that time to have these take the place of symmetry. The first Standards of that year were illustrated with outline drawings but were soon abolished as unsatisfactory.

Remember in judging symmetry that it is "the harmony of all the parts or sections of a fowl, viewed as a whole."

WEIGHT OF BRONZE TURKEYS

Weight is the next section under the scale of points and it is valued at 15 points. This section is of a good deal of importance whether the breeder intends to exhibit his fowls or whether he is raising them merely for commercial purposes. The Standard weights for Bronze turkeys are:

Adult cock .... 36 lbs.   Cockerel .... 25 lbs.
Yearling cock .... 33 lbs.   Hen .... 20 lbs.
       Pullet .... 16 lbs.

In scoring turkeys the Standard instructions are to cut 2 points for every pound less than Standard weight, using one-fourth pound as the minimum.

For example, if an adult cock weighs thirty-five and one-fourth pounds it would be cut one and one-half points (See Fig. A.). Any one can easily see that a turkey which is not up to weight and is handicapped by a cut of one and one-half, will stand a poor chance of winning in close competition.

Though many of the Bronze turkey breeders are exhibiting specimens weighing nearly fifty pounds and have been trying to get the Standard weights raised, it was not deemed advisable by the last revision committee.

The market demands a turkey even below Standard weight and they sell at a higher price than the exceptionally large ones. While the large specimen makes a fine exhibition bird, there is such a thing as getting them so large as to be useless as breeders; there is little call for them on the market except for use in large hotels, and they use them merely as "soupers."

CONDITION

This section is valued at four points, and refers not alone to the health of the specimen, but also to the condition of its plumage. Of course a bird should not be shown unless it is in good health, and its plumage should receive careful attention. Turkeys should be handled with great care when getting them ready to send to a show, as they are naturally of a wild disposition and broken wing and tail feathers and mussed and crumpled plumage due to rough handling and lack of room are things that handicap a specimen and it will be cut for such defects. A fowl showing signs of disease such as roup, cholera, etc., should be debarred from competition. These diseases are contagious and the judge should see that any such specimens are removed from the show room to save other birds from being infected. If a bird shows signs of a

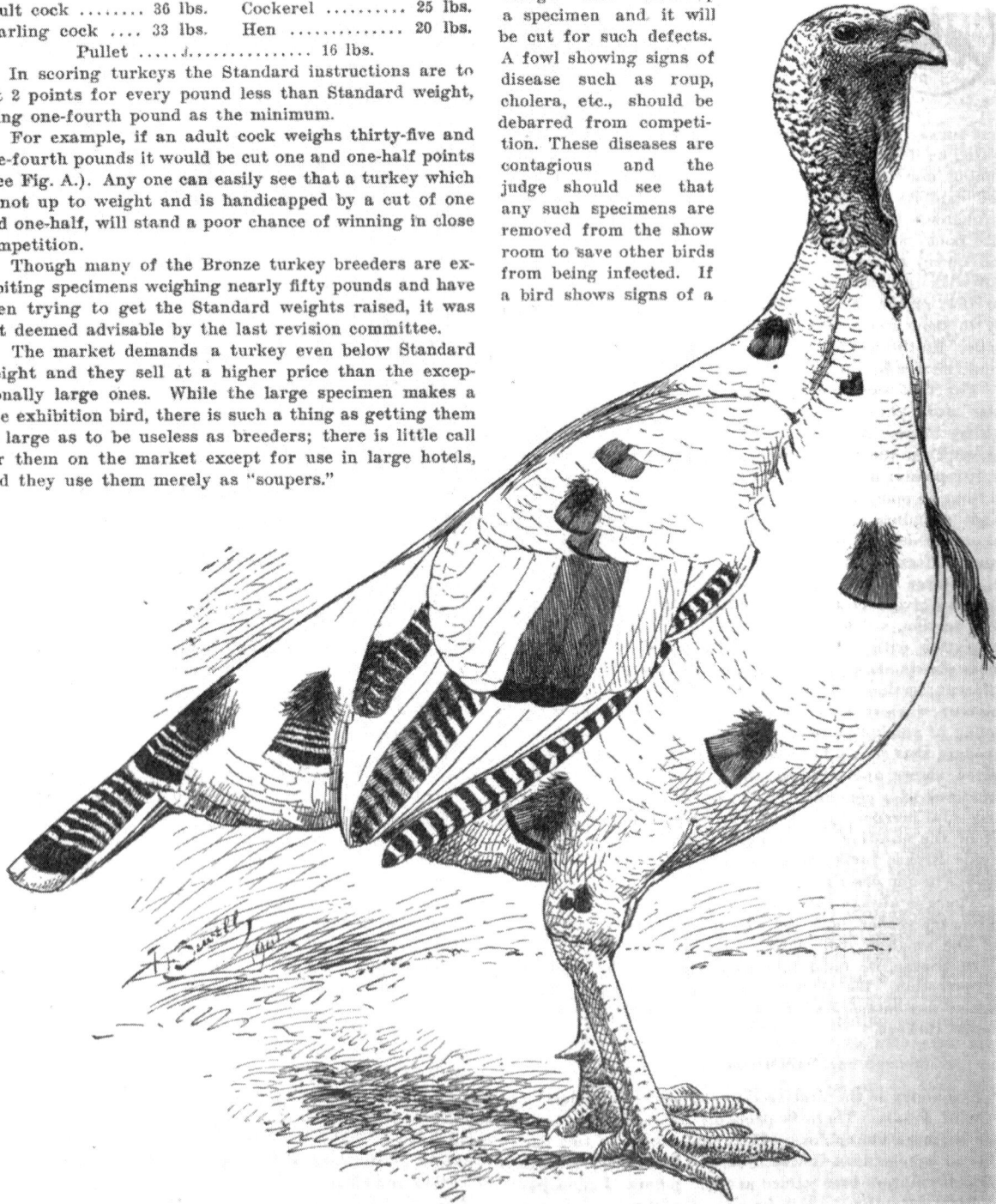

Ideal or Standard Bronze Turkey Male

Fig. 1. Chart drawn by Franklane L. Sewell, showing outline and markings of Ideal Standard Bronze Turkey Male.

cold or canker it should be cut at least one-half point. If it is rough and dirty from careless handling it should be cut one-half point; if the bird is cut and bleeding from fighting or other injury the cut should be from one-half to one. Specimens which are dirty and show that no care has been given them should be cut one-half to one point.

HEAD

The head is valued at five points, just the same as in the old Standard, and is usually good, both in shape and color. The Standard says that in shape the head should be: "Long, broad, carunculated," and in color should be: "Rich red, changeable to bluish white." This section is generally good and it is very seldom that we find a specimen that has to be cut and if we do, it is usually for being a little too short or having as it is commonly called, a bullet head. If such a head is found it should be cut one-half to one point. If the beak is too long or straight or injured, a cut of one-half is generally sufficient.

The eyes are included in the head section and should be "broad, clear," and dark brown in color. They were formerly known as hazel eyes but the last revision committee seemed to think that "dark brown" was the better description.

THROAT AND WATTLES

This section is valued at five points as of old, and is usually passed without a cut or discount, especially as far as color is concerned. The Standard calls for "Heavily carunculated." Once in a great while we see a specimen that is rather smooth in this section and it should be cut one-half to one, but such cases are very few.

THE NECK

The neck section is valued at six points and is divided three for color and three for shape. In shape it should be long and curve backward toward the tail. In color it should be "Light, rich, brilliant bronze." Please note that it must be brilliant and show a bronze sheen and that the Standard says it must be "light." The bronze shading is not as deep on the neck as it is in some other sections and so it has a lighter appearance. It is very seldom that a neck has to be cut; perhaps once in awhile one will be found that is a little too long and straight, but not often. The color occasionally shades off to a brown on the back of the neck and if it does cut one-half to one.

THE BACK

The back retains the same valuation as in the old Standard, ten points, but is divided differently as shape is now valued at four points and color at six points, while formerly it was divided evenly, five for each. This section in a turkey, as in any other variety of fowl is of great importance, for without a well balanced back the specimen is of little value as a breeder. In shape it should be broad and somewhat curved, rising from the neck and descending in a graceful curve to the tail. The color "from neck to middle of back, should be a light, rich, brilliant bronze, each feather terminating in a narrow, black band extending across the end. From middle of back to tail coverts, black, each feather having a brilliant bronze band extending across it, near the end."

We have heard some breeders object that the Standard does not give some definite length of back. This would be a pretty hard thing to do. In order to come up to Standard weight and still have a nicely proportioned and well balanced body, without appearing too flat, the back would have to be of good length and we might be safe in describing it as "rather long." We must remember that the shape value of this section has been reduced one point and is now only valued at five points. If the back is too straight, failing to show the curve above referred to, the cut should be from one-half to one and one-half. If the curve is too prominent, giving the bird

Fig. A

POULTRY ASSOCIATION

January 10, 1910 Date

Official Score Card American Poultry Association

Exhibitor _Samuel Smith_

Breed _Bronze Turkey_ Sex _Cock_

Entry _1_ No. Band _100_ Weight _34¼_

	Shape	Color	Remarks
Symmetry			
Weight	1½		
Size			
Condition			
Comb			
Head			
Beak			
Eyes			
Lobes			
Wattles			
Neck			
Back	¼	¼	_Flat—Dull_
Tail		1	_Brown edging_
Wings		1	_Poor barring_
Breast	¼		_Not full enough_
Body and Fluff			
Legs			
Toes			
Crest and Beard			
Sharpness of Feather			
Outs	2½	2½	Score 95

D. E. Hale Judge

F. L. Bradford Secretary

Reproduction of Score Card, Showing Sample "Cuts" for Defects

the appearance of having a humped back, the cut should be the same. If the back is deformed or crooked, the specimen will be thrown out of competition.

In color, if the feathers lack the narrow black bands across the ends, the cut should be one-half to one. In the males especially a shading of brown will sometimes appear in this section. It generally is a narrow edging just inside the black. When this is found it should be cut from one to two points.

THE TAIL

The tail is another important section and one in which the color defects are as prominent as in any section of the bird. It is now valued at twelve points, divided four for shape and eight for color, while formerly it was worth but ten points, divided four for shape and six for color. The valuations are the same as for wing and both are important color sections. The Standard merely says that tail should be "rather long." It should also be well spread, for a pinched tail on a turkey would look as bad as on any other fowl. By studying Fig. 1 you will get a good idea of the markings which the Standard describes as "Dull black, each feather evenly and distinctly marked transversely with parallel lines of brown, each feather having a wide black band, extending across it near the end (the more bronze on this band the better) and terminating in a wide edging of white. Coverts, dull black, each feather evenly and distinctly marked transversely with parallel lines of brown, each feather having a wide black and bronze band extending across it near the end and terminating in a wide edging of white, the fewer larger coverts extending well out on the tail having a little bronze on them. The more distinct the whole plumage throughout the better.

The black band near the end of the feather should be a sharp distinct black having a shade of bronze, and the white band at the tip should be a clean, distinct white and not a gray. When these two bands are sharp and distinct as they are on a well bred bronze turkey male, no prettier contrast can be found on any bird. Should the white band be more of a gray than a white, it should be cut from one-half to one. The coverts should be transversely marked or barred with brown, ending in a wide black or bronze band, extending across the feather, with an edging of white.

While the ground color of the tail feathers is black, they should be well barred the full length. You will note

upon examining Fig. 1 that part of the tail is covered by the covert feathers. In judging the specimen the judge examines well down toward the roots of the feathers for sometimes they are found to be solid black under the coverts. Should this be the case the section should be cut one-half to one and one-half points. Sometimes broad bands or bars of pure white will be found at the base of these feathers. Some breeders claim that this is caused by trying to breed too wide a band of white on the tail coverts and on the ends of the tail feathers. Too much "white blood" crops out at the base of the tail, and it will sometimes show at the base of the wing primaries.

Where we find these white bars at the base of the feathers, the cut should be one-half to one. Where the barring is irregular on the tail proper the cut is one-half to one and one-half. Where the white outside lacing is mixed with gray or brown the cut is one-half to one and three-fourths. Where the coverts fail to show a clear edging, the cut is one-half to one and one-half; if mixed with brown or dirty gray, the cut is one-half to one and three-fourths. A tail that shows a decided edging of brown or red should be severely discounted in the show room and the bird should not be used at all in the breeding pen, for it is indicative of an outcross with the wild turkey, and is not, in color, a pure bronze.

Fig. B on page 29 showing the outspread tail of a bird owned and bred by Mr. W. J. Bell, shows what excellent white edging is being bred.

This half tone does not do justice to the bird's penciling or barring, for it was much plainer and more distinct than in this picture.

THE WINGS

The wing section is another important one especially as regards color. It, too, has been raised in valuation, being now valued at twelve points divided, four for shape and eight for color, while formerly it was valued at ten points divided four for shape and six for color.

It is seldom that we see a perfect wing. We wish again to call your attention to Fig. 1 and to ask you to study the markings of the wings. The Standard says:

The Pride of the Farm

"Bows, light, rich brilliant bronze, ending in a narrow band of black; primaries each feather evenly and distinctly barred straight across, with parallel bars of black and white throughout the length of the feather; secondaries, dull black, evenly and regularly barred across with parallel bars of white, (the more distinct the better) the color changing to a bronze brown as the middle of the back is approached and the white bars become less distinct; an edging of brown in secondaries being very objectionable; coverts a beautiful rich bronze forming a beautiful, broad, bronze band across the wings when folded; feathers terminate in a wide black band, forming

irregular showing zig-zag tracings across the wing, the cut is one-half to one and one-half. If the barring appears only on one side of the quill, the other side showing black or a mixed up muddy color, the cut should be one-half to two. If the secondaries show a slight tracing or edging of white or brown, the cut should be one-half to one, but if this edging is prominent enough to mar the beauty of the wing, the cut is one to two and one-half. If the coverts fail in the black band at the end of feather, causing what would be termed an unfinished wing, the cut is one to two.

In order to illustrate what good wing barring is, we

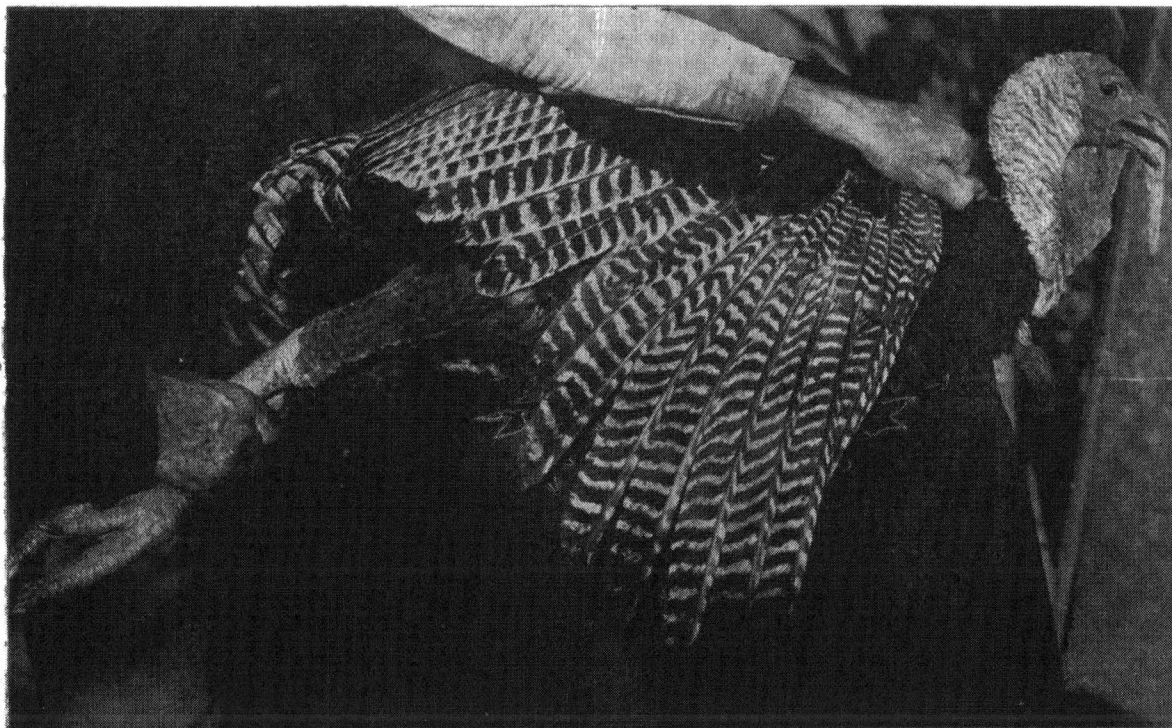

Fig. 2. Reproduced from photograph, showing Standard Barring on Wing of Bronze Turkey Male.

a glossy, ribbon-like mark, which separates them from primaries and secondaries. The flight coverts are barred similar to primaries."

Note carefully the tracing of bronze on the wing bow. Up near the top the feathers are solid black, but as they approach the wing bar the bronze edging deepens, giving the wing when viewed in the sunlight the color of burnished bronze. It might be well to go a little farther and say that the last bar on the primaries and secondaries should end with black. We should also remember that the barring should extend to the end of the feathers. We quite often find a specimen that is unusually good in color, especially in primaries and secondaries, except that near the end of the feathers the barring will stop and the last two inches will be solid black. When the wing of the male is perfect in color, except this black, mate with him females that show more white than black in their flights, and should you have one that has a wing with the last bar white, instead of black, she will be all the more valuable as a breeder.

In scoring the wing of either male or female, when this black appears at the end of the feather, the cut should be one to one and one-half. If the barring is

call your attention to the half tone picture Fig. 2 on this page.

Note the sharp, distinct barring, also that it extends well back on the secondaries.

While the tips of the flight feathers show as being black, we are reliably informed that this was the fault of the photographer and not of the bird, for they were well barred to the tips.

THE BREAST

The valuation of the breast section has been raised one point by the last revision committee and is now valued at eleven points being divided, six for shape and five for color, shape valuation having been raised one point.

From a commercial point of view this is as it should be, for there is no part of the turkey that is more popular at our national Thanksgiving feast than this section, unless perhaps, it is the well-known "drum stick."

This section is seldom passed without a cut as it is very liable to be undeveloped or a little too flat, unless the specimen happens to be an old tom and fully developed. In shape it should be "Broad, deep, full and well rounded." In color it should be "Light, rich, brilliant bronze; feathers on lower part of breast approaching the body, terminate in a black band extending across the end."

If the breast is too narrow or too flat the cut should be one-half to one and one-half. If it is too shallow or not deep enough through from the shoulder to point of breast bone, the cut should be one-half to two. If the color fails in the narrow edge of the black, giving the surface a dull, dead sort of color, the cut should be one-half to one and one-half. Should any of the feathers on the breast show an outside edging of white the cut is one-half to one and one-half.

BODY AND FLUFF

This section, the same as breast, has been raised one point and given a valuation of eleven points, being divided, shape six, color five, shape getting the added point. The Standard description for shape of body is very clear, viz; "Long, deep through the middle, finely rounded." The color is given as "Body, black, beautifully shaded with bronze, but not so decided or so rich as breast. Fluff, black, each feather having a wide, brilliant, bronze band, extending across it near the end and terminating in a narrow edging of white." If the body is too short or too narrow, the cut should be one-half to two; if flat, failing to show a nicely rounded outline, the cut should be one-half to one; if not deep enough from back to base, the cut should be one-half to one and one-half. If the keel is crooked, the cut should be one-half to one.

We should not advise the amateur to breed birds with a crooked breast bone. While we read a great deal about them being caused by the birds roosting too young and by being kept on a board floor and several other things, we are convinced that it is bred in them the same as any other deformity and we certainly should not use one for breeding if it could be avoided.

The color of the body is usually pretty good; once in awhile we find one that loses its bronze and has a dull brown look and these should be cut one-half to one. Sometimes gray tips are found, which should be cut from one-half to one and one-half. See that the fowl has plenty of length back of the legs. If not well balanced and the bird has the appearance of having too much weight in front of the legs the cut should be one-half to one.

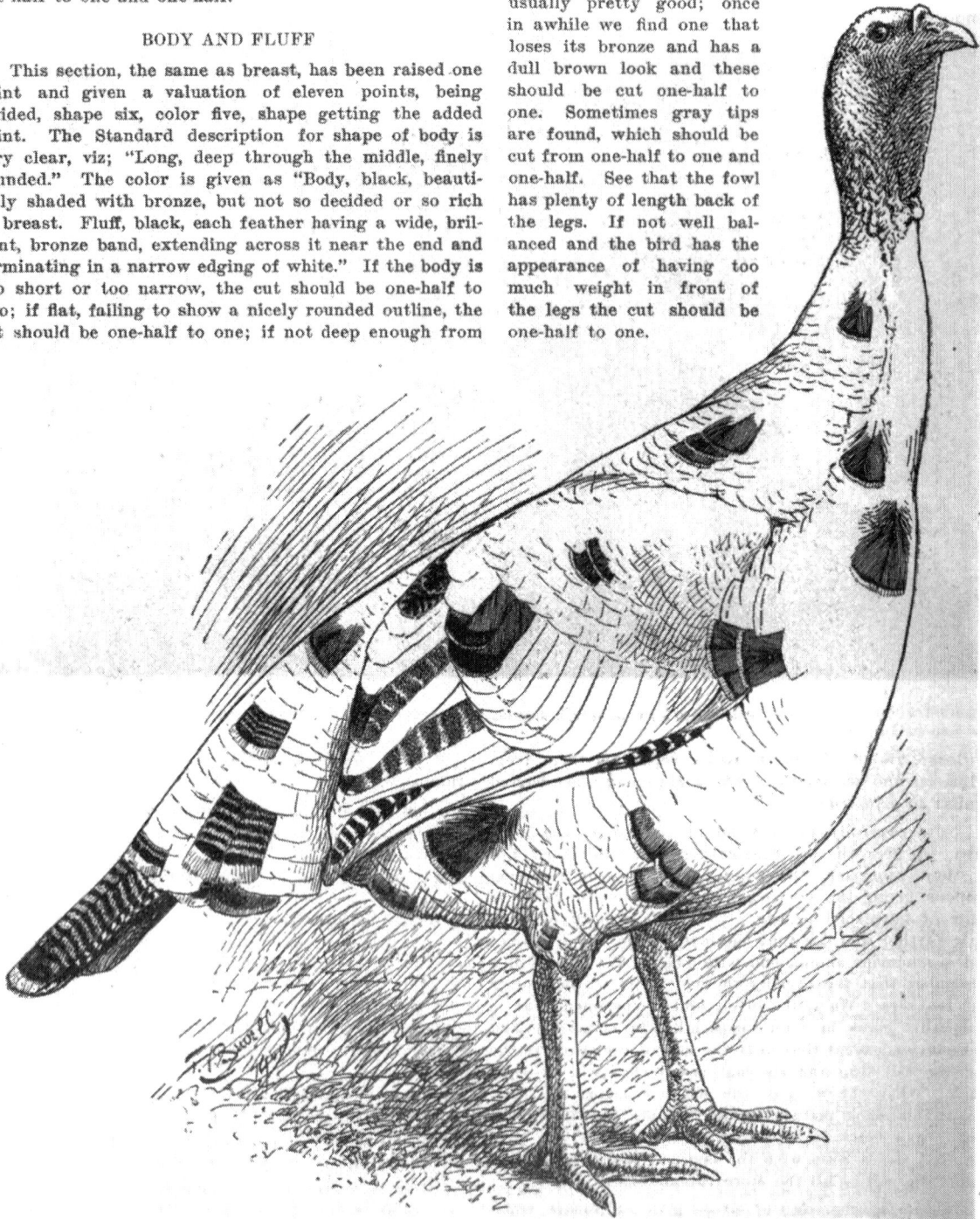

Ideal or Standard Bronze Turkey Female

Fig. 3. Chart, drawn by Franklane L. Sewell, showing outline and markings of Ideal or Standard Bronze Turkey Female.

LEGS AND TOES

This section retains the same valuation that it had in the old Standard, but is divided, three for shape and two for color. They should be, "Thighs, long, stout; shanks, large, long, strong. Toes straight, strong." Fig. 1 gives you an excellent idea of what a good turkey leg should be. Here we have a thigh that is of good length, and stout, the kind that carries lots of meat and muscle. The thighs should be the same as the breast, only less brilliant in shade. The shanks should be pinkish, in old birds, and in young birds will be dark, approaching black. They should stand well apart, giving the specimen a broad, massive appearance when viewed from in front.

The toes should be straight and well spread. The legs should be as described by the Standard, of fair length so as to hold the specimen well up, but not so long as to make him look leggy or lanky.

If the legs are too fine in bone making the bird look feminine, the cut should be one-half to one; if too short or too long, the cut should be one-half to one and one-half; if too close together or knock-kneed, the cut should be one to two. Crooked toes should be cut one-half each. If the legs are faded, dirty or scaly they should be cut one-half to one and one-half; if off-color they should be cut one-half to one and one-half.

THE BRONZE TURKEY FEMALE

In Fig 3 is shown one of the best turkey drawings ever produced by any artist. Every breeder that has inspected this chart conceded it to be the outline of an ideal female. Although Mr. Sewell drew this picture several years ago, we have never seen any that could take its place.

It is not necessary to go into a detailed sectional description of the female, for she is similar throughout to the male, except being finer in bone and not so coarse looking. In regard to color the Standard says; "Plumage similar to that of the male, except edging of white on feathers of back, wing-bows, breast and body, which edging should be narrow in front, gradually widening as it approaches the rear. Beak, eyes, throat, wattles and shanks and toes same as male."

A common defect in the female is a brown color that shows on the outer edge of white lacing on the feathers of the back and breast. When this is found it should be cut from one-half to one and one-half. The back of the neck is more apt to show this than any other section and it occurs oftener in the female than in the male. We do not, of course expect as brilliant or bright a bronze in the female as in the male. Breeders by carefully mating together each year the best of the flock are improving the female to such an extent that it will not be surprising in time to find the same brilliant bronze on wings and tail coverts that we do on our best exhibition males.

If the amateur will study well the charts shown herewith, also how each section is valued and how the common defects are cut, he ought to be able to pick out his best exhibition specimens and be better qualified to select his breeders.

TURKEYS—THEIR CARE AND MANAGEMENT

An American Wild Fowl that in Domestication has Been Brought to an Advanced Standard of Excellence and Serves
Highly Practical Purposes—Standard Requirements of Different Sections—Mating to Produce
Exhibition Specimens—General Advice on Care of Flock

S. B. JOHNSTON

THERE are a number of turkeys bred in this part of the state, so that we are generally well acquainted with the different varieties, although our work has been confined to the Bronze variety. There are six varieties besides the Bronze in the Standard, namely the Narragansett, Buff, Bourbon Red, Black, Slate and White Holland. Then there is a white sport from the Bronze that is nearly as large as that variety and that has more desirable features than the White Holland, which is the smallest variety in the Standard. The White Holland is a good bird, but is too small and will not bring the marketman as profitable returns as the Bronze or Narragansett. I believe fewer people raise the Black Turkey than any other variety, as it is not liked by shippers on account of black pin feathers. Bronze, White Holland or Buff Turkeys are easier dressed and pin feathers are not evident.

The Bronze Turkey is the largest of all varieties. It matures quickly and by the holiday season will attain its full weight. It is docile and easily kept at home. It is said by some that the Bronze Turkey is not easily kept at home, but I have found that turkeys of any variety not having proper care will stray away. In hardiness and vigor there is no variety that can surpass the Bronze when properly bred. The wild turkey is so near in color to the Bronze that by carefully introducing new blood by wild hens the breeder can get hardiness and vigor unequaled. Turkeys that are hatched in April, May and June will begin laying the latter part of March or the first of April the next year. I believe that all varieties of turkeys in the same latitude begin laying about the same time. In this latitude they begin about the first of April more generally than in March. There seems to be always a good demand for turkeys of all varieties. It takes the Bronze variety about three years to get its full weight—in other words, to get its heaviest weight, while most other varieties attain their full weight by the second year. There are more Bronze Turkeys raised than all other varieties combined, which fact is proof enough that the Bronze has more good qualities than any other variety.

RANGE AND HOUSING

Turkeys do not do well in small and crowded quarters. They can be raised to some extent on a small range, but such specimens generally are stunted in size and of poor color, just as is any other stock that is ill-kept. When the turkey was first found it ran wild in the forest, hence the love of range is about its first instinct and it will attain nearer perfection in size and color when it has freedom. Some writers advocate the housing of turkeys, but in my experience I have not found this best. I have learned that a turkey hen can take care of its young better that either a domestic hen or myself, as the turkey mother seems to understand the little poults' chirping and knows what they need. I have tried raising turkeys in coops and pens, keeping them close to the house, but with poor success. When the season is not too severe, turkeys can be given the run of the place, and if they have good quarters in which to roost at night, under bushes or something of that kind, and are looked after during the day for a few weeks, they will not need much food, but will do better and grow faster than those kept close to the house and fed from five to six times a day. Turkeys raised in this way are less trouble, have better plumage and are more vigorous, and in the fall when the corn is being gathered they can be toled to the house to roost. Turkeys kept close to the house and not extra well fed will stray off, hence the advantage is all with the one who raises his turkeys away from the house.

I have found that a roost built close to the ground is of great advantage to young birds that are growing fast, as it often happens that promising youngsters are injured in flying from high roosts. I believe that a shed open to the south and closed to the north, east and west is of great advantage in severe weather in keeping turkeys dry and free from drafts. Such a shed makes a good feeding place when there is snow or mud, and would make a good roosting place if the turkeys could be induced to roost in it. The great trouble is to keep them from roosting on top of the shed, but this can be prevented by running a two-foot wire netting around the top. I should not attempt to raise turkeys on one or two acres of ground, but with proper care a forty-acre farm will give ample forage for five hundred birds. In these days it is a large flock that contains more than one hundred turkeys. They do best when divided into flocks of about fifty.

MATING BRONZE TURKEYS FOR PRIZE WINNERS

If I were asked the most essential point for breeders. I should say first of all vigor, then size, then fine markings of plumage. The fancier must consider size, because nine out of every ten want size first. It is not the rule, however, that the biggest turkeys are the highest scorers, no matter how well they may be bred. To improve size, weight and markings, select the finest marked tom of good big bone, with typical carriage, strong and vigorous, and mate him with the largest hens possible, no matter if they are not so well marked. Then the next season reverse the order and if you are so fortunate as to get well marked birds of both sexes, mate them in the following manner: For the females, select tall, rangy birds, with long, deep bodies, broad backs, and full rounded breasts, with as big bones, feet and legs as possible. In color, the head and wattles should be a rich red, but under different circumstances the head is changeable to bluish white. The plumage of the neck and breast should be a rich, lustrous bronze, the breast and back in front of wings showing a narrow lacing or edging of gray. The back is somewhat darker in color, as it shows a narrow black band across the feathers as they near the lesser tail coverts, these ending in a white or gray edging. The primaries and secondaries of the wing feathers must be as near Standard as possible. I take it for granted that every breeder has the Standard, for it is the book of authority, and sets forth clearly the disqualifications. I would say, however, that the white or gray bars should be about three-sixteenths of an inch in width with the black or brown bars about three-eighths of an inch. They should be even and straight across the feathers. The tail should be long and black, with pencilings of light brown across the feathers, the feathers ending in a broad, black band with an edging of dull white coming right up to the black. The feet and legs should be dark, approaching black. This is of less importance in the females than in the male.

The tom has more influence on shape and color of offspring than has the female. He should be as near perfection in carriage and color of plumage as it is possible to get. He should be of medium size and of good vigor. In my opinion, the Standard makes a mistake in calling for larger birds, as this detracts from their profit as egg-producers. A good vigorous tom will mate with eighteen or twenty hens. As to the best age for breeding fowls, I use a two-year-old male and female one year old, or vice versa. Yearling turkey hens will lay more eggs than an older hen, but the two-year-old hen's eggs will hatch stronger poults. Hens are profitable as a general thing until they are four years old. I have kept some good layers until they were six years old. As a rule turkeys are not profitable after they are four years old. Three to four-year-old tom turkeys usually become cross and irritable and are dangerous to have about where there are children.

I have the best success with pullets from sixteen to twenty pounds, and old hens from eighteen to twenty-three pounds. They lay more fertile eggs than larger hens, are more active and healthy and make better mothers. Turkey hens do not all commence laying at once, and generally by the time the first layers want to sit the last ones to lay are ready to begin. Turkey hens should be carefully fed at the laying season if fed at all, as they will pick up on the range nearly all the food they need. If allowed to get too fat they will not lay until late. It is a good plan to feed meat two or three times during the month before you want them to lay, as it will have a tendency to make the eggs more fertile. Turkey eggs as a general thing are sure to hatch. I have had hens lay as many as four clutches of eggs in a season. Turkey eggs will hatch in twenty-eight days, but with medium sized turkeys it usually requires twenty-nine days, and eggs from very large hens frequently run over to thirty days. I have an eight-foot fence around about two acres on my home place that I use for the laying turkeys in the spring. I use boxes and barrels turned on the side for nests.

AT HATCHING TIME

One should be very careful in setting turkey hens, as they are of a wild nature. It is best to try a hen, if one has valuable eggs, by giving her a few nest eggs for a day or so, then at night taking the nest eggs out and putting the good eggs in. Be careful to have the bottom of the nest firm and solid, so that the eggs will not roll about. Have the nest so formed that it fits the shape of

the hen. In this way the eggs will all be the same distance from the hen's body and receive the same amount of heat. Sprinkle the eggs at sitting time and two or three times during hatching time with Lambert's Death to Lice, or some other good insecticide. If your hen is gentle you might take the poults out of the nest as they hatch. This leaves more room for those that are to hatch. If the hen is inclined to be irritable, it is best to leave her alone, as she may get excited and trample on the poults. I have successfully used incubators for hatching turkey eggs, but when it comes to putting the poults in the brooders it is another matter. It is all right to hatch them in an incubator if one has hens to which he can give the young poults to be raised. I never feed my young turkeys until they are twenty-four to thirty-six hours old. They are first given grit, then some oatmeal or groats. I use very little soft food. When giving soft food it is best to mix it with sweet milk and give only what they will eat up at one meal, as turkeys should never have sour food. Give table scraps and any green food you may have. Cottage cheese is a good food for poults and is particularly good with cut onion tops, salted and peppered to taste. Oat groats are highly recommended as a dry food for poults. Give millet seed, kaffir corn, wheat and then cracked corn. Feed these grains alternatingly.

A Flock of Bronze Turkeys on the Farm of S. B. Johnston

AT MARKETING TIME

I have found that winter feeding differs from summer feeding, as in cold weather poultry needs corn on account of its heating and fat-producing qualities. Turkeys on the range in warm weather do not require much corn. If one has a large range the turkey crop is almost clear profit. Turkeys intended for market should not be fed heavily until within about two weeks of selling time, when they should be given all the corn they will eat, with a change of food as often as possible so that they will not tire of the corn before they are fat. Make corn their main food.

The average price for turkeys on the market is eight cents per pound. When stockmen get five cents per pound for hogs and cattle they make a good profit. It does not take anything like the amount of food to produce turkey meat that it does to produce cattle or hogs, and it is very seldom that the turkey grower gets less than eight cents per pound. On the other hand, it is seldom that the cattle grower gets more than four cents per pound for his beef or pork. When turkeys are properly raised they are a benefit to the crop instead of a waste, as they destroy numerous insects. In California turkeys are rented out to men who have vineyards, who turn the turkeys loose among the vines to destroy insects. Turkeys do not require to be fed on a grain ration until within a few weeks of marketing time, as they get their living from the gleanings of the field. In this way they get a large frame, which the grower can fatten when selling time comes. Turkeys should be fed away from other poultry. Sandy or gravelly land is the most suitable for turkey raising. Low, swampy land is not desirable, as it creates rheumatism, to say nothing of the filth.

SUCCESSFUL TURKEY RAISING

With the Minimum of Labor—Laying House for Turkeys—Hatching the Poults—Housing Turkeys with Poults—Feeding
Young Turkeys—Roosts for the Young Birds—Shipping Crates for Pairs, Trios and Pens

MRS. M. L. SINGLETON

AM AWARE that no two breeders manage their turkeys exactly alike, in fact, there are no iron-clad rules in turkey raising. Our surroundings differ so from those of others, that it is useless to formulate rules that would be impossible for them to follow, but there is one safe rule for beginners. No matter what your environments may be, start with the very best stock you are able to buy. If you have money enough to buy a good pair only, do not spend it for a trio or pen. If you can spare the money for first-class birds, of course a trio or pen is desirable. To the thoroughly equipped breeders who have years of experience behind them, my methods will appear crude, doubtless. It is not for the breeder of experience that this article is written, but for those whose advantages are not great and who must struggle perhaps for years to gain the knowledge that will make them successful turkey raisers.

I learned several years ago that I had neither the time nor strength to follow the hens around and hunt their eggs in fence corners and hedge rows, so I had a laying house built for them. It is not a very elaborate affair, but it accommodates them very comfortably. A week or two before I think it time for them to hunt nests, I have them driven every morning into this house. In this way they become accustomed to going in and usually by the time they begin to lay they will go without being driven. When the turkeys lay from twenty-five to thirty eggs, I set them under domestic hens, putting nine or ten under each hen. We find that there will be as many poults as one turkey hen ought to carry. Of course you have to use a great many domestic hens where there are many turkey eggs to hatch, but it pays, I think, as they hatch so much better for me than do the turkeys. I do not set the first turkeys that get broody, but break them up and let them lay a second clutch. By the time the first turkey eggs have been incubated two or three weeks, the last hens will probably be getting broody.

SETTING THE TURKEY HEN

In the meantime, I arrange my turkey nests, which are empty barrels, as I consider them among the very best nests. I saw out two or three of the staves about half the length of the barrel, that is, just below the middle hoop. I stand the barrel in the corner of one of my poultry houses with the open end up, because I think setting the eggs on the ground causes bad results. By making the nest on the closed end of the barrel the eggs do not come in direct contact with the damp ground, and they are yet near enough to obtain sufficient moisture Tack an old piece of carpet or gunny sack on the barrel over the opening and another over the top. Put in a lot of new straw and shape it into a solid, but rather shallow nest, and it is ready for the turkey. In the evening I remove her from her old nest and putting her gently in the barrel, drop the curtain over the opening. I have previously put a few chicken eggs in the nest so if she is restless and inclined to stand up at first, there will be no harm done. The second day I raise the curtain and put food and water near the barrel, but if she does not

come off, I let her alone for a day longer, and if she still refuses to come off, I lift her out. After she has eaten, I see that she goes back on the nest. When she has become accustomed to it, I lift the curtain up so that she can come out into the poultry yard and dust and pick around, always being careful to see that she goes back on the nest. I arrange a number of these nests in the different houses to accommodate the different broods that come off. A day or two before the little ones are due to hatch, I remove the eggs from one of the chicken hens, putting them under the turkey hen. When the little poults appear she is just as proud of them as though she had done all the work of incubating. As the little poults get dry and strong, I remove them to a flannel lined basket in the house. When evening comes, if the turkey is a very gentle mother, I carry them back and let them remain with her, as the warmth from her body strengthens them, but if she is a foolish old hen, I wrap the basket warmly and keep them in the house. When they are all dry and strong enough, I remove the mother turkey and her little ones to their future home. It is this home I wish to tell you about most particularly.

HOUSING THE TURKEYS AND POULTS

I do not remember to have read an article on turkey raising in which the writer did not suggest that a nice, shady orchard was a desirable place for turkey coops. Now I admit an orchard is all right, provided it is located where you can run out and look after the young turkeys at all times, but when one has all the work of a large house on one's shoulders and cannot get any help that is worthy the name, then I say most emphatically, don't. Here at Elmhurst is a large, shady yard at the west side of a building which has a porch almost the full length of the dining room and kitchen. A door opens out of each of these rooms on the porch. At the end of the porch is the pantry, which has a window in the west side, so if I am in either the dining room or kitchen, I can step out on the porch and see my turkeys, but if I am in the pantry, I can look through the window and see them, for it is in this side yard under the elm trees that my turkey coops are placed. "Turkey coops in the yard!" I hear some housekeeper exclaim. Yes, for my turkey coops are very neat affairs and do not detract very much from the beauty and neatness of our yard. The coops are renewed each year, that is, I turn the last year's turkey coops over to the chickens and get new ones, because for some reason my turkeys always thrive better in new coops. These coops cost only twenty-five cents each and a little work, for they are dry goods boxes sawed slanting, so that they are only about half as high at the back as they are in front. There are boards nailed on to extend over the front and rear. The lower boards are taken off the front of the coop and battens nailed on for the door, which slips back in place and is fastened with a wooden button which is just above the door. About six inches above the door another board is removed and screen wire nailed on to ventilate the coop.

FEEDING AND CARING FOR POULTS

Now we have the turkey hen and her brood in a nice new coop under the elm trees where just enough sunlight fliters through to keep the ground dry, and not enough to hurt the tenderest poult. The next thing is to feed them. For the first day or two I give them nothing but light bread soaked in new milk, and pressed as dry as possible, with plenty of black pepper sprinkled over it. After that I feed them almost entirely on egg corn bread soaked in sweet milk, in which is mixed raw egg. Right here I want to say, there is nothing better for young turkeys than raw eggs. I learned several years ago that they are far superior to boiled eggs. I know that curd or clabber cheese is highly recommended by a great many persons, but I have found it a very injurious food for poults. I have believed this for several years, but nevertheless, I commenced to feed sparingly last spring, and in less than two weeks I lost five or six poults, and in every case but one I found the curd packed in the entrails. The other case was enlargement of the gall bladder, caused from indigestion.

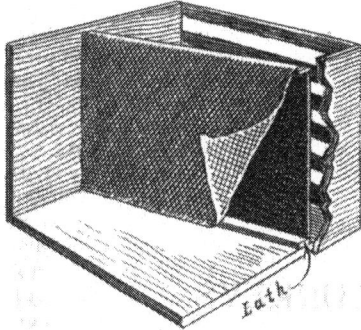

Fig. 1. Coop for two turkeys, showing lath at top, over which the cloth partition hangs, and the lath at bottom to which it is tacked.

Before putting the hen and her brood in the coop, I cover the bottom with hay or straw, otherwise there is danger of the hen injuring herself from slipping on the boards. I once had a valuable turkey almost ruin herself in this way. The young ones, however, get injured much more easily on the straw. I keep the mother and turks in the coop for a day or two, unless the weather is very mild, and then I stake them out in an open place in front of the coops. This is done by tying a stout twine, such as fleece or wool is tied with at shearing time, to a short stake and driving the stake even with the top of the ground. I measure the twine so that it will not be long enough to wrap around any tree or shrub, but near enough to the coop so that she can go in, but not around it. The string I tie on the leg, just above the foot. The hen will work and pull at the string for awhile, but she soon becomes accustomed to it, and when I take her out to tie her each morning she seems perfectly satisfied. This way has a great many advantages to me over the old way of putting them in a pen in the orchard. In the first place, the hen cannot kill the poults by jumping in and out. Secondly, they are right in sight, where I can give them my personal attention at all times. Third, if a rain comes up, I run out, untie the hen and put her inside the coop. The young ones rush up for the food I give them and I put as many in with each hen as I think she ought to have, because you see I have several of these families in the yard and one mother is the same as another to them. By the time the rain comes, the hens with their broods are all safely housed, for it only takes a few minutes to attend to all of them. Fourth, by the time I give them their liberty, which is not till the poults are three or four weeks old, they have become accustomed to their roosting place, and the flocks are usually running together. The hens never separate, but all come in at night, bringing the whole drove with them. It is very seldom that they fail to come up, but if they do, I go after them and drive them up, because if they form the habit of staying out, it is almost impossible to break

them. When they outgrow their coops and show signs of wanting to fly up to roost, I drive them into the turkey house, which is well ventilated, where I have roosts made about two feet from the ground. I do this for fear of sudden rains in the night, for I am not strong enough to get up and carry turkeys in out of the wet. I used to do such things in the past when my coops were kept under a shady tree in the orchard, but I realized that it was only a question of time when I should be compelled to give up the business entirely, or keep the turkeys where they could have my personal attention at all times.

When they are a few weeks old I feed them any small grain that I have, but the principal food is corn chops dampened just sufficiently to cause the fine part to adhere to the coarse. As they get older and until they are sold, they are fed almost entirely on corn. They must be well supplied with grit and oyster shells. When I first commenced to raise turkeys in such close quarters, I was told by all my neighbors that I would stunt them so that they would never recover from it, but as I raise the heaviest turkeys that have ever been raised in this part of the country, my friends have quit talking.

I have been asked what preparation I give my turkeys for the show room, and my answer is, none whatever. From the time they are four or five weeks old until they are shipped to customers, they have the range of a one-hundred-and-sixty-acre farm, and as soon as they are old enough to withstand the hard rains at night, they are made to roost outside in the open air. If during the winter we have deep snows, and protracted cold spells, we drive them into the barn and allow them to roost there until the weather moderates. Managed this way, there is no danger of them contracting colds and roup when being shipped a long distance.

SHIPPING CRATE FOR TURKEYS

Seeing the forlorn and bedraggled condition of turkeys shipped in pairs and trios to our station, made me wonder if the turkeys I shipped to customers looked the same when they arrived at their destination, and I determined to devise some means of preventing them from picking each other and breaking their feathers while on the journey. The crate I use is my own invention, as I have never seen one anything like it, and while it is a very simple affair, it answers the purpose admirably. I use narrow cloth-lined crates for shipping turkeys,

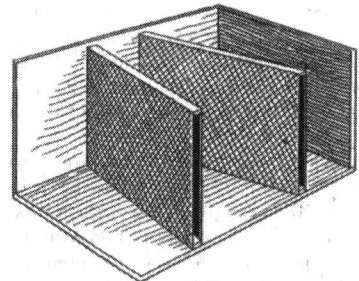

Fig. 2. Showing coop for trio, with cloth partitions in place.

making the crate for a pair just a little wider than for a single bird, and for a trio a little wider than for a pair. Any style of crate will do, but the ends should be upright pieces so as to have something to nail partitions to. In making a coop for a pair, after the frame is made and before it is lined, nail on two laths lengthwise of the crate, one the width of a lath below the top, the other against the bottom. Nail them firmly to the upright piece at either end. These laths are just slanting enough to show the space at one end to be about twice the width of the other. When you have the laths firmly in place, take a piece of your lining twice the depth of the crate, drop it over the top lath, tacking it firmly to the floor on each side of the bottom lath. Now you have a good, firm partition, one that will sway gently with the motion of the birds, but keep them apart as effectually as a stone wall. If you wish to ship a male and female, have the space on one side of the partition a little wider than the other side, as the male is always broader across the back. Make it just wide enough for them to rise up and sit down comfortably. When putting them in the crate, place the tom with head toward the wide space at one end and the head of the hen toward the wide space at the other end, having their heads at opposite ends. There is no danger of fighting, and the space being wider at one end and narrowing down at the other, there is no chance for them to turn around, which I have seen them do in a narrow crate that is the same width. In shipping a trio, follow the same general directions, having the wide end of the wide compartment and the narrow ends of the side compartments at one end of the coop, and at the other end, the narrow end of the center compartment and the

wide ends of the side compartments. Have the middle space somewhat larger than the side spaces and place the tom in it, with a hen on either side. I believe the same plan could be followed in shipping a pen, making the crate wider and adding two more partitions. The crate must not be lined until the partitions are put in, because there is no room to nail.

No matter how you raise or ship your turkeys, be honest in your dealings with your customers. In corresponding with them, describe your birds honestly, sending a tail, wing and covert feather. If your birds are well marked, the customer can tell it by the feathers, but they have to depend on you for correct weight, shape, etc. Remember always, the golden rule and judicious advertising are the only safe rules to follow in poultry culture. If you do not sell all your birds this year or next, you will some time, and if you do, you will not be ashamed to look your customers in the face if you should meet them.

BREEDING MAMMOTH BRONZE TURKEYS

Selecting the Breeders—Setting the Eggs—What to Feed at Different Stages of Growth—Remedies for the Dreaded Blackhead or Cholera—Hints on Turkey Rearing from One Whose Experience Covers More than a Quarter of a Century

JAMES E. LORD

EARLY in the spring of my eleventh year my father sent me to an adjoining farm on which our family was to locate in a few weeks, my duty being to stay with the turkeys, to watch for their nests and to gather their eggs. If my memory serves me well, this was my first responsible share in the management of the flock.

The March winds were fierce and cold, but with undiminished interest I resumed the task each morning. The flock was made up of practically all the breeds and crosses known at that time and their wild natures were in strong contrast with our stock of to-day. I remember following one of those cunning creatures for the greater part of a day, but she finally eluded me by taking wing and alighting in a woods nearly half a mile away.

Two years later I was sent to a distant school. I recall distinctly the heartache I experienced in parting with "Old Yellow," a gentle house turkey that was all my own. The frequent allusions to this old bird in my correspondence with my mother attest my fondness for this part of farm life, which though interrupted from time to time, has been resumed as often with all the ardor of those days.

Raising fancy stock was not very general then and showing was not even thought of, but our turkeys were sent to market in prime condition, were neatly dressed and sold at a premium even at that early date.

Improvement in blood was first suggested to the writer twenty years ago when he received a present of a number of beautiful Bronze Turkeys from a friend in Vermont. They formed the nucleus of our present flock.

The old tom became a wonder in intelligence and he was taught several tricks. At picking one's pocket he was an adept. While showing off one day he stumbled and his neck was broken.

From time to time the best blood obtainable was secured, with the result that our birds were sought by ex-

hibitors and many prizes were won at leading fairs. Then we decided to show our birds, with results so gratifying that since 1902 the greater part of our stock has been sold to fanciers and breeders.

SELECTION OF BREEDING STOCK

Much may be written on the selection of stock for breeding. Somewhere I have read that it is easier to breed a turkey up to the requirements of the Standard than any other variety of poultry. I am not prepared to say whether this statement is true or not, but of one thing I am positive. Never yet has there been a perfect specimen of Bronze Turkey taken from the show room, and so long as this is true none of us needs to be less earnest in his efforts.

It has been our practice to keep as near the Standard as possible, size being the first requirement, shape next and color last. The defects in the female we try to overcome with the male, which must be good in all sections.

Fanciers should bear in mind the fact that the larger part of our turkeys goes to flocks bred for the market, and that in order to furnish satisfactory breeders we must aim to have birds of large size and those that mature early. To produce this result, select females of large frame and mate them with a cockerel, the largest and best of the breed that one can afford.

Lately pullets are coming more into favor. They lay earlier and lay a greater number of eggs than hens, make quite as good mothers and are less wily.

It is also desirable to have the broods off reasonably early. A few days give the early poults a long lead over their later fellows, which is as great an advantage to the market man as to the fancier.

Bear in mind that the male is one-half the flock, therefore do not stop at a few dollars for a tom that suits. An undersized tom from a standard-bred fowl is to be preferred to one overgrown where the quality of his ancestors is unknown.

The matured toms are often too heavy and unless

one can give them closer attention than is customary, the hens will be injured by them. It is a safe plan to keep such old toms apart from the flock, except when they can be watched. They are a necessity in standard flocks, but it requires a great amount of patience and perseverance to be successful with these extremely large sires.

It is a safe rule to place one tom with ten to fifteen hens. It sometimes happens that a valuable tom is not inclined to mate. This difficulty may be overcome by securing another one, preferably smaller. When the two meet in the flock, jealousy will open the eyes of the old bird to his duty.

For many reasons the hens should be induced to lay near home. Ours are so domestic that it is not unusual for them to nest in the buildings and often one is found in the hay loft. Collect the eggs each day, place them in a cool room and turn them every day or two until wanted for setting. The hen should then have a thorough dusting with some good lice powder. As a heavy turkey hen is liable to break the eggs, it is better to hatch them under common hens. Put a few china eggs under the turkey until such time as the poults arrive, then slip one or two of the little ones under her over night and by morning she will be in a mood to mother the whole brood. By another day they will be ready to be taken to the field, at which time they should be carefully dusted. We have found one application sufficient for the season, but it may be necessary sometimes to apply the powder several times. At any rate, use it as often as required, because poults cannot thrive where lice abound.

A slatted coop three feet square and two feet high placed where the grass is short and pulled gently to fresh ground each day serves as a home from two to four weeks. Occasionally a hen will not take kindly to being confined and in her efforts to free herself will injure if not kill her young. We know of no better way than to let her go and rear them as instinct teaches her.

During pleasant weather two feeds a day are enough. From the very first this consists of a mash of wheat, bran and corn chops with a sprinkling of chopped onion tops, cabbage or lettuce, dampened with milk or water. Fine sharp grit is put where they may get it at pleasure and it is very essential.

Make an iron-clad rule never to overfeed during the first two months. If you do, liver trouble will be the result and it will prove fatal to most of those that are affected. About the fifth week cracked corn, whole wheat, barley or other small grains may be included in their diet to advantage, but the mash described above constitutes the main ration throughout the season, supplemented later by crushed ears of corn scattered about the yards. Mangels and cabbage make the best green foods for winter and they are greatly relished.

It may be well to say right here that Indian corn is the chief food on most of the turkey growing farms during the fattening period preceding Thanksgiving and continuing up to the holidays. The superiority of the Rhode Island turkey in our large markets is due to its plump condition and pale colored flesh—results of being fattened on the native white flint corn—and its neat appearance the result of being carefully dry picked. New London County probably furnishes half the so-called Rhode Island turkeys and from one of the many flocks there the choice bird for the president is usually selected.

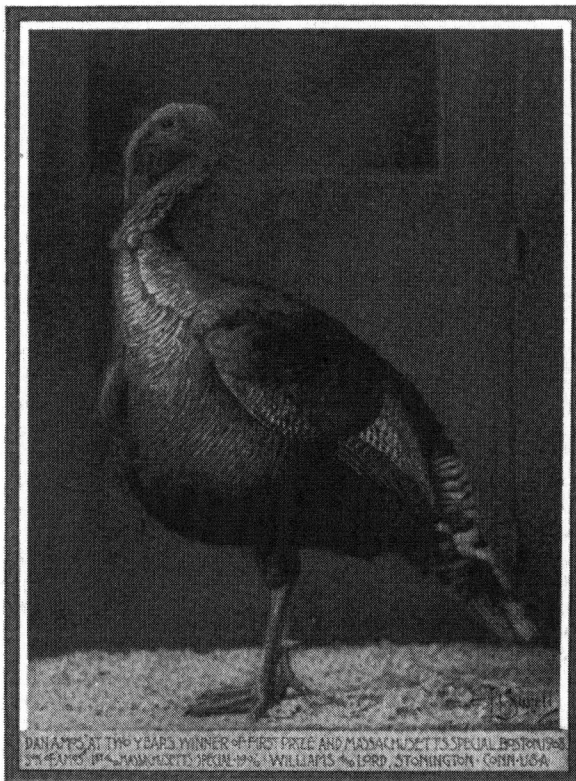

Bronze Turkey Cock

Mr. F. L. Sewell, the artist who photographed this bird, wrote of it: "Judges and breeders at the Boston show admired Dan Amos not for his unusual weight of forty-six pounds but because his great size was modeled into such a beautiful form and on account of his majestic carriage and fine color. Those who are used to studying the exceptionally fine turkeys each year at Boston Show know that those winnings represent the best in the East."

CARE OF TURKEYS

Early roosting on perches should be discouraged for the reason that the tender breast bone is liable to become ill shaped and the market value reduced.

The best roosts are those that are low and nearly on the level, otherwise there will be continual strife for the highest perch.

Turkeys are healthier in the open air. On rare occasions one may be blown from the roost during a cold snow storm and perish, but we have yet to learn of any being frozen while clinging to the perch.

TURKEYS ON FISHERS ISLAND

Turkey Raising Profitable—They are Not Difficult to Breed Under Proper Conditions—Wide Range Essential—
Half-wild Turkeys—Selecting Breeding Stock—Hatching and Raising Poults—Profits

E. M. & W. FERGUSON

T ALWAYS gives us great pleasure to write anything pertaining to Bronze turkeys, and especially to our turkeys, for our work with with them has been productive of much satisfaction, not to speak of a very considerable profit.

While we shall make this article chiefly a history of efforts in turkey breeding, rearing and exhibiting and a brief treatise upon our methods, we realize that all turkey raisers have not the same environment and will endeavor to write in such a manner as will be interesting and instructive to every breeder wherever he may be and by whatever conditions surrounded.

It seems to be an established fact that turkey raising in this country, particularly in the east, is on the decline; where years ago a flock numbering one or two hundred was a profitable adjunct on the majority of country farms, now these birds are found but rarely and then in flocks of a dozen or less, tolerated rather than fostered. The cause is hardly apparent; the thickening settlements have not yet encroached upon the solitude of many a back-lying farm where green pastures and sheltering woodlands offer ready for use, the best possible food and shelter. True, they may damage to some extent the growing crops, but they will render services much more valuable than what they destroy, in the wholesale destruction of bugs and insects which threaten the farmer on every hand and which they incessantly pursue as the principal article of their diet.

We are sometimes told that turkeys are difficult to raise and lack a strong constitution, but common sense, backed by our actual experience, tells us that such is not the case. In fact if they be allowed to indulge their natural desire for a wide range and outdoor life the year round, and are properly bred, anything but strength and hardiness in their make-up, would seem well-nigh impossible. But where such cases exist it seems to us that the cause must be found in the absence of one or another of these conditions.

We believe that a wide range is very essential and that although turkeys can be reared and kept in an enclosure of moderate area, a much less percentage will reach the highest development in size, shape or color. With this condition provided and a lack of vigor prevailing an inherent weakness must be present in the blood of the parent stock. This may be traceable to indiscriminate inbreeding or unwise mating. In no other domesticated fowl does deterioration so closely follow careless breeding, and for a farmer to breed the same small flock year after year with no further attention than is required to select the largest and fattest for his Thanksgiving dinner, is to invite failure by the most expeditious course.

Mistakes in adding new blood may prove equally demoralizing; in fact, we can cite cases that have come within our own observation where a breeder has sadly depreciated the value of his stock by adding a bird which, apparently strong and healthy in itself, had an inherited weakness caused by poor breeding. We speak of these matters not to discourage the prospective breeder or the disheartened farmer, but to emphasize the advisability of close adherence to the methods that have proved successful and the value of a careful study of the principles involved.

Some years ago we managed to secure at heavy expense a flock of genuine wild turkeys, which, although purchased for the purpose of crossing with our Bronze to make a better foraging market bird, have proved to be of inestimable value for infusing new vigor into run-down flocks, and we sell every year a large number of toms for this purpose. The half-wild make a market fowl par excellence; they are rapid growers, carrying a considerable amount of fine-grained meat, and support themselves almost entirely throughout the year by foraging. When crossed on the pure Bronze as a strengthening agent, reducing the wild blood to one-fourth, the increased stamina is the only apparent effect.

SELECTING BREEDING STOCK

The selection of breeding stock with us begins as soon as the young turks are given their first food in the fall, say the first of October, when any bird that gives particular evidence of lusty good health and sturdy growth becomes an object of especial interest to be carefully watched as it matures and finally selected for use if it has constantly maintained its robust health; but it is discarded if the slightest evidence of weakness has been detected.

The final selection is made usually in January when the stock is at its best. We have found that one male to every twelve females is about the right proportion, and we advise that at least two males be allowed to run in the same flock in view of the fact that occasionally a hen will refuse to mate with a certain tom, but can readily agree with another, and also to safeguard against loss should one of the males be, or at any time become, wholly or partially impotent. When one recollects that the female is served by the male only once in a season, the wisdom of this plan is obvious. But care must be taken to use toms that have been accustomed to each other's society and that agree, else it will be necessary to confine one each day while the other runs with the hens, changing them every night.

We endeavor to get our breeders in a condition of medium flesh, as a fat bird never gives satisfactory results. For this purpose we consider oats to be the best food, and it is fed exclusively so long as food is required during the breeding season.

When we began with turkeys we did all manner of things supposed to contribute to their welfare, but we have gradually given up trying to do what they are better able to do themselves, until now we leave them pretty much to their own devices and find the results far more gratifying.

THE TURKEY AND HER POULTS

Occasionally it happens that two or three hens are found laying in the same nest, a proceeding which is usually discovered by the slightly different color of the eggs. In this event we remove all eggs as laid, substituting a couple of china eggs or duck eggs to guard against a change of nest. When one hen begins to sit we give her a full quota (fifteen to eighteen eggs) and confine the other hens for a few days, after which they will begin laying again in another nest. If, however, the discovery is made after incubation has begun, we prefer to let them sit together unless we can ascertain unobserved that there is but one sitting of eggs. And we will here state that we always try to make our visits at a time when the hen is absent, otherwise she may become worried and give up her nest. When the hatch is complete, we provide a little nourishment for the young turks in the form of stale bread moistened in milk; this will assist them to gain strength until they are well on their feet, after which time they get their food from the earth and air. Occasionally we find one weaker than the others, by reason of slowness in hatching, which is unable to leave the nest with its mates; such a one we care for until it is strong enough to go with the hen. After they are all able to hustle about, we put poults and hen out in the low bush with which the island is plentifully supplied, and pay no further attention to them until well into the autumn, when we begin to get them together for the fall feeding.

As they grow and develop through the late summer and early fall they gradually form into several large flocks, which wander about together under the guidance of the old toms, each flock having its own roosting place, generally at least a mile from that of any other. In October they are found to be in excellent condition and require but little feeding to fit them for the Thanksgiving market. At this time they are very suspicious of any one who tries to approach them, but soon become reconciled to the presence of the feeder and will surge around him with such force as to endanger his footing. Corn is the only food given at this season, and as killing time approaches we feed them all they will eat.

The greater part of the market stock is devoted to the Thanksgiving trade and is shipped to private families all over the country; but there is always a certain number that are not fit at that time and which are reserved for the Christmas season. By furnishing each year a very fancy grade we find ready sale for all we have to dispose of for table use at a considerable advance upon the highest market quotation. These are carefully picked and drawn, the heads, shanks and last joint of wing being removed, and are then packed in clean boxes, in which they are shipped direct to the residence of the consumer.

December usually ushers in the advance orders for breeding and exhibition birds, in which we always do a large and satisfactory business. Having so large a number to select from (all of which are selected specimens from the hundreds that we raise), we find little difficulty in filling the most exacting order, and it is seldom that we receive a complaint.

Although our business in turkey eggs for hatching was very satisfactory, we decided to discontinue their sale three years ago and have had no cause to regret our decision. We find it far more profitable to set every egg ourselves and sell the stock instead. In shipping the birds we know that the purchaser will get full value for his money, while in selling eggs too much depends upon various conditions.

PREPARING FOR EXHIBITION

Our method of preparing turkeys for the show room is simple indeed. It consists wholly in taming the bird and getting it accustomed to being handled. Our turkeys coming from a range of over five thousand acres are as fit as only a free, wild life can make them, full of rich,

red blood, which sustains their vigor and spirits through the longest trip and the tedious, weakening confinement of the exhibition hall. They have a hard, smooth and wonderfully brilliant plumage, together with that robust development and noble carriage that is never found in a turkey raised in confinement.

We select the birds that we are going to show about two weeks in advance of the time when they are to be exhibited, and always take up more than we expect to show to insure having our full entry in case one or more

"Miss Alice"

A Bronze Turkey Hen, that traveled two thousand miles to shows and never was defeated. Owned by R. M. & W. Ferguson.

of the birds becomes damaged in plumage or otherwise. These are handled with the utmost care, as it is very easy for a struggling bird to break a number of wing flights or to strip feathers from its thigh, where a careless handler is almost sure to get his grip.

PROFITS

To any one who has read the foregoing paragraphs it must be evident that turkey raising as it is managed here —and we know of no reason why our methods and success can not be duplicated in almost any locality—is much more profitable than any other farm crop that the farm can produce. Any one who is apt at figures can easily figure out the possible profit to be derived in his own locality, which will be governed by the cost of food, the area of the range available, and the price that can be obtained for the product.

We would say in concluding that as many questions will doubtless arise in the mind of the reader which have not been clearly answered in this article, we shall be glad to see them at our farm, where we shall always be pleased to explain every detail of the business and where we can give far better instruction verbally with the birds and their home to illustrate our words.

A Typical Forty-Pound Bronze Turkey Cock

The above splendid specimen of Bronze Turkey was Second Gobler at Madison Square Garden, New York Show, exhibited by Mr. George W. Salsbury. Forty-pound Bronze males are not rare at the leading shows; however males that are so much above standard weight rarely possess such rounded form in all sections. The great fault in most large poultry is coarseness, the medium-sized birds of the breed as a rule being nearest the ideal form. We present the above as one of the most symmetrical males shown above 40 pounds. The size, general form, character of head, and color points of this typical Bronze Cock are worthy of imitation on the best turkey ranches and where show quality is sought.— F. L. SEWELL.

CARE AND MANAGEMENT OF TURKEYS

Raising Bronze Turkeys in Canada—Best Soil for Turkeys—Inbreeding and Line Breeding—Shape, Color, Markings—
Roosting Houses Used with Success—Young Hens as Breeders—Setting the Hen—Care of
the Young—Diseases—Catching and Weighing—Selling Stock

W. J. BELL

ALTHOUGH I am aware that turkeys are raised successfully on all kinds of soils and in nearly all locations, I believe that sandy land or clay with an abundance of gravel is a better place than heavy clay soil, especially if the latter is not well drained. On two of my turkey farms the soil is gravelly clay and there is running water all days of the year and from those farms have come my largest turkeys.

When I moved to my present farm in 1893, which has no sand or gravel in its composition, I noticed the poults a day or two after they were moved out on the ground from the nest commenced to look sickly. I could not imagine what was the matter, as they were free from lice and their treatment was the same as previously given on the home farm. In watching them going around I noticed they were picking at small substances. I immediately procured some fine gravel for them, and an improvement was noticeable in about a day's time. This shows what is gained by close observation and also that the dying of poults is caused—not by the food given, which is usually the cause assigned —but through overlooking what may seem unimportant matters. I consider a fifty-acre range necessary for even a small flock.

BREEDING SHOW STOCK

Some writers say that to mate Bronze turkeys you have only to "discard all specimens disqualified by the Standard." After thirteen years spent in breeding these birds I must say I disagree with them, for I have found the selection of the largest specimens and inbreeding them to certain extent will increase the size instead of decreasing it, but when carried too far inbreeding will impair the vitality and produce deformities. Therefore, to properly mate these birds is, I claim, as much of a problem as mating any of the Standard breeds of fowl. I wish the reader to remember that I am referring to the production of Bronze turkeys for breeding and show purposes.

In regard to the shape of the male I like one that stands well up. By this I mean one that carries his breast high, the same to be moderately full and well rounded. I have no use for the bird that carries his breast and body in a straight line parallel with the ground. Fig. 1 is my idea of a good shaped bird, either for the breeding yard or show room, except that the feathers on the rear part of the back were raised a little when the photograph was taken. Select a bird with good, heavy bones, and see that the toes are straight.

COLOR

When you examine the different birds in the show room you will find on breast and neck almost as many shades as birds. There is the green bronze, the black bronze, a dull brown bronze and a yellow bronze. The latter is my preference, and what I think is called for in the Standard, although plenty of judges favor the black bronze color. The body and back will be darker, with bronze reflections. The legs should be pink.

In the wings and tail are where the faults appear. Spread the wing and look for solid black feathers in the primaries, irregular barring in both primaries and secondaries and also a white edge along the bottom of each feather in the latter. They are bad faults. Fig. 2 is a good wing. The tail, which includes tail coverts, is seldom perfect; in fact, I have never seen one. The black bars near the end of the tail coverts (I mean the row of feathers lying farthest out of the tail proper) are generally missing, and two center feathers of the tail proper always have the white tip, the black bar and the brown barring more or less mixed. I have noticed the latter peculiarity in the wild partridge. Spread the tail coverts apart and look at the bottom of the tail proper and in a great many cases you will find white barring the same as on the wing. This is another serious fault. Some breeders are satisfied with a tail which is all speckled with black and brown so long as it has the black band near the tip and a white tip. Now I am satisfied that

Fig. 1. Showing a Well-Shaped Bird for Breeding or Show Purposes

Feathers on rear of back were slightly raised by the bird's excitement at having his picture taken.

a feather regularly barred with brown and black, with the broad black band and dull white or gray tip, is the proper color. Fig. 3 is as good in color of tail as I have seen.

I do not refer to all the shape or color sections, but only to those which are usually faulty or in dispute. The above will give you my idea of a good male to head a pen, except on one point, and that one in my estimation is the most important, viz., you should insist on having a line-bred bird. If you use a bird produced from two strains entirely different in build and in a great many sections in color as well, what can you expect? My advice is to have a good male sired by good males of one line of breeding.

What I have said in regard to shape of male will apply to the females also. The Standard says of the female. "The entire plumage is similar to that of the male, but the colors are not so brilliant or clearly defined, and the edging of the feathers dull white or gray." Now some breeders say that hens should have a gray edge to breast and back feathers, and I must admit that the great majority of hens are marked that way; still the meaning I take from the "color of the female" section in the Standard is that they should have the same color as the male, and I claim that the females in all our shows are scored too high. It is not impossible to produce them, for I have produced quite a few and find a great demand for them.

Young hens in my experience have proved the most satisfactory breeders. The old hens in a great many cases (and young hens sometimes) will lay soft shelled and misformed eggs in spite of all I can do. I have starved them; have had an abundance of old mortar and lime before them; have given them free range and everything I could think of, but I cannot stop them entirely. I consider it the only fault the Bronze turkeys have. Usually I mate seven or eight hens with one male, but I think more than that number would still give satisfactory results. Any shed or building not too warm will do for a

roosting place for breeding stock. They should be given free range during the daytime in all weather. I would advise feeding the male pretty well, but the hens only lightly.

SETTING THE HEN

At this stage it is a good plan to have nests prepared, as I have noticed hens looking up nests a month in advance of laying. Have them roomy. so the hen can turn and come off without breaking the eggs, and place them

Fig. 2-B. The wing of a present day Bronze Turkey. Shows the improvement in markings made in the past decade. Bred and Owned by Mr. W. J. Bell.

in all the corners and secluded places that you can find. By doing this early I save myself the trouble to a great extent of hunting the turkey nests. It is a good plan to watch which hen lays in a certain nest, and mark the eggs as you gather them, placing them in bran in a cool room until the turkey wants to sit. Then dust the nest well with insect powder and give them to her—about seventeen eggs if she lays that many. Some advocate placing the first laying under domestic hens and forcing the turkey to lay a second lot, but here in northern Ontario the late July hatches are seldom a success. About two days before the eggs are due to hatch dust the hen and nest well with insect powder. I consider this one of the most important things to do, as a young turkey cannot stand a dose of lice the first thing.

CARE OF THE YOUNG

When you bring the young from the nest mark them on the web of the foot with a small poultry punch. If marked when about twenty-four hours old they seldom bleed and the hole never grows together. By doing this and keeping the hens' eggs separate you can ascertain which hen is producing the best birds. I now come to a period in which my treatment of turkeys radically differs from other successful breeders, but I have had very few casualties under this system and so I intend to continue following it, and, further, I can raise them by this system just as easily as chickens. About twelve hours after the last poult is hatched I take them to a larger box—turkey and all. I feed them bread soaked in milk. They

Fig. 2-A. Ten years ago this was considered an exceptionally good wing Bred and Owned by Mr. W. J. Bell.

will not eat much at first, but by sticking a little of it around the sides of the box and working it on your hand among them, they get started. I keep them in this box from one to two days, depending on the weather, and get them taught to eat off my hand. Then I change them to an A-shaped coop with no bottom, and a lath front, and gradually I substitute shorts for the bread in their food.

I feed them their shorts entirely out of my hands until they are sold. I am very often told by my customers that they are surprised at the tameness of my turkeys. Another advantage gained by feeding out of your hand is that there is no food left on the ground to sour—a fruitful source of bowel trouble.

Up till five weeks of age I feed five times per day and cut dandelion leaves fine and mix with the shorts nearly every meal. I occasionally cut onion tops instead of the dandelions. Give plenty of milk—any kind—to drink, and keep fresh water before them all the time. Something which should never be neglected is to move the coop the breadth of itself every day. In mixing the shorts it is important to have them quite damp, but not sticky. There is one fine grade of shorts it is impossible to mix properly. I am aware some claim that feeding five times per day will kill the poults, but they surely have not tried feeding shorts and milk. Shorts digest very fast and I believe is a preventive of bowel trouble. At any rate I have found it a very slow-killing process.

At about five weeks old I give the hen her liberty and let them have free range of the farm and roost on the fences or buildings until fall. I only feed twice per day during the summer—shorts mixed with milk in the morning and clean wheat at night. If grasshoppers are plentiful they will oft-times refuse the wheat, but with me they never refuse the shorts.

HOUSING

When I first started I found great difficulty in getting them to roost in a shed at night during winter. I would spend over an hour keeping them from going on the

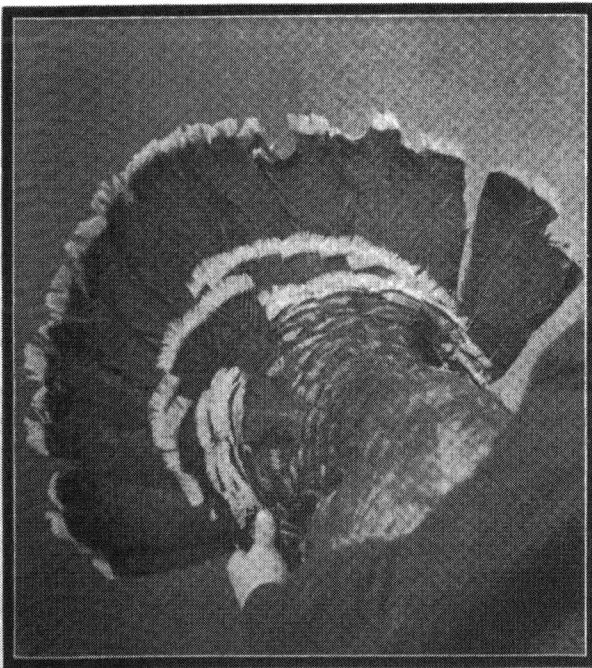

Fig. 3-A. A tail considered fair ten years ago. Bred and Owned by
Mr. W. J. Bell.

fences and buildings, so I thought of a plan which has worked satisfactorily ever since. I built a lean-to on the south side of my farm barn. Twelve feet from the barn and parallel thereto four posts were placed twelve feet apart and seven feet above ground. On these were placed a four by four-inch scantling. Then to the side of the

Fig. 3-B. A Modern Bronze Turkey Tail. This tail shows the improvement made in Standard marking during the past ten years. Bred and Owned by Mr. W. J. Bell.

barn, twelve feet from the ground, another scantling was spiked, and on these were placed the rafters. The two ends were then boarded up close and also the front, except what was required for doors and windows.

Now the rafters were not cut close to the building, but extended over about four feet. Straight under the points of rafters I placed four short posts twelve feet apart and two feet above ground and boarded this two feet up solid. From these boards to the point of rafters was strung poultry netting. One and a half feet from the ground and against the two-foot boarding was nailed a V-shaped trough the entire length, thirty-six feet, and a door placed on the end of this "run." The inside or house proper can be divided into two or three compartments as required, with roosts, and a large sliding door and a window for each compartment. I advocate placing the roosts on a level and about four feet from the ground. All I have to do now is to place food in the trough, drive the turkeys into the "run," leave the sliding doors open and they have plenty of light to see their food and are compelled to roost inside. Then, again, if the weather is warm the windows can be raised and the sliding doors left open all night, and if cold all can be closed. Figs. 4 and 5 will give an idea of this building. Of course the rafters are boarded over and shingled.

DISEASES

I shall touch very lightly on this part of the subject. I have had very few turkeys die from disease. At one time I housed them in a building much too small, and they contracted roup. I tried doctoring, but found it was not a success, and now use all my energies in preventing disease. I firmly believe if you let your birds have free range in daytime, feed at regular intervals and keep them free from lice you will have no more trouble than in raising any other line of live stock. My greatest troubles have been soft shelled eggs and foxes.

CATCHING AND WEIGHING

While our Provincial show was judged by score card and all birds were weighed, I was generally asked by competitors to catch their turkeys and place them on the scales, as I could handle the birds more easily than any other. In catching a turkey, if on the ground, I stand on left side, place my right arm over its back and grab both legs. Lift by placing left hand under the breast. It may try to break loose for a second or two, but hold steady, and it will give up. If the bird is on a perch, grab by both legs from behind—right hand for right leg and left hand for left leg—and draw quickly from the perch so its breast or wings will not strike it; then hold steadily while it flaps, afterwards it will remain quiet if held by the legs. In placing on the scales hold its feet toward you with the right hand and breast with the left. Lay it on its right side and pull its right wing down towards its breast as much as possible when withdrawing your left hand. Make your movements gradual and quiet and you will have very little trouble. It is almost impossible to get their weight while standing on their feet. In weighing as above if small counter scales are used it is advisable to place a box of the same size as the scales and about one foot higher under the scales, as the head and tail of the turkeys will droop a little on each side and having the box under the scales prevents them touching the floor.

SELLING STOCK

It would require a whole book to treat this subject properly, as it includes advertising and making coops. I think the best advice I can give is to be perfectly honest and truthful. I have found more persons lie about the weights of their turkeys than about any one thing in this world. I have bought turkeys at different times to be a certain weight and in almost every case have found them five to ten pounds short. I am aware that turkeys will lose about two pounds in transit, no matter how short the distance, but seldom more. Then again you will notice prominent breeders using cuts that have been in existence for years, as if said cuts were from photographs of their stock. A case of this kind which amused me and caused me not to trust a leading breeder with my order was to find a cut on his envelope and underneath labeled "S—3rd, 1st prize cockerel at C——, 1899," and right in front of the cut in small type was "F. L. Sewell, 1897," which showed that the cut was made before the bird it was supposed to represent was hatched.

Fig. 4. W. J. Bell's Turkey House
With roof cut away to show interior arrangement.

In regard to advertising, I would say try small ads in different papers and then increase the space in those papers which give best results. Do not try to make people believe you have the only good ones on earth, but state just what you have done in the show room and what you have to offer. Showing comes under the head of advertising, and I find it must be done or we drop out. I would say exhibit at the largest shows, as it is not the amount of money you can "clear" at the show, but the amount of reputation for good stock that you can gain. Answer all correspondence promptly and be careful to answer all questions asked as far as it lies in your power. Upon receipt of an order acknowledge by first mail, stating what day you will ship.

For shipping coops I use dry basswood. Take four pieces one and one-half by one and one-half inches and thirty inches long for corner posts. Nail two pieces three inches wide, two feet long and one-half inch thick on each end, and two pieces three inches wide, three feet long and one-half inch thick on each side. This will give you a light square frame. Nail on a bottom of one-half inch basswood and two pieces three inches wide, one-half-inch thick on top. Tack factory cotton all around the coop and after the cotton is on nail lath about four inches apart around the coop. This makes a light, strong coop in which to ship a pair of young turkeys.

For old birds it would have to be larger in every way, and for a single bird it could be narrower. I generally try to ship by night trains, as the birds are quieter at night and do not abuse themselves so much by breaking their feathers and bruising their flesh.

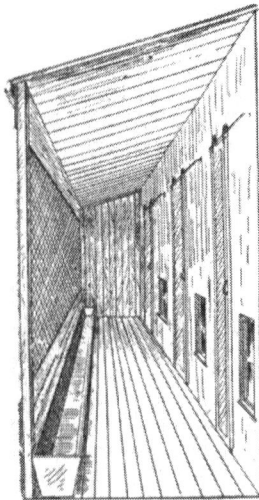

Fig. 5.
Runway in Turkey House.
Showing Feeding Trough and Wire Netting.

HATCHING AND REARING BRONZE TURKEYS

A Successful Breeder of Mammoth Bronze Turkeys Gives Valuable Advice for the Beginner with Turkeys—Importance of Properly Conditioned Breeding Stock—Management of Layers and Care of Eggs—Housing, Feeding and Rearing

RALPH S. MOSELY

THIS article being composed particularly for the benefit of the beginner, or amateur, who is starting in or who has trouble in raising turkeys, I will try to write so anyone can understand how I have raised Mammoth Bronze Turkeys, year after year, and what I have found the most practical way to hatch and rear them.

How often one hears people say that turkeys are hard to hatch and raise. It is a settled fact that turkeys cannot be raised under the same conditions as most chickens are, as we know that the turkey is not domesticated the same as a chicken, but we do know that if turkeys are given range and a place to thrive, with good, sensible care, they become as easy to raise as chickens.

Before saying anything about the hatching of eggs, let us consider the breeding stock that produces the eggs. The question arises, "Are you sure your stock is in the best condition to breed from?" The best condition means that they should be well matured, vigorous and free from diseases. As the breeders are the foundation of your flock of young turkeys, this coming year, you should note carefully this important point, as those who breed from the late hatched, or scrubs, are as a rule, the ones to complain that turkeys are hard to raise.

FERTILITY OF EGGS

Some amateurs say "My turkey eggs don't hatch well. What is the trouble? I feed them all they want to eat and give them the best of care." There are quite a few reasons for eggs being infertile; some, on account of the turkeys not being healthy, others, because the stock is confined in too small a yard, but the principal reason is because the turkeys are too fat, not having been reduced in flesh during the winter after they were selected from the flock that was fattened for market.

MANAGEMENT OF LAYERS AND CARE OF THE EGGS

My breeders are fed oats and Canadian peas, once a day, during the winter and spring, and about a month before I think they will lay, I begin to feed some ground bone, once or twice a week.

The ground bone tends to make them lay earlier, and makes the eggs more fertile, especially if there is no green food to be obtained in the fields.

About two weeks before they commence to lay, I place some salt barrels on their sides, along rail fences

near brush heaps, a little way from the house, and put some straw and leaves in each, with a nest egg. By making nests in this manner, I have no trouble in keeping the turkeys from running to the other end of the farm, thereby losing a part of the eggs.

I gather the eggs every day, marking upon each egg the date and name of hen laying same. By doing this, I know how old each egg is, and can keep the pedigree of each turkey when hatched. As quickly as the eggs are secured, they are put in a room where the temperature ranges from 50 to 60 degrees and turned once in one or two days, until I want them to set.

SETTING AND HATCHING

Those who have observed carefully, know that generally when the first turkey commences to sit, the last one of the flock begins to lay, and to keep the first turkeys laying, I break them up and make them lay a second litter.

When the turkeys are half through laying (about twenty days from the time the first egg is laid) I gather all the eggs laid up to that time and set them under chicken hens, giving eight or nine to each hen, according to her disposition and size. The nest is made one foot high and fifteen inches square on the sides. In one side there is an opening for the hen to enter. A frame of muslin is hinged on the top for a cover, ventilation and convenience.

The nest material is a sod about fourteen inches square and two or three inches thick, and to make the nest concave, the bottom of the sod is scraped a little in the middle, then a thin layer of straw is placed on top. The sod makes the best nest, as it gives the eggs the right amount of moisture, to give the best results. As previously stated, I set my turkey eggs under hens, so I can get more eggs from the turkeys, and because there will be no disturbance from foxes, skunks, etc. Two or three times the sitting hens are dusted with insect powder until I am sure there are no lice left to disturb the poults. Enough gentle sitting turkey hens are kept in reserve to take care of the poults when hatched.

When the eggs are about to hatch (about twenty-seven days) I give a few of them to each turkey to hatch, so that she will own the young poults. I have had turkeys that, after sitting only three days, became the best of mothers. I leave the poults in the nest, fixing

Victor seven and a half months old, weight, 35¼ pounds. Bred and owned by Ralph S. Mosely.

the opening so they cannot drop out and get chilled. At the expiration of forty-eight or fifty hours, I look the poults over carefully and if I find any of them with the yolk sack not absorbed and digested, I leave them in the nest, taking out the rest and giving twenty poults to each turkey in their respective coops or houses.

HOUSES, FEED, REARING, ETC.

There are two ways of rearing turkeys, one by putting the young turks out with their mothers at the other end of the farm and letting them shift for themselves until fall, while another (and better for me) is partial confinement when young, giving them free range when older; feeding once or twice a day to induce them to come home. The latter way produces larger boned turkeys, and insures more freedom from foxes, etc.

My turkey houses for the young poults are 10 by 20 feet, divided by partitions into three apartments. The south end of the house has four windows, and the east side two. The four windows in the south are kept open except when it storms they are covered by muslin curtains. When forty-eight hours old I give the first feed of fine chick grit, charcoal and water. The grit gives the poults teeth for the next feed and starts the machinery going; second feeding is stale bread soaked in sweet milk squeezed dry, part of a hard boiled egg and enough powdered charcoal to give the food a darkish color. Feed this every two or three hours for three days. Once a day feeding green food, such as onion tops, lettuce or dandelion leaves, chopped; grit and fresh water is kept constantly before them. It is very important that they do not have all they will eat at each meal, as their systems cannot stand the strain of continual gorging—it causes liver trouble or diarrhoea, when about four to six weeks old. When three days old I let the hens and poults out in the middle of the day, if pleasant; after a week they are able to stay out all day, and they are then fed three times a day on bread, eggs and charcoal, until two weeks of age, when the egg is left out and wheat

fed at night until three weeks of age. After this they are gradually worked on to johnny cake and curds in the morning and wheat at night. The johnny cake is composed of two parts white middlings, one part corn meal, one part ground oats, a little pure beef scraps, mixed with skim or sweet milk, and baked until thoroughly done. When fed take as much cake as will be required at one feeding, mixing with one-third milk curds giving them only what they will eat up quickly. I continue this feed for one month, after that feed oats, peas and skim milk to give growth. By this method of feeding have raised young toms that would weigh 37½ pounds at eight months of age, being just in ordinary breeding condition.

LICE

Young poults should be looked after very often and see that lice are destroyed with good insect powder. Look sharp for they are hard to see. Lice will kill a poult in a very short time.

INDIGESTION OR WHITE DIARRHOEA

It is generally caused by over-feeding, letting them out when the grass is wet, thereby getting chilled, filthy drinking water, or irregular feeding. I have found powdered charcoal, mixed in with the feed an excellent remedy for this, at the same time keeping them dry. Sweet milk scalded in which a little nutmeg is grated is also a good remedy.

SUMMARY OF SUCCESSFUL TURKEY RAISING

1. Breed only from vigorous, well matured stock.
2. Keep stock in healthy condition.
3. Do not let poults run in wet grass.
4. Do not over-feed or starve young poults.
5. Make war on the lice.
6. Prevent disease by disinfection.
7. Use your best judgment and common sense.
8. Give plenty of range. The turkey is naturally a wild bird and will not thrive in confinement.

SOME PRACTICAL HINTS

O. E. SKINNER

WHILE I have not had as much experience in raising turkeys as a good many others, I have had continued experience with them for over thirty years, but my remarks on the turkey will be from a practical standpoint and I shall leave the fancier's portion to some expert judge.

In the first place, everybody knows that turkey eggs, as a rule, hatch well, but the rock that wrecks all hopes is the art of raising them after they are hatched. One of the most successful turkey raisers I ever knew handled her young turkeys about as follows: She never let them out while there was the least particle of danger of getting their plumage damp, even if she had to confine them a whole day. I was there once after a heavy rain and she had them closely confined in a small box. I made the remark, "You will surely kill every one of them confining them in such a place." But upon visiting her a few months later she still had every turkey that had hatched. I believe this is the great secret in turkey raising—keep them absolutely dry and free from lice and nature will do the rest.

Another neighbor who is just about as successful handles his the same way, only he uses turkey hens for mothers. He follows the same plan about keeping them from getting their plumage damp when young. He has domestic hens sitting on the eggs, but he keeps giving them at night to the turkey hens until they have some twenty-five or thirty each.

WELL SHAPED BIRDS COMMAND A PREMIUM

The cry nowadays is for as large turkeys as possible. This is all right provided you retain the full breast and good shape generally. If you will observe the daily market reports, you will notice that the quotations say that scrawny turkeys (poor shape) are either not wanted or will be taken only at a big discount. So after all it is the shape that sells the turkey rather than the overgrown size. I have always made it a point to breed for full breast and good shape more than for oversize.

As to feed, I do not believe it cuts much figure if the other sanitary conditions, noted above, are closely followed. Plenty of sharp grit I believe necessary for best results however.

POINTS ON TURKEY BREEDING

Loss of Vitality in Turkeys and Lack of Fertility in Eggs—Injured Females—Food for the Young—Danger from Lice—Their Causes—
Care of the Layers and Sitters—Indigestion and Diarrhoea—Preparation for Market—The Poults—
Feeding the Breeding Stock—Advantages of Roosting Outside

J. F. CRANGLE

RONZE turkeys are more raised than any other variety, for several reasons. First, they are the largest; second, they are hardy and well adapted to this climate; third, they are good layers and the best of mothers; fourth, they are most satisfactory for marketing, being full-breasted and possessing the desired color of flesh. They will lay eighteen to forty eggs a season under proper care.

Generally it is considered that one male will mate with six to ten females. I have used one male for twenty-five hens, but I do not think it well to risk using only one male with your entire flock (especially if you have more than eight or ten females) for the following reason: A female usually allows the male to tread once. If from any cause the male did not effect proper connection, the eggs would not be fertile and the best part of the season would be lost because the first litter is considered the best.

The hen after connection selects a spot for her nest and a few days after it is made. This is usually done by scratching up the earth so as to make a hollow place to keep the eggs from rolling out. A great deal of the risk of males not fertilizing the eggs could be avoided in the following way: Use two toms alternately every day, but under no consideration allow both toms to run with the females at the same time. If you do you will, as a rule, have bad luck, as the males will fight and at times hurt themselves, also the females.

The lack of fertility in eggs and vigor in young poults is one of the main reasons for the decline in turkey breeding in the eastern states, and perhaps all over the United States. In many of the eastern states, where a few years ago hundreds of tons of turkeys were raised, they now have to import mostly from western states, to meet the demand, as it seems almost impossible to raise them. I think the main cause is in-breeding. There are many farmers who in the past have not thought it necessary to obtain new blood, and who thought they could save a few dollars by borrowing a tom from a neighbor, in this way using the same blood year after year. This has been done for so many years that the vitality has been about bred out. For the past few years turkey breeders no doubt have seen their folly, because many of them are now looking months ahead for a good male. The vitality had gotten so low that it created disease, and I am sure that many of the turkey diseases with which we have to contend have been caused by lowering the vitality of the turkey. I believe there is no other variety of birds in which the vital forces decrease so rapidly by in-breeding as in the turkey.

I think it possible under proper management to raise turkeys in every state in the Union, and I believe if farmers in general will be more careful about in-breeding and will see that they have the proper kind of males to breed from, such as will introduce new, strong, hardy blood into their stock, they will be able to raise turkeys as they have in years gone by. To people who are having trouble in raising turkeys I advise using a half wild male if they have large range. It is almost impossible to get a pure wild tom in this country, although you may hap-

pen to run on one by accident. About all the people who claim to have wild turkeys have nothing but half-breeds, yet with a half wild tom you can get enough new blood to make the offspring very much stronger, and this will be noticeable the first season.

THE LAYING AND HATCHING SEASON

After the turkey commences to lay, in many sections of the country, the nights are cold and in many places the thermometer goes down to the freezing point. When hens are laying and you are afraid of frost, the eggs should be gathered every evening and marked with the date. Then they should be placed in a pan or basket in common wheat bran with the big end of the eggs down, as by so doing you will keep the air cell in good condition. Put them in a cellar or any cool place and turn them every day. It is not best to turn them completely over; turn them only part way over each day. It is safe to keep them ten or twelve days, but I would not advise keeping them any longer than possible, as they are liable to get stale, in which case not so many of them would hatch. When the eggs are removed from the nest a glass egg should always be put in. If you do not put glass or wooden eggs in the nest the hen will probably leave her nest and lay elsewhere.

A good mother will cover her eggs when she leaves her nest; usually this is done with dry grass or leaves, so that in looking for a turkey nest it is always necessary to be careful, as otherwise one might step on it. An ordinary hen will cover eighteen eggs. If she lays more than that number, take the extra ones and put them under a common hen, setting this hen and the turkey at the same time. If you have a good hatch and get out more than eighteen, leave a few of the poults with the common hen. The turkey hen can brood eighteen poults with safety. Above all things, see that there are no lice on the hen when she hatches, as the poults are very tender when hatched and if the hen has lice the poults will have them on their bodies within a few hours. When you transfer poults from common hens to turkey hens dust them well with a good powder, as you want to be sure there are no lice on them.

It takes twenty-eight to twenty-nine days to hatch turkey eggs. If the turkey does not leave her nest at that time do not disturb her for at least twenty-four hours, because oftentimes a few of the eggs are slow in hatching and she stays on the nest several hours after they are hatched for the poults to gain strength. It is always well to take a piece of stale bread moistened with milk and put it near the nest, near enough for the turkey hen to reach it. If the poults are hungry, they will also eat. This food is very important because if the hen is hungry she may leave her nest before she should, looking for food. We must remember she leaves her nest only three or four times in twenty-eight days. If she does not appear inclined to move to get the food, do not disturb her, as it is a very easy matter to find out whether she has hatched any young, for as a rule, broken egg shells will be seen near the nest. At the expiration of thirty days, if you see no signs of the young turkeys, it will be well to investigate the matter by raising the turkey off the nest and ascertaining whether the eggs are fertile or not. If they should prove to be infertile, shut up the female for four or five days in a coop large enough for her to get a little exercise. Give her food and water and a place to dust herself and in three or four weeks she will lay again.

One of the best places in which to let the hen turkey run with poults is a field where the grass is short. As a rule, a pasture is very good; woodland is also suitable. Keep them out of long grass and grain fields when there is a heavy dew or it is rainy, until after the grain and hay are harvested, because the wet vegetation is bad for the young poults. It chills and sets them back in their growth and often is fatal. You will always find the largest and finest turkeys where they have free range. As a rule, turkeys will wander some distance from home during the day, but will come back to their home every night. Under proper management you can place turkeys anywhere you wish on the farm, and by teaching them to roost in one particular place, they will come to regard this as their home, and will know no other; you will always find them wherever they have been taught to roost. This can be done by watching them a few nights in succession and driving them to the place where you wish

shell, it will be porous. I have known many germs to die on this account.

DISEASES AND INJURED STOCK

Under no consideration breed from a diseased turkey. It is much safer to kill a sick turkey than to let her among your flock of healthy birds.

When the males mate with the females and they are extra heavy and clumsy, it is well to see that the male does not tear the female or hurt her back. A very good way to prevent this is to file down the toe nails of the male. I have seen them many times slip off of the female and rip open the hips or side. It is very easy to discover an injured female by her actions, more especially the next day, as she will be lame and her wings will droop. It is best to catch her at once and examine the wound, as generally they can be saved by sewing up the tear. This is not a very difficult matter. Let one person hold the turkey and another do the sewing. Pull all the feathers from the edges of the wound, and with warm water moisten them so they will stay back while you are putting in the stitches. Before sewing, the wound should be washed thoroughly with castile soap, using a small, soft sponge; then take a long, fine needle and with white

A Mixed Flock

them to stay. Just before dark they will go up in the trees or on a roost that has been put up for them. With the right kind of breeding stock turkeys at Thanksgiving time should weigh about as follows: Toms, sixteen to twenty pounds; hens, twelve to fourteen pounds. I have dressed at six months old, turkeys weighing twenty-four pounds, but they are rare.

FEEDING THE BREEDING STOCK

There are two things which have to be done in order to have success in breeding. One of them is to get the right kind of breeding stock, and the other is to feed them properly. These are the two main things. The proper way to feed breeding stock is to be careful not to overfeed them. After your breeders are selected, feed almost entirely on oats (scalded). I find they do better on oats than on any other food. For a change, feed whole corn about twice per week, and at no time feed more than they will eat clean. Where turkeys have a barnyard to scratch in, you will have to be careful not to get them over-fat, and as a rule, it is only necessary to feed them at night. A good accompaniment to the food for turkeys is charcoal ground coarse. Put it in a box where they can find it. They also need shells—oyster shells are the best. On a farm they can ordinarily find all the grit that is necessary for them to have. If the hen turkey has not enough lime to properly supply the egg

silk thread draw the edges of the skin around the wound so that the parts meet as they were. Commence at one end of the wound and gradually draw the edges of the skin together over the wound as you stitch, until the tear is all closed up. Many times I have taken as many as fifty stitches in one wound. Bathe the wound with witch hazel every day for four or five days. It is well to keep the hen in a small pen or coop for three or four days where there is quiet, and where you can catch her without running. If you gave her free range she might tear out the stitches. The period of confinement depends entirely on the size and nature of the wound, but as a rule, after three or four days she can be liberated with the rest of the flock.

FOOD FOR YOUNG TURKEYS

As a rule, many young turkeys are killed by overfeeding. On large farms where the hen turkey and her poults have plenty of range, it is best to feed them only twice each day, once in the morning and again at night. Young turkeys can live on insects and many little grasses which they relish. You will always find that food they get in the fields will keep them in better condition than anything you can give them. During the berry season, especially, when wild strawberries are ripe, it is a pleasure to watch the little turkeys pick and eat them. In seasons when there is a good supply of grasshoppers, the turkeys will live almost entirely on them.

When young turkeys have to be fed the best food I know of is stale bread, but be sure the bread is not sour. By stale bread I mean wheat bread three to ten days old. Moisten the bread with sweet milk, but do not get it too moist. I usually press out all the milk that I can with my hands. Clabbered milk is also good for young turkeys. Put it in a dish on the ground where they can get at it easily. During the warmest weather of summer it is best to keep all turkeys. young or old, on the hungry side, for if you do not, there is great danger of their having bowel trouble.

I have told you how to care for turkeys on a large range. If you are on a limited range, or for any reason you have to keep your birds confined, I mean young poults, take three boards twelve or fourteen inches wide and ten or twelve feet long and make a triangular pen. In this pen put the old turkey and her poults. Do not confine the hen. She will jump out and in over the boards and will not leave her poults. It is best to leave the poults in this pen for fifteen to eighteen days, and then let them range with their mother. Many persons think it is necessary to put the hen turkey in a coop to keep her near her young, but this is not the case, as the mother will stay with the poults; you could hardly drive her away. When the young poults are confined in a pen as above described, it is necessary while so young to feed them four times a day with stale bread moistened with milk. If the weather is rainy and wet, it is sometimes well to use red pepper enough to make the bread quite warm. If any of your poults are drooping it will tone them up. Clabbered milk is also good for them. Should you find that the young turkeys are drooping and do not seem to pick up, the very first thing to look for is lice. If your poults have lice or ticks they will not do well, and it is almost impossible to raise them. You will find at times a large blue tick on turkeys and turkey poults; they are on the neck and head only. If you should find any ticks on your poults, pick them off, then use clear lard on the head and neck. It will kill the nits that would hatch if you did not use some preventive. For the two other varieties of lice, use any good insect powder, but always be careful that none gets in their eyes. Hen turkeys generally keep free from lice if they can find any place to dust themselves, but some are very lazy and if these hens have poults they will be sure to be infested with lice, too. In looking for lice it is best to examine the little wings, as generally you will find them at the base of quills, also around vent. For the terrible ticks, which are almost sure death, look upon the neck, push back the feathers carefully until you reach the top of the head. You can easily see them, as they are good sized, and the older ones are dark blue in color, usually full of blood. If you keep your poults free from lice you will have overcome almost all danger of loss.

Stale bread moistened in milk should be fed to the poults for three or four weeks, then gradually get them to eat wheat and fine cracked corn. This grain should be scalded, as it will then assist digestion, but do not feed it until it has thoroughly cooled. Indigestion is very prevalent among turkeys, both young and full grown.

If your poults should have diarrhoea from any cause, one feed of boiled rice will usually stop the trouble. Another common but sure relief is to give them red pepper, say one tablespoonful. Mix it with about two tablespoonfuls of wheat middlings, then moisten it with water, but do not wet it enough to make it sticky. Cut it up in about four to six parts and roll the parts into pill shape, put them in an oven and bake them hard. It is well to have a few always on hand, as after baking

they will keep for a long time in a dry place. If I have a turkey, either old or young, with a bad case of diarrhoea, I give one pill three times a day until the droppings are improved. Then give a tablespoonful of castor oil if the turkey is full grown, or a teaspoonful to a young poult. It is very seldom that I cannot stop a case of diarrhoea with this treatment.

FALL FEEDING

I commence to feed all turkeys the first of October to get them ready for Thanksgiving, as we all know there is more demand for turkeys at that time than at any other. They should be fed morning and night, but never more than they will eat within a few minutes. Most of the trouble we have in the fall is caused by overfeeding. At the time you commence to feed for fattening use common sense and feed lightly for the first ten days, gradually increasing the food. The principal food from October to January first should be corn, not cracked, and the older the corn the better, as new corn will cause bowel trouble. I have seen large flocks of turkeys knocked out by feeding new corn. If you get their bowels out of order, it takes weeks to get them in good condition again. As a rule, most of your turkeys will be fat and in good condition to dress at Thanksgiving. There may be a few late hatched broods that will be improved if carried over to Christmas.

Many people advocate putting turkeys in a closed pen to fatten. I have given this method a good trial many times and under all conditions and find it a failure. Let them have all the range they want. The results will be better and you will avoid the sickness they will have if you confine them. Many persons do not understand why their turkeys are not so fat as they should be, but almost invariably you will find that they have fed them in confinement and the turkeys could not stand it, especially for a period of several weeks. They get off their feed and will not eat. In the fall when the weather is cold, turkeys will not range far from the farm buildings. They will eat their morning food, then roam around after a little grit to help them digest it and then lie down in a warm place out of the wind. Drive all the turkeys you wish to kill in a barn or shed so as to confine them twenty-four hours before killing with no food of any kind. To look well when dressed, their crops must be entirely free from food.

THE BEST ROOSTING PLACE FOR TURKEYS

Many persons who keep turkeys think they need shelter in the way of a building. That idea is entirely wrong. The best possible way of keeping turkeys in good health is to have them roost away from buildings, in trees if you have them. By roosting in trees they will not be in draughts, as they would be if allowed to roost in sheds or buildings. I have known turkeys to roost in trees with the thermometer fifteen to twenty degrees below zero, and be much healthier than turkeys that were inside a building. A turkey can stand any weather we have in the United States if they are roosting in trees that are partly sheltered from the wind. I have seen turkeys in trees during a snow and rain storm with the wind blowing sixty miles an hour, and they did not appear to mind it in the least.

A great improvement has been made in the size of turkeys, especially Bronze, in the past twenty years. The ordinary turkey of some years ago, as bred by the average farmer, would weigh about as follows: Toms, twenty pounds; hens, eight to ten pounds. Today Bronze turkeys will weigh: Toms, thirty-five to forty-two pounds; hens, eighteen to twenty-five pounds. This shows

IN NATURE'S WAY

Selecting Breeders—Introducing New Blood—Raising Breeders—Avoid Crossing, but Judiciously Inbreed—Poults in Nature's Way—
Range—Food—Housing—Difficult Sections to Breed Correctly

B. F. ULREY

S I BREED only the Bronze variety of turkeys, and a limited number of them for exhibition and breeding purposes, and as I have had no experience with any other variety and never sell on the market, except the culls of my flock, I cannot give you much information on raising turkeys for market. However, if I were to breed turkeys for market purposes, I should employ the same methods as I do in breeding exhibition fowls, except that I should not discard a good bird if it were faulty in color. Most farmers, I notice, sell all of the early hatched turkeys on the market because they will bring more money and they retain the late hatched and immature poults for breeding purposes.

The consequence is, they do not raise many next season, because the breeding stock has no vigor and the poults no strength when hatched.

I have bred Bronze turkeys for ten years and my method of raising them is entirely different from that employed by anyone with whom I have talked, or from the methods of poultry writers which I find printed in the poultry journals from time to time. In the first place, I keep about fifteen females in each flock, seven hens and eight pullets, headed by an adult tom, assisted by a cockerel, and I always have fertile eggs. The Bronze turkey commences to lay when she is about ten months old and she will lay from twenty to twenty-five eggs before she offers to sit, then if confined for about a week or ten days she will commence to lay again and will lay from twelve to sixteen more eggs before she becomes broody. Most hens lay two clutches in a season, though I have known some hens to lay all summer, and I have one hen that laid ninety-seven eggs from April first to September tenth. In selecting my breeding stock I take females as near Standard weight and color as possible, having large frames and bones and such as are not too fat. These are mated with toms that are a little above Standard weight, the cockerel weighing from twenty-eight to thirty pounds at ten months old, the yearling cocks from thirty-five to thirty-seven pounds, the adult from thirty-eight to forty-two pounds. I am particular to have males of the best color and shape I can get. I find that the female gives us size, while the male governs the plumage. In changing males and breeding for exhibition purposes, I always try to get a tom that is extra fine in the sections in which my females are defective. The best way to introduce new blood is to purchase a female from some successful breeder and mate her with the tom that heads your own flock. Save her eggs and mark her poults, and if they prove good, you can use them successfully. On the other

hand, if you buy a tom of another strain (the male counts more than half of the flock) to mate with your hens, and such mating results in poor birds, you have lost the season. I often see advertisements in poultry journals in which breeders offer stock for sale produced from twenty-seven to thirty-one pound hens and forty to forty-seven-pound toms. Such claims are intended to catch amateurs, for any breeder of experience knows that a hen that weighs twenty-seven pounds never lays fertile eggs, and a tom that weighs forty-seven pounds never fertilizes an egg.

HATCHING AND RAISING POULTS

I allow the hens to have their own way about their nests, although I place barrels on their sides along hedges and in secluded places in the orchard and fence corners, in each putting a small quantity of straw. The hens generally nest in the barrels and I remove the eggs every day until the hen is ready to sit. I then give her seventeen eggs and at the same time put ten eggs under a domestic hen to hatch. All the poults are given to the turkey hen to raise, as I find that a turkey knows more about taking care of poults than I do. I give her a good feed of corn and a drink of water and then let her go where she likes. If there is a meadow or pasture within three-quarters of a mile, that is where she will go. I have

Two Winning Hens, The Property of B. F. Ulrey

Indiana Queen (at left), score 97½; Pride of Shawnee (at right), weight at ten months old, 23½ pounds

one hen that hatched sixteen poults and I gave her nine more hatched by a domestic hen and she raised twenty-two of them. I have never seen a fence that will confine turkeys unless one wing is clipped, then a four-foot netting with a barbed wire above will keep them confined, but I do not wish to confine my turkeys except occasionally for a short time. Once in a while I have a hen that wanders too far from home to build her nest. I have an orchard covering about two acres which is inclosed with netting and barbed wire and in which I keep my Silver Laced Wyandottes during the breeding season. I bring the wandering turkey home, clip her wing and put her in the pen described until she lays out her clutch. If a hen and her brood get to running away and going to a neighbors', I put them in the chicken yard for about ten days, after which I have no further trouble with them. I look after the hens with poults on bad days when I cannot work in the fields. If I find any weak poults I examine them for lice, and if I find any lice I give the poults a good dusting with insect powder. If the weather is dry, the poults find enough dust in which to wallow to keep down the lice, but if it is wet weather you must look out for lice. I am satisfied that nine-tenths of the poults that die are fed to death or are killed by lice.

RANGE—FOOD—HOUSING

I give my turkeys unlimited range and feed nothing until July 15th, then I drive them home every night and give them a little corn. In about a week they will come home at night for food and to roost and I have no further trouble with them until I am ready to sell or show. Some writers claim that wet weather and heavy dews are fatal to poults. If such were the case I should not have a poult today, as the past season was the wettest we have had in several years. Still I have more poults now than I ever raised before in one season. I have never had but two sick turkeys during the years I have been in the business. One of these was crop-bound. I poured about a pint of warm milk down her throat and kneaded her crop with my fingers for about ten minutes, then gave her a tablespoonful of castor oil and she was all right the next day. The other was a three-year- old tom which dropped

not eat a half bushel of corn a day during the week I fed them.

Never discard a good bird because it is getting old. I have known hens to be first-class breeders when seven years old. The best tom I ever owned, both as a breeder and an exhibition bird, I sold when he was three years old because I thought he was getting too old for a breeder. The person to whom I sold him used him two seasons and he proved a successful breeder. Then this man sold him, thinking he was too old for breeding or showing, but his new master thought differently and showed him at Madison Square Garden, New York, that winter when he was five years old, and won the blue ribbon. Old "Champion" has a record of eighteen first prizes. He weighed thirty-five pounds as a yearling, forty pounds as a two-year-old and forty-three pounds when four years old. He was the sire of the first prize

Champion Jr. One of B. F. Ulrey's Chicago Cup Winners. Score 97 Points, by B. N. Pierce

off the roost dead. I commence feeding my turkeys all they will eat about November first and continue feeding until about February first, then I let them hustle for their living and they will be in good breeding condition.

I never house turkeys, as the trees and fences are the natural roosting places for turkeys and I think that the nearer they are raised as nature does the better the results. Turkeys cannot be raised successfully without plenty of range, as they must have exercise and a variety of food, which they cannot obtain except on an extensive range. If you will examine the crop of a poult after September first that has had plenty of range, you will find grasshoppers, bugs and worms, together with several varieties of weed and grass seeds, but very little grain. Some persons claim that a turkey will eat more than a hog. I had a chance to test the matter last winter when I had sixty-five turkeys on hand and there came a severe snow storm which prevented the flock from getting anything to eat except what I fed them. The sixty-five did

cock and second prize hen at Chicago, January, 1900, and to my knowledge, was the sire of eleven turkeys that scored 97 points or better.

STARTING THE BUSINESS

If I were to start in the business of raising turkeys, having the experience I now have, I should purchase three or four of the best females I could find that were near Standard weight and as nearly perfect in color as I could find. I should also buy their sire if he had proved to be a good one and should mate them to him. If I could not get the sire, I should get a cockerel from the same mating that the females were from and should mate him to the females. Then I should save the eggs from the best hen, mark her poults and save a tom from her to mate with my flock the next season. The pullets I should take to another farm and mate to a tom from the home flock. In that way I could line-breed and not in-breed too closely. When I saw there was need of new blood, I should purchase a female from the breeder of whom I purchased my original stock, and in that way I would keep the same strain, but my birds would not be near enough related to affect their health and vigor. As surely as you introduce a new strain in your flock, you will lose both shape and color and it will take at least three years of careful mating to get back where you were when you made the cross.

I find that the breast and back are the most difficult sections to breed correctly in regard to shape. As a rule, the back is too narrow and too short. We want our birds broad across the shoulders with a long back and full round breast, rather long legs and large feet. In color we have the most difficulty with the wings, tail and back. The Standard says in regard to color of wings: "Primaries —Each feather evenly and distinctly barred across, with

parallel bars of black and white extending the entire length of the feather." Of the color of the tail it says: "Dull black—each feather evenly and distinctly marked transversely with parallel lines of brown, each feather having a wide black band extending across it near the end (the more bronze on this band the better) and terminating in a wide edging of white." Now I find if we get a clear white barring in the wings we are sure to get white barring in' the main tail feathers, which is a serious defect. In fact, I should not keep a bird for a breeder that had white barring in its tail. I also find that if we get a clear white edging on the tail and tail coverts we do not get a rich bronze on the back and tail coverts, and if we get a good bronze where the Standard demands it, we are sure to get smutty white on the end of the tail and smoky white on tail coverts.

TURKEYS RAISED WITHOUT HOUSING

Confining and Housing Turkeys—Turkey Eggs—Care of Poults—Feeding Corn—Diseases—How to Begin

B. F. HISLOP

A FEW years ago when we finally concluded to try turkey raising, we had already decided that the Bronze was the variety which suited us best, and we bought a trio in the fall in order to be ready for business the following spring. We had no experience, so we began to read up on the subject and to question our neighbors about their methods of caring for the young. We found that most of the neighbors allowed the turkey hens to do all the work, and when winter came, if there was a large flock of turkeys the farmer's wife claimed all the credit, but if the turkey hens failed to raise large families, they had all the blame. At first we raised the poults with domestic hens and later decided to try the turkeys, but found the old ones so unruly that we again gave the poults to the domestic hens. We worked according to rules, kept the coops well scrubbed, etc., and we succeeded fairly well, raising as large a percentage of poults as we have ever raised since, but the work we did that year, if applied to some other calling, would have obtained us far more money, and we concluded if raising turkeys required so much work we had better quit the business. The time we wasted doctoring colds that season would have discouraged most amateurs. We were afraid these colds might develop into roup, and so labored most patiently. We wish to say that we do not believe turkeys ever have roup as chickens do. We think the birds become debilitated from injudicious treatment from the time they are hatched, and when autumn comes the birds take cold, which develops into chronic catarrh. We do not believe it is contagious, but a flock will be more or less affected, as all the birds are exposed to the same causes. It is hard to cure such colds, for if a man does not know how to prevent his flock from taking cold he is hardly likely to know how to cure them. There may be flocks that have the roup, but we have never seen any, though we have seen birds whose owners thought they had roup, but which we believed to be suffering from a severe cold.

This year not one of our turkeys has a cold, although this is the season for it, and we think we understand why they have escaped. In the first place, we changed the blood, as we believe inbreeding produces weak stock, although one does not need to make too great a change.

We do not think the turkeys are as liable to be off in color as chickens are, and so we have no hesitancy in putting a fine tom at the head of our flock without tracing his pedigree. A tom will do a large part in elevating a flock, but he cannot do it all, because much depends on the females. The male, so our experience teaches us, has much to do with the size, with the length of the bones, markings of the tail and wings, and also the shape of the body, but if the females are too small and poorly marked, one cannot expect anything first-class from such a mating. A large percentage of judges are very particular about the markings of the tails and wings of turkeys, so one has to look after these sections. Some judges are very particular about having a good bronze, although shape, size, etc., will help one out, but the best judges want a bronze, not a black or brown. Many breeders cannot see bronze in any but their own birds, but when the birds are all together in a show room, a person, if he has an eye for beauty, can select the bronze birds, and so can the judge—which is one good point for comparison judging.

CONFINING AND HOUSING TURKEYS

We do not think turkeys can be raised in large flocks without a large range, although we have never tried raising them in confinement. A turkey is naturally a forager and in roaming about procures its proper food. Even if a person has solved the food problem (we do not think we have) and confines his turkeys, intending to feed them, he would prevent them from taking the proper exercise which they require as much as they do food, if they are to attain the greatest possible size and vigor. We find that the lack of size and vigor is to be seen in poults raised by domestic hens. We have been asked if it is best to house turkeys. We have never housed them ourselves. They have always roosted at night in the trees and lived around the buildings during the day, but we intend to try housing them sometime because from what we have learned we think it would be a good plan. We shall use sheds open to the south, with trees for protection on the open side. We have a grove that is a great protection to our flock, but we think they need more. When a bird stands around on a cold, bleak day, all drawn up and then goes to sleep on a naked limb, with the wind blowing a blizzard around him all night, we cannot see that it is of any benefit to him. He has the same sort of body that other stock has and if he has no shelter to keep him warm, his food has to do it. Plenty of fresh air does not mean that birds must be out of shelter. We do not think that over seventy-five turkeys in one flock will do well and we prefer fifty or less. It does not matter how early turkeys are hatched. The hens in this climate will not commence to lay much before the first of April, and the later hatched will lay about as soon as the early ones, unless very late hatched.

IN REGARD TO TURKEYS

We do not keep the young birds for breeders because they are not matured enough. Breeders should be at least ten or eleven months old, the older and more mature the fowl is, the better the breeder. We may not get so many eggs from the females, but we get better ones. The one draw-back to two-year-old turkeys and older is that we let them get too fat in this corn country during the winter. We have never been able to secure such large clutches of eggs as some claim. We get an average of twelve in the first clutch and about ten in the second. Some hens will lay more, and some will lay three clutches, but they are less in number and we never count much on them, for the hens usually hide their nests and we seldom bother about them. Occasionally a hen will lay a large number of eggs, in fact, will lay all summer, but such eggs are seldom fertile. We have mated fifteen females with one tom with good results, and we do not believe there was any larger percentage of infertile eggs than when we mated a tom with two females. Turkey eggs are usually fertile if the hens are not too fat. We put our hens on "starvation rations," as we call it, when nearing the breeding season. At that time we feed mostly oats, meat and vegetables. Turkey eggs incubate in twenty-eight days, and when the weather is very warm a day or so less time is required, but we do not remember ever having one sit over twenty-eight days. Turkey hens seldom hide their nests for the first clutch. In the second they make the attempt, but we watch them and if they want to go too far away we drive them nearer home and thus get them to commence laying in a nest more convenient to us. We gather the eggs and keep them in a cool place, placing them on the small end, and if we should keep them long, we turn them, but as a rule, we do not keep them long enough to take that trouble, for if we do not set them ourselves, our customers are waiting for them. We have generally had better success in putting eggs under domestic hens, but we do not let them raise the poults. We always have a turkey hen waiting to take them. If a turkey hen has been sitting two weeks, or even less, she will take the young if they are put under her when a few hours old. We have tried putting pipped eggs under the turkey, but too many of them get mashed, so this year we waited until the poults were a few hours old. If a turkey chooses to sit in the proper place, we put eggs under her and set a domestic hen at the same time, but give all the poults to the turkey.

First Prize Young Tom
Chicago and Indiana State Fair. Bred and Owned
by F. B. Hislop

CARE OF POULTS

We used to keep the poults and the mother hen penned up for about ten days or two weeks, feeding the young turkeys three or four times a day on boiled eggs, dandelions, curd and bread soaked with milk. They did very well, but we think now it was a mistaken kindness, for we lost a larger per cent of the young in the fall. We think that with all our care we invariably overfed, but they did not show the effects until fall. Now we make a practice of keeping the hen and poults penned up four or five days, feeding very sparingly on boiled eggs, dandelions or any green plant, such as onions or lettuce, and a little bread. We have discarded curds altogether as we think it is too much work for the benefit, in fact, we have almost concluded that it is a detriment to the turkeys, for when we fed it we were bothered by the fowls having worms more than we are now. This season we went to very little trouble to feed them after the hen was set at liberty. If it were convenient we fed them twice or three times a day, but if not, we looked after them at evening to see where they roosted, and fed them, giving then some kind of cooked food, oatmeal, and bran, and later a mash composed of equal parts of corn meal, middlings and bran, with a little meat meal, bone and venetian red. The food we gave them was so little that we did not consider it necessary, and as they grew older they did not have use for it, but we still fed them in order to keep them tame and teach them that they had a home. Nevertheless, we frequently had to drive them home. A turkey on a farm range will take care of her flock and raise them strong and vigorous with very little food from the house.

There is much ado about young poults being killed by damp weather and by being out in the dew. By the time a turkey hatches in this climate it is not likely to be very cold, and unless the ground is so low that the land is flooded, there is little danger from rains. This has been a very wet summer in our locality, and we had hens out in heavy rains when the poults were but a few days old and we did not lose a poult nor did the young get wet. We have a large orchard and grove that furnishes a great deal of protection, but often the hen sat out as far from the trees as she could get, not to entirely leave the orchard, still there were no poults drowned. We think during such wet spells that the poults need to be fed more regularly, as they cannot hunt for their food. We have lost more young by having the old hen go into a coop with a part of the flock, the other part being left out and drowning, than we ever did when the hen was out with the flock. After the frosts kill the bugs, grasshoppers, etc., the turkeys require more food, and we feed them morning and night a small ration, increasing it as the food in the meadows and pastures decreases. In the morning we feed a mash with the same ingredients that we fed to the poults while young, with the addition of charcoal and oil meal in small quantities. We also give them cracked bone and grit, all they will eat of the latter, and at night coarse cracked corn and soaked oats. Now if the young poults are not fed to death, so to speak, there will be little, if any, indigestion, and if a case now and then appears lessen the food, and in individual cases give the fowl a full tablespoonful of castor oil with from five to ten drops of turpentine in it. If one dose is not enough, give two or three, or even more, one dose a day, and search for lice. We have invariably noticed that the debilitated fowl always becomes lousy and generally has worms, as these pests invariably follow indigestion.

FEEDING CORN

Do not begin too soon to feed corn. Last year we fed our chickens considerable cracked corn in the outside scratching pens. Our turkeys soon learned this and were on hand by three or four o'clock, if they had not hung around all day waiting for evening, and they got a large share of the corn. As a consequence, we lost a lot of fine birds from indigestion. We could not cure it, as we did not remove the cause. We wanted fat chickens and we paid for them with our best turkeys, but we learned our lesson. Keep your turkeys going out on the range as long as possible. Drive them away in the morning if they will not go. When the weather becomes cold and the proper time for fattening comes, then feed corn and heavy grain. We would never fatten the birds intended for breeders if the purchasers did not demand heavy weights, as fat is a detriment to the birds. We cannot blame the purchasers, as this is about the only way they can be sure of getting a large fowl and so they call for actual weights; but the tall, rangy, well-shaped, long, coarse-legged turkey, even if he does look slim in the fall, is the one that will be a large bird. Our first turkeys purchased were low, blocky birds, and they were almost as heavy in the late fall as they ever got. We thought them fine at first, but it did not take us long to change our minds, so that the next autumn we purchased a trio of birds from a well-known breeder. When they came the fowls were but a pound or two heavier than our old stock, but they were long legged, awkward, green looking birds, and we were pleased with them, for we could see into what they would develop and we were not disappointed. Since then we have known better what to purchase. Turkey raising is like a great many other things. One can read a great deal about it, but the actual experience is necessary. More than that, it can never all be learned, nor does one person possess more knowledge than all other turkey raisers combined. The longer one is in the business the less conceited he becomes if he has any success.

MARKETING TURKEYS

In catching poults or old turkeys, one must catch them by the legs, holding them just below the hocks with the legs together, laying the birds across the arm if you wish to carry them, or on something else if you do not. The cost of feeding a turkey on a farm does not amount to more than 50 cents per head, even with all the extras a breeder needs, and the farmer's wife who lets the turkey do the raising is out so little one cannot estimate it. We purchase food for all our poultry together, using as we need it, and consequently when the time to balance comes we simply count up our expenses and income from all our flocks and look for the gain or income. When turkeys are raised for market, the heavy ones will pay the most profit fattened and sold for Thanksgiving and Christmas, but the younger and lighter weights that are not in as good condition as they will be later, can be marketed any time during the winter, as the turkey market does not fluctuate so very much for good stock. We have had dressers of poultry tell us that the Bronze turkeys were the finest they handled, but we do not believe they command a higher price than other varieties, all conditions being equal. Good dressed turkeys bring from eleven to twelve and one-half cents a pound in Chicago. Every breeder should dress his own fowls, as it will pay him in all instances. Have the fowls fat and do the work nicely and you are sure of the top price.

LICE ON TURKEYS

We have not touched the lice question in regard to young poults. We are not much in favor of greasing, except in using a little lard on the old hen when first taken from the nest and on the tops of the poults' heads as a preventive of head lice. We dust the old hen two or three times while she is sitting, and thoroughly when we give her the poults, then watch the young and as soon as we see lice on them, dust them with good insect powder, avoiding the white, as it makes them look shabby. We do considerable dusting, once a week for a few months, but oftener if the lice compel us to. Dust the old hen, too, for when the lice are destroyed in this way at the beginning your trouble is over. We catch the young by having a box trap. Feed them in a bunch and when they commence to eat set the trap over them, the top of the box being laths with a little trap door in it so we can take the poults out one by one, dust them and let them go. In this way none are missed. It is not so easy to catch the old bird. Occasionally she escapes a dusting, but we manage to get her often enough to prevent trouble. We seldom have a sick poult, so we never experienced pulling wing feathers. Our trouble heretofore has been, as we said, in the fall, and we think we can steer clear of that better than we have.

DISEASES OF TURKEYS AND RANGE

In our experience the diseases of turkeys are brought about by impaired digestion. If one can build up the constitution and remove the causes of the trouble one can cure many of them, but when the constitution has become thoroughly broken down you might as well use the ax and stop the misery. Do not be too hasty, however, as many of them may be cured and marketed. Colds are not necessarily fatal, nor is rheumatism, although the latter is worse, but when a turkey gets the black head he is often dead before one gets a chance to doctor him, so the best way is to begin right and avoid such trouble. A large flock is more difficult to handle than a small one. We do not aim to raise over seventy-five in our home flock, as the range is not good on the prairies and the pastures are too small. We all know that a large cattle pasture is an ideal range, but they are not to be found in a locality like ours, where land is high and it is all under cultivation, besides one's neighbors do not like to see another man's turkeys in their oat fields or corn fields in the fall, although it is a well established fact that turkeys eat more injurious insects than they do grain and they are a benefit rather than a detriment, but you can not make many farmers believe it, and it is useless to try. We are trying to console our neighbors by compensating them in some way for the imagined damage, but with all that the yellow cur puts in his appearance occasionally and chews up a fine bird. It is not all clear sailing in the turkey business, and as we are located, if it were not for the pleasure we take in seeing a fine flock of the mammoth beauties, we should quit the business.

We do not think swampy ground would be a good place for turkeys, especially during a wet season. There has been a great deal said in regard to the size of the Bronze. Many think the present Standard weights are high enough and we have heard of judges cutting birds (toms) for being too heavy, same as too light. Now this surely is carrying matters too far, as size is one of the main features in a turkey (or any domestic bird that is cut when under Standard weight for that matter) as long as we retain shape and plumage. We have never struck such a judge in our exhibiting, and when we do, there will surely be a noise. Hen turkeys may be too large and masculine to be good breeders, but even they can be from two to four pounds over Standard weight when in good flesh and yet be very desirable breeders. As for an adult cock, we don't think 40 pounds would be too heavy for Standard weight, and birds that reach 45 or 46 pounds are just as good breeders as those of Standard weight.

One cannot expect to retain size in his flock if he does not stick to large males for breeders. An occasional use of a small cock with large females may be necessary to secure some desirable feature that the breeder is more in need of than size, but the latter has bothered us more than any other point, as our customers are always looking for the big birds, even at a sacrifice of other qualities; especially is this true of the market breeders. We fanciers are always looking for the birds that win the blue ribbons at our shows, but nevertheless we cannot afford to let the market qualities go unnoticed, as all our birds after all are bred for the common market in the end. One thing the prospective purchasers, old breeders as well as amateurs must learn, is that weight does not always mean size. For instance, two turkey cockerels may each weight 25 honest pounds, but one may be a large bird and the other small. The birds may both be scored and taken on an average. There is very little difference as far as the score card speaks, but compare the two. One may be worth twice what the other is to a breeder that wants size as well as other points.

A score card show will not do justice to Bronze Turkeys, and the breeders of our most popular birds, the large, fine ones that are in demand all over America, know this; if they don't, they will soon learn it.

The kind of turkey judges we want are those that consult the Standard for plumage, shape and size, but for the latter we want a man that can see size without putting the bird on a scale and weighing it, as the scale has to consider the fat along with the bone and muscle. Nor does it tell you how much of each there is in the bird considered. The Standard has no other way of fixing the size, save by weights. The rest is in the hands of the judge, and he is supposed to know the meaning of size.

FOR THE AMATEUR

Were we to start in the turkey business, knowing what we do now, we should buy the best breeders we could find that were for sale at a price we could stand and would not be afraid of a few dollars if we could afford it. We should build a shed for them, and if we did not have some kind of a grove we think we could ill afford not to build. We should start with the Bronze, for considering all we know of other breeds, we still like them best, and think that we can make the most money out of them. The market man prefers them for their size and the fancier for their beauty. Judging from the numbers shown in our exhibitions, they are the most popular variety.

A word to purchasers—when you wish to buy, first select a reliable breeder and if you want breeding birds you can easily purchase them at a reasonable figure, but if you want show birds for breeders (which are the best) do not expect them at common breeding stock prices, for no man's whole flock is composed of show birds, even if many of his old breeding stock were once show birds. If the breeder tells you that his birds were never beaten in the show, immediately learn where the birds were exhibited, whether in a local show or in a show like Chicago, New York or Boston. No person has made a clean sweep at many large shows unless the competition was very small indeed.

A Part of the Range over which Mr. B. F. Hislop's Turkeys roam

MATING STANDARD-BRED BRONZE TURKEYS

Desirable Qualities in the Males and Females—Number of Females in Pen—Evil Effects of In-Breeding

J. T. THOMPSON

IS THERE any kind of live stock on the farm that is more beautiful to look on, or more profitable to raise, than Mammoth Bronze turkeys as they are bred today? I believe that you will answer in the negative, for they bring more per pound than other live stock and their flesh costs no more; in fact, I do not believe it costs as much to raise them. They are great rangers and they obtain most of their living from foods that you would not otherwise realize on. Males weighing from forty to fifty pounds each, females of twenty pounds or more, that are beautifully and delicately marked, and with that rich bronze color and proud carriage, are certainly admired by everyone.

History tells us that in the winter of 1620—about a year after General Bradford and the pilgrims landed on our eastern coast, and after having endured hardships that only the strongest and bravest could survive, they set aside a day to offer thanks to Him for bringing them through such discouraging times—on their first Thanksgiving, the pilgrims ate wild turkey, in preference to the meat of the elk, the deer, the bear or any of the other wild animals that were plentiful. While that is nearly three centuries ago, I am glad to know that from that time to the present the flesh of the turkey has been more honored than any other fowl that we raise.

The North American forests being their native home, they were, nevertheless, raised in many parts of Europe within three years after they were discovered here. This proves that the people of the old world like those of America, were not long in discovering the fine flavor of this royal fowl.

BREED FOR EXHIBITION QUALITIES AND SIZE

When we began raising Mammoth Bronze turkeys years ago, our object was to breed them for exhibition qualities as well as for great size. We believed that in order to make the greatest success of the turkey business, and to realize the most money from it that we must combine the exhibition and utility qualities. For the past seven years, our toms have weighed as yearling birds from forty to forty-five pounds, and our hens of similar age, twenty pounds or more. The high honors

that we have won at the leading poultry shows, certainly proves that our efforts have not been in vain.

MATING TURKEYS

In mating turkeys select those that have large, broad heads, long necks and bodies, big feet, and as well heads, long necks and bodies, big feet, and are as well as well marked as you can get them, at the same time, never discount a poorly marked hen if she is of good size and shape, for if the tom is well marked, he will, to a great degree, overcome this defect. The same is true with a poorly marked tom mated with well marked hens.

Never breed from a short turkey, for while they fatten more quickly and look larger than the rangy one of the same age, it is the latter when fully matured that makes the big ones—the kind that we all want.

If your turkeys are large, but not as well marked as they should be, or perhaps they are a little off in color, and you have a strong colored tom that is somewhat small in size, it is all right to use him once to breed out such defects. However, you cannot afford to continue to breed from small males, for the size of your stock will certainly decrease. As the breeder who raises for market purposes demands size, and since the Standard cuts more on size than anything else, it is evident that it is the main consideration.

NUMBER OF FEMALES IN PEN

Never mate more than twelve hens with one tom. In my opinion eight is the right number for the average male. I have known of cases where good results were obtained by mating twenty and twenty-five hens with one tom, but such cases are exceptions and not the rule. Never let two males run in the same yard. If you have too many hens for one tom, and do not wish to mate two yards, you can arrange it by having one of the males in the yard and keeping the other penned up for three or four days. The birds should then be changed, and the one that was in the yard should be confined and the other placed in the pen.

Never breed from the same tom more than two years. It is better to change every year, for there is nothing

Exhibition Mammoth Bronze Turkey Tom
Bred and owned by J. T. Thompson

that will decrease the vitality of your stock more rapidly than close inbreeding. In buying a trio or pen of turkeys, demand that the male is not related to the females. We have two flocks, each on a separate farm, and in filling the orders of our customes we always select the tom from one flock and the hens from the other. We thereby start our customers on the right road to success by furnishing them with good, vigorous stock that is not related.

Many breeders, in selling off their stock in the fall, dispose of their largest turkeys—because they bring more money and keep the late hatched specimens to breed from, thinking that by spring they will be sufficiently old and large enough for breeders. This is a mistake. You cannot raise large, vigorous turkeys from small, late hatched birds. By all means keep your earliest hatched turkeys for the next year's breeders.

Some breeders advocate mating an old tom with pullets, but I prefer mating the pullets with a good, young tom, as an old male is sure to injure and probably kill some of them.

If you have only a few turkeys by no means yard them, for they will do much better when they are given the entire range of the farm. During the laying season

One of J. T. Thompson's Turkey Toms with Tail and Wings Spread to Show their Markings

it is sometimes difficult to find their nests when they have so much range, but if you will pen your hens until the afternoon, they will go straight to their nests.

THE FARMER'S BEST FRIEND

The Mammoth Bronze Turkey So Proclaimed by One Who Formerly Would Not Allow a Turkey on His Farm—Turkeys as Pest Destroyers—Selection of Breeders—Hatching and Raising Poults

MRS. J. M. RANDOLPH

CONSIDER the most important thing in turkey raising is good, healthy breeding stock. In selecting a tom I look for good markings on wings and tail, a long body, large legs and feet and as the Standard requires heavy weight, as large a bird as I can get that meets these requirements, although in my own judgment a thirty-two pound tom is large enough. I think most old turkey breeders will agree with me that there was a great mistake made in demanding such heavy weight toms. As I believe the poults get size from the hens and markings from the tom, I select the hens with regard to size first, but with markings as good as I can get on large hens.

About the middle of February or when the hens begin to call—a sound familiar to all turkey breeders—and show signs of mating, I remove them to a young orchard enclosed with poultry netting, and clip the right wing of each hen, but I never clip the tom's wing, as he will not give trouble by trying to fly out as a hen will do if her wing is not clipped.

In this yard they have plenty of range, blue grass and clover and I never let them out until the breeding season is over. I believe every breeder should have an enclosed yard or park for turkeys. Much as I should dislike to give up raising turkeys, I would do so before I would go back to the old way of letting them have the run of the farm. I cannot forget long, weary, ofttimes fruitless searches I have had trying to find their nests, only, perhaps, to have them move again in a few days.

We have a great many osage orange hedges in this part of the country and these hedges seem to be a favorite place for turkeys to hide their nests. I have had them follow the hedge more than a mile and then make their nests. Being in an enclosure not only ensures your getting all their eggs, but they can be gathered often and thus avoid having them chill during the early spring months.

TURKEY NESTS

Turkeys in this locality usually begin to lay the latter part of March. After confining them to the park I take some evergreen boughs and lean them against the poultry netting which adjoins a hedge fence on one side of the park, thus making a secluded place for them to nest. I do not leave a very large opening, but let them creep in, and they think they are hiding their nests. Usually I keep about twenty-two hens and most of them will lay their first clutch of eggs in two of these nests, but later on when the grass grows knee high they will steal their nests and sometimes elude me for several days or a week, but by that time it is warm enough so that the eggs will not chill.

HATCHING THE POULTS

Although turkey hens seem to be expressly designed to take care of their offspring and know how to do this part of their work to perfection, I have not found them to be as good sitters as domestic hens. For several years I have not waited until I had a turkey want to sit, but as soon as I have enough eggs for several sittings I place them under domestic hens. About two weeks before they are due to hatch I put some hen eggs under a broody turkey hen and when the turkey eggs begin to hatch I placed one or two eggs under the turkey and she would own them without any trouble.

Last spring I kept breaking my turkey hens from sitting in order to keep them laying and so at one time some turkeys were to hatch in a few days and there was no turkey mother for them. About that time I had another turkey want to sit, so I gave her, without moving her from the nest, two or three small Barred Rock chickens to see if she would own them, placing them under her just at dusk. Next morning she was hovering them and was very proud of her suddenly acquired family, so the next night I moved her to a building and gave her eighteen little turkeys, of which she seemed just as proud as if she had sat four weeks. This was a new idea to me, but I thought why not use that plan altogether and thus keep the turkey hens laying. I did so the balance of the season with eight or nine turkeys, giving them broods when they had sat only a few days and in some instances only over night. Just one hen out of this number refused to own and care for her brood, the others acted as if they had sat the allotted time. I shall try it again this season and I feel confident that it will work all right.

The best success I ever had in raising poults was in a small lot with very short grass and a very large coop or small building in which they could roost. They were kept shut in on rainy days and in the mornings until the dew dried off, until they were four to five weeks old. Then they were turned out to range, being driven back to their coops at night. For the first few weeks I find clabber cheese and green onion tops, pinhead oatmeal and millet seed to be good food for them. A little bone meal and small sharp grit also is put in their food once a day. I find sand and old plaster is good for them and a load of sand is hauled and placed where they can run to it. No one has any idea what a lot of sand young poults will eat until he undertakes to carry it to them as I did one spring.

At this season we always have plenty of milk and so I give them new milk every day, first boiling it to prevent bowel trouble. When the little poults are just one week old I pull out all the flight feathers in their wings. By the time they grow out again the little birds have more strength to stand the strain of growing them. Since following this plan I have had much better success in raising them.

I also go over them once a week and treat them for lice, rubbing a very little lard on top of the head, in the quill feathers on the wing and just below the vent. I lost a great many turkeys before I knew that when lice and mites were around the last named place they were most fatal. Remember I said a very little lard, for smearing the body with grease is sure death, as I learned by sad

experience. Occasionally I use some good insect powder instead of lard.

After they "shoot the red" and can be driven to the pastures and meadows it is surprising to see how they will thrive and grow with only a little food to induce them to come home at night. A more beautiful sight in poultrydom than a large drove of Mammoth Bronze turkeys with their bronze plumage glistening in the sunlight, I cannot imagine.

TURKEYS AS PEST DESTROYERS

Years ago I used to raise the old fashioned mixed turkeys, but my husband grumbled so about what they destroyed that I gave up raising them when he said if I would do so he would give me his note to pay me as much each fall as a drove of turkeys would bring. So I did not try to raise any for several years. Then a neighbor wanted to exchange some turkey eggs for some pure-bred Buff Cochin eggs and I made the exchange to accommodate her, besides I wished to raise a few to have for Thanksgiving and Christmas. I raised five very nice ones and killed two of them, but decided I could not manage any longer without turkeys and so kept a tom and two pullets to raise from the next year. The next fall I sold them all and bought six pure-bred turkey hens and a fine tom and went at it in good earnest so that the next year I had a fine drove.

Near the house we had forty acres in clover and the grasshoppers were so plentiful that the turkeys seldom went more than half way across the field until they had all they wanted. The result was that when the clover was cut for seed it was found that only the part where the turkeys had ranged was of any account. The grasshoppers had ruined the other part. That convinced my husband that turkeys were a good thing to have around, in grasshopper season at least. It was wonderful how those turkeys grew.

This season we had our clover for seed on another part of the farm a mile or more from the house, and I had a drove of over one hundred turkeys. The grasshoppers ate up all the clover seed. Every day my husband would say, "I do wish those turkeys could get to that clover field, for the grasshoppers are ruining it, and I shall have to buy my clover seed." And so he did and he had to pay a good price for it. He said that after this experience he would try to have his clover for seed near the house. A prominent turkey breeder told me afterwards that I could have trained the turkeys to go to the field if I had begun to do it when they were first turned out to range. In a case of this kind again, I am going to try it.

I hope this article may help some farmer's wife, whose husband, like mine did, does not think turkeys pay, and who, like myself, has need of some loose change. Perhaps the husband, like mine, will become convinced that turkeys are the farmer's best friend.

Markings on the Wing of one of J. T. Thompson's Mammoth Bronze Turkey Males

SUCCESS WITH TURKEYS

Time and Method of Making a Start—Housing and Feeding Breeders—Nests and Food of Sitting Turkey,—Care of Poults—Lice—
Fattening Stock for Market—Preparing for the Show Room—Diseases of Turkeys

MRS. BETTIE GLOVER MACKEY

TRULY there is more interest taken today in poultry culture than ever before in the history of the American people. There seems to be an awakening to the fact, long proclaimed by a few, that there is money in poultry. The question is seldom asked now, "Does poultry pay?" The form has changed and the question now is, "How can I manage my poultry to get the best returns?"

It seems to me that the poultry business, and especially turkey culture, is one belt which reaches around the globe. America is sending fine turkeys to foreign countries, and the west is furnishing the east with her best turkeys. I have shipped turkeys and eggs from ocean to ocean, from Canada to Mexico. The turkey is one American bird that will thrive in any land, will grow on any soil, or in any climate, and is considered a luxury by all, from the king on his throne to the humblest laborer in his hut.

There are more specialty fanciers than ever before and in no department of poultry culture is there more interest taken than in the turkey department. Of the many varieties, the Bronze is the leading one now bred. It is hardy, easy to breed to Standard, has fine style and is a beauty in color. It is of quick growth and will attain immense weight if fed for flesh. The objection is urged that the Bronze is more roving in disposition than other breeds. This disposition to roam is not confined to the Bronze alone, and the roaming turkey is more healthy than the one which hangs around the back door. Whether any other one will ever supersede the Bronze in popularity remains to be seen. Of one thing I feel assured, and that is that no breed now in existence will ever rival them. What may be produced by a cross we do not know.

While there is general admiration for the turkey, and a desire to raise them, there seems to be, among those who have never handled them, an impression that turkeys are very hard to raise, very expensive to keep, and difficult to manage as to disposition, that is, that they are such a roving and wild nature it is almost impossible to keep them at home or tame them. This last impression has grown out of the first. For years it was the custom, when turkeys hatched on the farm, to take them as far from the house as possible and put them in

Mrs. Mackey and Her Turkeys at Home

a place of security from vermin, and the only person who went near them were those taking them food. This was said to be the only way in which they could be raised, for if they were kept near the house they would be sure to become unhealthy and die. I well remember when I thought this true. Of course, turkeys thus raised became timid and ran away from every thing or person they saw. They were generally fed until six or eight weeks old and then allowed to make their own living. Naturally of a roving nature, they did not seek quarters near the house, and I have seen them fly to the highest trees whenever they were approached. They would tear down shocks of corn, for how else were they to get their living? No one thought of feeding them.

WILD TURKEYS IN VIRGINIA

I do not agree with persons who think turkeys are hard to raise and keep healthy. But they cannot be raised in a haphazard manner. Follow nature as nearly as possible, and the poults will do better.

Wild turkeys abound in warm, woodland countries. In the pinelands of Virginia (my native state) wild turkeys grow in large flocks. This is a mountainous region, rocky, abounding in springs of crystal water. The pine trees are in all forests, and it is said that there is more or less of the properties of turpentine in the water. Even in rainy seasons the rocky hills are not very wet and there are such large, sheltering trees the hen turkey can protect her young in the hardest storms. The seasons are mild and the pine trees are said to be a preventive of vermin. As turpentine is sure death to lice, I think it reasonable that the pine will prevent them. There are abundant seeds and wild food for the fowls, with plenty of insects and grit.

Following this lesson in nature (where the wild turkey thrives and large droves of tames ones are raised) I draw the conclusion that a hilly, rocky slope is a good locality; that turkeys must be kept dry, have plenty of pure water and fresh air, and at the same time not be allowed to become chilled. Either they must have a place where there is plenty of grit or it must be supplied to them. I do not favor giving poults or chicks hot feed. It is not the natural way and we cannot improve on nature. I have succeeded in raising strong, vigorous, gentle turkeys.

That it is their nature to roam cannot be

denied, but this may be greatly overcome by the treatment they receive.

BEGINNING WITH EGGS

Frequently I am asked which is cheaper to begin with, eggs or stock. This question can be truthfully answered—Eggs and stock. Circumstances and surroundings largely decide which is cheaper. If you have the money buy a trio of turkeys; if not enough for a trio, then a pair; but if you have not money enough to buy the turkeys, buy a sitting of eggs. I have made some very profitable investments in eggs.

I have been asked if turkey eggs will hatch after being shipped? I reply that where eggs are rightly packed and fairly handled there is nothing in the shipping to prevent a hatch. But there is a great deal in the hen under which they are set. From exactly the same lot of eggs set at the same time one hen will hatch several hours before the other and will hatch every egg, while the other hatch will be very poor. If you break the eggs decide whether it is the fault of the egg—an infertile egg will not rot, but will be as clear at the end of the hatch as when set. Turkey eggs are usually better fertilized than chicken eggs.

Follow these directions when setting shipped eggs: Allow them to rest twenty-four hours after receiving them; longer will not hurt if kept in a cool, dry place; put them under a quiet hen in a quiet place and disturb her as little as possible. If the weather is dry sprinkle the eggs with warm (not hot) water a few days before they are due to hatch; be sure they are clean. If an egg should be broken the others must be washed with a clean cloth in clear rain water; be sure there is no grease about it, as grease will prevent the eggs from hatching.

BEGINNING WITH STOCK

I should advise the beginner not to buy more than a trio. The mistake of almost all beginners is that they want to start with too many.

When writing for breeding stock state just what line of business you are in. Do you wish to sell your stock on the market or as breeders? Do you wish to raise exhibition birds or simply good pure birds? Much of the unpleasantness between customers and advertisers would be obviated if each inquirer would make his wants clear.

I think from the 25th of November to the first of February the best time to buy breeding stock. The sooner it is purchased after the first of December, the better, for at that time fanciers have plenty of good birds, while later you may have to take what you can get. Turkeys always pay, and while it may seem expensive to pay for a tom to change blood, it will pay in the vigor of the young turkeys next year.

Do not hunt for the cheapest, but try for the best. This is not always the heaviest in weight, but the best bodied and the best in quality. Look out for healthy, vigorous stock. Do not wait until the weather is too cold to have the birds shipped without getting the roup. You may think this strange advice when I tell you my turkeys roost in trees all winter, but I have noticed that if you take a turkey that has been used to the cold and put it into a warm place and then expose it to the cold it is liable to take cold. This is what is done when turkeys are shipped in bitter cold weather. They are put into warm cars and exposed to the cold after being taken out and changed into a new home. Buy your breeding stock early and turn it out and let it get acclimated and used to the new home by breeding season.

The most important part of turkey culture is to start with strong breeding stock. I will not breed from a fowl of any kind that is delicate. If I have weakly chicks or poults hatched I am always glad when they die. Yet it is true that a chicken or turkey may take cold and have a sore eye or head for a short time and not be materially injured as a breeder. But when the disease becomes very bad or chronic, better kill the bird, for the progeny from a bird with a chronic disease will never be of any account.

IN-BREEDING AND LINE BREEDING

In selecting or buying breeding stock, do not buy inbred turkeys. If you do you will lose by it. Possibly you may get better markings, but can you afford to sacrifice the vigor of your flock for these?

I have been asked if I think it will do to breed from the same tom two years. The question, I presume, has reference to using a tom with his pullets. There may be circumstances where this could be done to advantage. In order to secure certain points it might be done, yet I think not without loss in the number of turkeys raised. Demand, when ordering a trio of turkeys, that the breeder send male and female not related.

I advocate line breeding and practice it. But this may be done very easily without close inbreeding. I do it by mating on different farms every year. By looking up every sale and the yard from which the stock was taken, I avoid selling related stock. If a pen or trio is ordered, the tom is taken from one yard and the hens from another. These are booked, and if the same customer orders again he gets new blood. To introduce new blood, I buy eggs and use the toms in one yard, the pullets in another, thus keeping my own line, but introducing new blood. If necessary, I import a tom at the breeding season.

One who has common turkeys would like to know whether it would be best to grade them up or start with thoroughbreds. I think this is simply a matter of what you wish to do with them. If only for market, the cross with a full Bronze tom will increase the size and beauty as well as the vigor of your flock. But why not get the best and sell your toms as breeders to your neighbors? If you have the full blood and are the first in your neighborhood to get them, you can more than replace the cost in the excess of the price over market turkeys.

Another asks, "How can I get larger turkeys? I have the Bronze, but they do not get as large as some I see advertised."

Very often those advertised are never seen except in the advertisement. But it is a fact that the size of turkeys may be increased by breeding from not only good individual birds, but from birds of good stock. The greatest reason for production of smaller turkeys is in the breeding. To save the price of a tom, a breeder decides to use one from his own flock, year after year. I do not know that using the same tom two years would cause the turkeys to degenerate in size, but the habit of inbreeding is injurious.

Again and again comes the question, "Do you prefer an old tom or a young tom?" I can truly say, yes and no. It all depends on the conditions. I let the purchasers have their choice, but I always give to customers preferring young toms those which were bred from either yearling toms or yearling hens, and often both. Where young toms are bred with yearling hens or pullets of large bone and large ancestors, I see no difference in the size of the young. Still in my own breeding yards I use the old toms, for people want eggs from the largest stock to be found.

VIGOR, SIZE AND FANCY POINTS

Several have written asking which I think is the most important point to consider in breeding stock. My reply is, first vigor, then size, and then fancy points. The reason I consider strong, vigorous birds the first point to be looked after is patent. If the parent stock is not strong, the young will not be so. Mind, I do not say weight, but size. Turkeys that are not large framed birds may weigh very heavy, especially young stock, but after they are fully matured the little boned birds will not weigh so well.

Why do I say I consider size first? Simply because the Standard requires weight and cuts harder for lack of weight than for anything else, and if we have to be governed by the Standard we must come to consider size in breeding stock. If you were to ask my personal preference, I might give a different reply. The fancier must consider size in order to win in the show room, and then the turkeys are "cut all to pieces" on weight which they lose in shipping. Again, the fancier must consider size because ten customers require large turkeys where one requires fancy points. But the fancier must combine the size and fancy points and this takes study in mating. It is not the rule that the largest turkeys in the flock score the highest, be they ever so well bred.

I will never believe that the demand for immense weights required by the Standard and turkey raisers is wise. I have lost the heaviest turkeys I ever owned simply from being over fat, and I do not feed very much for flesh, either. It is not unusual for me to lose sales because I cannot quote as heavy weights as are demanded, yet I have as large turkeys as any fancier. I know over-fat stock is not good for breeding purposes, and so does every one who has given the subject any careful attention, yet a turkey must weigh so many pounds regardless of consequences. If the would-be purchaser would be satisfied with Standard weights then there would be some reason in the demands, but I have often received inquiries in November for young toms weighing from thirty pounds up to sixty, "sixty preferred." Now everybody with common sense knows, or should be taught, that in this climate it is almost impossible to make a young tom weigh thirty pounds in November or even December, and that to do so is an injury to breeding qualities. From January to March young toms may weigh from twenty-eight to thirty-two pounds without any special effort at fattening them. I prefer a pullet from sixteen to eighteen pounds rather than one heavier, and I know that I voice the sentiments of some of the best fanciers in the United States. The over large hen does not lay so many eggs, nor are those she does lay so fertile.

It will not be many years before this demand for excessive weights will be greatly modified. Market poultrymen say our Bronze turkeys are too large for their trade, and the market poultrymen must control the turkey trade. If we continue to increase the size of the Bronze, some other breed will take its place, and when this happens the Bronze turkey fancier who has tried to excel all others by breeding the heaviest weights will see this error.

I hope I will not be considered as advocating small turkeys, for I am not, and I could call hundreds to testify that I stand for large boned turkeys. The weights of mine as adults have not been excelled in the west, but what I do plead against is the demand for the pound of flesh, which is far easier to put on the short legged, small boned turkey, than on the tall, majestic fellow,

that will, as a yearling, weigh from thirty-five to forty pounds. The extremely heavy weights are fit only for the show room and the fancier's yard, while the medium sized bird is the better turkey for all purposes. I do not like to breed from excessively large turkeys, neither does any other fancier, and yet the fancier has created the demand for these birds by advertising excessive weights to catch trade, and the farmer has caught the spirit, and without really knowing what is best, demands what he sees advertised.

If I were a farmer raising market poultry I would want turkey pullets weighing from fifteen to seventeen pounds, good large-boned birds, not fat, and young toms weighing from twenty-four to twenty-eight pounds, or yearlings from thirty to thirty-five. I would hatch my turkeys early and in the fall they would be as good market turkeys as anybody would want. I would keep the pure Bronze turkeys, for nothing has ever equalled them. I would not do as some have done—inbreed until I decreased both vigor and size of my birds, nor would I save the late small, runty turkeys to breed from. I would save nice pullets and yearling hens and buy a tom from some fancier every year; or if I were short of money I might keep one two years, though I prefer changing stock every year. One tom is sufficient for twelve hens, and more may be used with perfect safety. I would keep more hens than most farmers' wives do, and instead of breaking them up from sitting, I would let them sit on their own eggs, or if preferred, I would set the eggs part under the domestic hen, giving all the young to the turkey hen, and if I did not care to keep over so many hens I would sell the surplus after they had laid the early eggs. I raise late turkeys, but if I were not a poultry fancier, and were raising market poultry, I should not raise late turkeys; early ones are much more profitable, they are much hardier during the summer, and are not so apt to be affected with the disease which takes off hundreds of young turkeys in the fall.

The farmer should learn that he needs good, strong, large-boned, vigorous breeding stock, such as will take on flesh when he wishes to market them. Nobody wants a poor turkey to eat and if the ten-pound one is fat and brings more by the pound than the twenty pound one it still pays to have the twenty-pound one, but when the marketman says he can scarcely use the forty-pound ones at any price because only hotels and large restaurants want them, the farmer has no need for forty-pound young turkeys, as some demand.

BREEDING FANCY TURKEYS

As to shape of tom and hens to breed from—I select large head and feet, long body, long neck, held well up, and a broad back and breast, with long shanks. A short turkey will fatten earlier and look larger when not fully matured than the rangy one, but the latter will make the weight at maturity much heavier, and will produce larger turkeys. I select hens the same way, yet if they are specially well marked and good in weight I would not discard them if not quite as tall as I like them to be when pullets. I am sometimes disappointed in pullets, but cannot remember that I ever have been in a tom—pullets sometimes are no larger at two than at one year old. They often stop growing at one year, while a tom never does. Other pullets grow until they are two and three years old.

My method of mating is simply this: Select the very best tom possible, and in females do not discard a very fine marked one because it is not quite as large as desired. By this I do not mean that I breed from small

Some of the Fine Ones Raised on a Missouri Farm

A Flock of Turkeys belonging to Miss Addie Brown

boned females. There are some larger than others in all flocks of the same age, and I should not advise the use in the breeding pen of an undersized female, or a runt. Nor should I discard from my breeding yard an extra large female because she is not quite up in fancy points for the reason that the tom will overcome to some extent the defects. The well marked female will produce large stock from the mating with a large tom, and the one not so well marked will produce evenly marked young from the mating with a well marked tom. Yet these must be exceptional cases, for it will not do for a fancier to have many females in his breeding yard that are not well marked and not very large. By undersized, we mean pullets, for if at two years old a hen is not of average size I should discard her unless there were some special point I wanted to impress on my flock. I think young turkeys get size from the maternal side, even more than from the paternal. Never should a fancier use a late, small-boned tom, or a poorly marked one. As a rule toms get very thin in summer if mated with hens, and they do not eat a great deal until cold weather. I have known a tom to weigh twenty-six pounds in November and thirty-five by January. Turkeys will gain two pounds a week in cold weather, unless there is snow on the ground, then they will stay on the roost and will not eat.

I once had a red legged turkey pullet. She was not large when young, but her legs were almost too deeply colored to be called pink. I bred from her as long as she lived, or, I should say, until she was stolen. I could tell the turkeys from her eggs. They were a good size and invariably had pink legs when young, though not as deeply colored as were hers. From this hen I got that line of breeding which gives in some of my yards pink legs in young stock. I can tell it wherever I find it. But this is the only female I ever kept that was undersize after she was a pullet. The rule is that the shanks are dark when young. Some of the best hens in size have dark shanks always, while others get very bright pink—I prefer the pink legs, other things being equal. But I

am candid when I say that I make size and not weight the first consideration in breeding stock.

Never breed from a turkey with a natural deformity. I once bought a sitting of eggs from one of the foremost fanciers I know. The only pullet raised had a crooked toe, but she was so fine I felt I could breed from her. Every year there would be a lot of turkeys with crooked toes, and these were the very best otherwise. It took several years to get entirely rid of crooked toes.

While there are fewer culls among turkeys than there are among chickens, it is also true that under the present Standard some of the very best breeding birds are not first-class exhibition turkeys. For instance, all turkey raisers know that there is a tendency to brown edging on tail coverts in some specimens, and it is a notable fact that these specimens are usually very strong in wing barring and that they are decidedly larger boned than those which possess the Standard gray and white edging. Now such a bird cannot be sold for exhibition, but if one is raising turkeys for market and selling toms to other market breeders, what better breeder would he want than this same brown tailed turkey, for as the market poultryman pays for pounds, it is the tom with size that one raising for market must get. Again, one may be poor in wing for exhibition and fine as a breeder. Yet I am sure that at least ninety per cent of the best bred Bronze turkeys can be put on exhibition when fully up in weight, and whether they win a prize or not they do credit to the owner. The main thing in breeding is to select healthy, vigorous breeding stock of good size and shape, with the very best markings possible. Don't expect perfection, but try to attain as near it as possible. Patience, perseverance and knowledge will bring success.

CARE OF BREEDING STOCK—EGGS

When once you have your stock, be sure that you get your turkey eggs. To do this I keep my turkeys penned. I would prefer letting turkeys run at large if I could do so with much convenience to myself. But to follow from twenty-five to thirty turkeys to their nests is too great an undertaking for me, and I keep them in a large pen until after they have laid. Each afternoon about 4 o'clock I turn them out in an orchard of blue grass. After a few days they will come to the gate and call to get out. If I forget, they do not; but they always go back to the pen to roost. I find grass very essential both to the fertility of the eggs and to increase the number, and also to keep the turkeys healthy. If I were so situated that I could not let them out to eat grass, I would feed wheat bran with flowers of sulphur in it every other day in small quantities. There must be sulphur to insure fertility, but the grass supplies it. Plenty of lime, gravel and grass, with wheat twice a day, is all turkeys need. If too closely confined turkeys will not thrive and I believe that the freer the range the more eggs the turkey will lay, but when they lay where you cannot find the nest and you lose both hen and eggs, as I have often done, you will prefer to get the eggs they do lay in the pen.

My turkey house is sixteen feet long, eight feet wide and has two partitions, making three rooms in it. It is made of barn boarding sixteen inches wide. Two of these boards are put together at the bottom, but as they go up cracks are left so that the air can pass through; however, they are too close for animals to get through. It is one-half foot high in front and three feet in the back and is set out in the orchard where the poults will have a seven acre range of their own. This turkey shed has proved a success, and my young turkeys have seldom failed to come up at night. I think the large, airy roosting place provided has had something to do with their coming up, for in small roosting places I was always compelled to drive them in, while all I do now is to turn them into the pen and they go to roost themselves.

The fence is the best I have ever used. It is made of straight farm fence wire, with stays and locks. The wires are only three inches apart at the bottom, and the distance apart is increased as they get higher.

I do not like to cut the wings of large turkeys for they often get up in trees and when they fly down they hurt themselves. My show birds are often spoiled by cutting the wings. They do not always grow out in time for the show. I do not cut the wings of the toms because they will stay with the hens.

The natural instinct of the turkey is to roost high and in ordinary weather I think it is best for them to be out of doors. My experience is that the first turkey to get droopy is one roosting low in the same place night after night, unless the droppings are either removed frequently or the impurities counteracted by frequent applications of either air slaked or quick lime.

I am often asked if one living on a small place can be successful with turkeys. If by small place is meant a town lot, certainly not. If an eight, ten or twenty acre place is meant, you may be successful with a limited number; and if you trespass on your neighbors and they allow it, you may be successful with a larger number. It is no longer a question whether turkeys can be kept on small space successfully, for so many overworked women are penning the birds and so getting eggs with much less labor, proving that with proper care the stock will

be just as vigorous. We do not claim they lay quite as many eggs, but we get more of them.

My experience has been equally divided between a farm and a small place for raising turkeys. I have lived seven years where my turkeys had unlimited range and seven years on an eight-acre place. I give the farm the preference after the turkeys are grown. Until they are six or seven weeks old they do as well on a small place, but from that time until they are grown the larger the range the better for the growth of the young turkeys, and yet the finest turkeys I have ever raised were raised on the small place; but this is not an argument in favor of it, for they could have been raised with much less labor and expense on a larger one.

HOW MANY HENS TO A TOM?

I make twelve hens the number for one tom, as a rule, but once I kept twenty hens with a tom that was two years old in May or June, and never had eggs hatch better. The question of how to manage when more than one tom is desired in the same yard, is a troublesome one. The most satisfactory way in which I have managed it is to let only one tom in the yard at a time. Let one stay in the yard several days, keeping the other where he cannot be seen or see the turkeys in the yard. Then change, putting the one in the yard in confinement and letting the other out. Some advocate changing toms every day where changing is practiced at all, but I prefer letting each tom stay in the yard several days at a time. Where more than twenty hens are kept, two toms should be used as above directed if all the hens are kept in the same pen. After the hens begin laying one tom may be disposed of if so desired. After the first clutch of eggs is laid I find that all the hens never lay at the same time during the season. Some are sitting, some stop laying and begin again, and some carry turkeys, so that one tom is sufficient after the first fertilization. But it is always safe to have the second one at command if one should die.

Getting Ready for Thanksgiving
Notice the fine, white edging on the spread tail of the tom in the center of the group. Miss Addie Brown's Bronze Turkeys.

How long can a tom be used, or when is he too old for service? I do not know. I use them two years and have sold yearlings that were kept three years. I never go to extremes in mating, that is, do not keep too old or too young breeding stock.

FEEDING THE BREEDING STOCK

The breeding stock should never be excessively fat. All stock raisers will agree with this assertion. There is nothing more productive of soft shelled and infertile eggs than over-fat hens and toms.

What to feed for the production of eggs has been a question. I confess that I have lost faith in hot mashes for either chickens or turkeys, and I never feed hot food to either young or old. Neither do I give hot drinking water. I was first forced to adopt the cold feed from sickness. I could not get anyone to prepare a mash that did not make it sloppy and I soon learned whole grain was far more healthful than sloppy food. If turkeys have free range during laying season they eat very little that you feed them. Keep grit and lime on hand in abundance and sow wheat for them. If it is laid in a pile they often leave it, but if scattered broadcast they will pick all day. Turkeys in their normal condition do not sit around during laying season; they are active and want to roam and pick as they go. I often scatter the food after they go to roost, as they are early risers and begin picking before I have time to give them their breakfast. One thing you may depend upon and that is, to have turkeys lay well, and lay fertile eggs, they must have an egg producing diet in some way. If they run at large they will get this without any trouble to the owner, but if they are confined it must be given them. One year I fed soaked oats with excellent results, but I would not give oats without soaking them. I mix shipstuff with them so they are not so wet. Wet food sours in the crop.

When should turkeys begin to lay? The rule in my yards is, about the middle to the last of March. I once had turkeys lay the last of February. My mother told me the "old-fashioned turkeys"—by that she meant the common ones—laid earlier than the Bronze. I think the climate may influence the habit of earlier or later laying. In a southern climate they lay earlier than in the northern.

If you want many eggs, you must breed from yearling hens and pullets. Old hens do not lay as many eggs, and extra large ones do not lay as many eggs as smaller ones. A tall turkey will lay more eggs than a short one. Why? I do not know. I think the last eggs laid by the hen before sitting sometimes produce poults with less vitality than the others.

Will the eggs from yearling turkey hens hatch as well as those from pullets? I think they will, the greatest danger of infertility lying in getting them over-fat. They must be kept vigorous and healthy, but do not overfeed in order to get weight.

I am often asked how many eggs a turkey hen will lay. One of mine last year laid eighty, which is the largest number I ever could vouch for. Of course she was not allowed to sit.

One asks, "Do you think July too late to hatch turkeys?"

We have two toms which weighed in March twenty-eight pounds without having been fattened; they were hatched July 3.

July and August hatched turkeys of large vigorous stock make good breeding birds the first year and excellent ones the second year, but unless scarce of breeding stock we usually farm out the late hatches the first year, and put them in our breeding yards the second. From these late hatches we give our turkey dinners during the winter.

I dispensed with the barrels this year, having only one. I put straw in the hollows and covered them over with brush, allowing the turkeys to think they were stealing their nests. From twenty-six hens I got seventeen eggs per day, showing that confining the hens as I do does not materially lessen the egg yield. When the eggs are removed as they are laid, and I think it should be done every day, either nest egg gourds, china nest eggs or real eggs should be put in the nest. Few turkeys will continue to lay in a nest after all the eggs are removed from it. I usually put three or four infertile eggs in the nest as soon as I find a turkey has laid in it. This often saves much trouble, and yet with all my care every year I lose both hens and eggs, for either a rain washes out a hole, a wind blows down the fence or they fly out after their wings grow out and steal nests.

CARE OF SITTING HENS—EGGS—NESTS

How many eggs will a turkey hen lay before she sits? Some lay more than others, but I never had a hen that laid more than fifteen or sixteen eggs before she wanted to sit and I have many more that lay only twelve than I have that lay fifteen. A turkey hen may easily be broken from sitting if she is taken in time, and by this means I often get twenty to thirty eggs before I allow a hen to sit. A hen will lay in ten days after she is stopped from sitting and some times in shorter time.

If you do not wish to make the nest as suggested above, then use not a flour or lime barrel, but a salt barrel. I turn the barrel down on the side, putting it under a tree or in a shady place. The turkey will scratch the nest up for the first few days, but the barrel is a temptation she cannot resist and she will lay in it. I always put down several barrels, though I find the turkeys all like to lay in the same one.

If the hen is thoroughly dusted with a good insect powder when set, and the top outside of the barrel lightly painted with a good lice killer, she will be free from lice when the hatch comes off. Be sure in using this that you do not put it where it will touch the eggs or feathers of sitting hens. If you do you will in all probability fail to get a good hatch.

I set from seventeen to nineteen—never more. If the hen is large and the nest well made, nineteen eggs may be put under her safely.

Usually I have a turkey and domestic hen hatch the same time and give all the turkeys to the turkey hen. I have not been as successful with domestic as with turkey hens until this season. I know two other breeders who raise turkeys altogether with domestic hens, and they are very successful indeed. As a rule, however, the turkey hen is the better mother, especially after the poults are seven weeks old, for other hens wean them too early. I think a very good plan is to let both chicken and turkey hens have young turkeys the same age, and when the chicken hens wean those under their charge the turkeys will let them follow them and care for them all.

Do not set your turkeys where there will be anything to disturb them. When they hatch be careful to handle them very gently. If I find I have one cross turkey about to hatch, and I have a gentle, kind one not due to hatch, I exchange the eggs and let the gentle turkey hatch the brood. I find to prolong the period of incubation tones the refractory disposition and often a turkey that will be fussy at the end of four weeks, will be gentle at the expiration of five.

Few people, comparatively speaking, know how to set a turkey or domestic hen, or how to catch either a turkey or chicken. When you find your turkey broody, let her alone until night. Have your nest prepared in some quiet place where she will be undisturbed by other fowls. Make the nest with care. I like the grass nest better than anything else, but as I do not have a bountiful supply of this I use wheat straw. I do not like hay nests at all. Make them very much the shape, but not so deep, as a wash bowl. If too deep the eggs will roll over each other and either be broken or they will not be kept of an even temperature during incubation. Make a full, thick nest, for four weeks' sitting will mash the straw down very much. Put two or three hen eggs, as they are not so valuable as turkey eggs, in the nest. At night go to the hen very quietly and put both hands under her, taking her firmly by the leg, close to the body and lift her straight up. Don't drag her out of the nest. Put her head under your arm gently, talking to her all the time. Place her on the new nest very gently and set a blind firmly in front of it. The next morning you may peep in. It will be an exceptional case if she is not sitting as well as she did on her old nest. I look at her again about roosting time. If I find her restless I let her off. If she is kept on the nest in this restless, nervous state, she will break the eggs and likely will not sit at all. She will probably try to get to her former nest, but as dark approaches she will go to the new one; or if she does not allow her to go to the old one and remove her as before. I have often had to do this several times with one hen. As a rule, however, the second time is enough. You may say that it is a great deal of trouble. I do not call it trouble. It is work, and I learned very early in life that to be successful in anything required patience and work.

After the hen has fully decided to accept the nest given her then put the turkey eggs under her. So many people waste by haste. What difference will two, three or four days make in the age of the poults? But what a calamity to have a sitting of turkey eggs spoiled by a restless hen.

I usually give my turkeys the opportunity of getting off the nest every day. I find this much more satisfactory than keeping them so long without allowing them the chance to get off. Often they do not come off for several days, and I had one hen that never came off in four weeks except as I took her off the nest. I then had to put the blind up in front of the nest and force her to stay off long enough to eat. I thought that I certainly would have a good hatch from this hen, but I had only ten poults from seventeen fertile eggs. She had smothered the turkeys by sitting so close. Turkey eggs hatch better than chicken eggs, but they require more moisture.

If the weather is wet I do not moisten the eggs, but if dry I sprinkle them the last week. When the eggs have been setting until within three or four days of the time to hatch, put them in clean, warm water—100 degrees is about right, or if it goes to 104 it will not hurt. All the eggs which have live poults in them will move very perceptibly. Those which sink to the bottom have dead poults, and those which float without any jerky motion are spoiled or infertile. However, the infertile eggs usually sink.

TURKEY EGGS IN INCUBATORS

Will turkey eggs hatch in an incubator? They certainly will. I once told a lady that from fourteen turkey eggs in an incubator I got fourteen turkeys. She in all seriousness replied that "a hen would do as well as that." If you expect more than one turkey from an egg an incubator will likely disappoint you. I do not hatch turkey eggs in an incubator because I do not wish to raise the young in brooders; but if an egg gets broken I put it in an incubator. Last season the finest young turkey I had hatched was from an egg with quite a large piece of shell broken off of the large end and I cut a piece of cotton cloth just a little larger than the hole and made a flour paste, just touched the edges of the cotton with it and placing it over the cavity, put the egg in an incubator and it hatched in due time. The reason I used cloth was—it is nearer the texture of the shell. Paper is not porous enough. Flour paste is better than glue; use only just enough to make the cloth adhere to the egg. With a clean, damp cloth I wiped off all surplus paste after the cloth was put on the egg. This would not have hatched under a hen, as she would have broken the egg.

Usually I do not care to have turkeys hatch until after the cold spell in May. But it is all right earlier if the weather is warm. Yet if they come out any time in May they will get the weight for the December and January shows. This is one advantage southern breeders have over western. We ship turkey eggs south as soon as the turkeys begin to lay. When one has a large number of early hatched turkeys I would not advise the raising of late ones unless they can be entirely separated from other fowls of every kind. But if for any reason you have failed to have early hatched ones, hatch them late. They make fine table fowls.

Years ago I bought a sitting of eggs from a prominent turkey fancier. I was sorely disappointed when I opened them as I had never seen such small turkey eggs. I made another order to another fancier and never saw larger eggs than I received. The turkeys hatched from the small eggs grew to be larger at maturity, though of course they were not so large when hatched.

One tom from the small eggs weighed forty-four pounds at two years old and one hen twenty-four. Those from the large eggs never got so large, though they were fine turkeys. In speaking of this to an old lady and my surprise at results, she replied: "I don't see why you should be surprised. Nature does not vary much, whether in lower animals, the feathered tribe or the human family. All depends on the blood." I believe the old lady was right. I prefer medium sized eggs, both in turkeys and chickens. I find the very large eggs hatch large young, but they are not generally as well formed and often are weak legged and while medium sized ones hatch smaller young they seem more vigorous and grow much faster. Of course there are eggs that are small to deformity—so are there those that are large to deformity. Often the last egg laid before a hen goes to sitting will be so small it will have no yolk at all. It is also true that the largest eggs are not always laid by the largest hens, though as a rule pullets lay smaller eggs than hens.

Many do not know the difference between an infertile and a rotten egg. A rotten egg is never clear and an infertile egg is always clear at hatching time and does not have an offensive odor. Eggs may rot from age or because they are not sufficiently fertilized and the germ dies before maturing, and they may rot under hens which sit well, but do not have sufficient body heat to hatch them. Again they may be set where there is too much dampness, which causes them to rot.

We are often asked if fanciers do not sell eggs too high. We think not, for several reasons. First, customers often write that from five dollars' worth of eggs they sell ten dollars' worth of turkeys and have a good breeding pen left. Second, fanciers are at great expense to hold stock enough to supply egg orders, and run much risk in holding over so many turkeys which could be sold in the spring. Third, the customers build their reputations on the fancier's work, and certainly this is worth something. You are not simply buying eggs from the fancier, but you are buying the experience of years.

CARE OF POULTS—FEEDING—LICE

I would by all means prefer a turkey hen to carry the turkeys. The natural mother is the turkey hen. She seems to understand turkey nature better than the domestic hen. There is only one advantage gained by letting the domestic hen carry the poults; they do not wander so far from home, though I think this is counteracted by the disposition of the domestic hen to wean them when they need a mother's care as much as when first hatched. And the turkey hen never begins to wander so far until the poults are as old as they are when domestic hens wean them. I find that it is the poults which lead the mothers away; they go and the mother follows.

It is a mistake to give a turkey so many poults; of course she may raise them all, but the chances are much better for her to raise all of twenty than they are for her to raise thirty to thirty-five.

When the poults hatch be careful in your management of both the young and the hen. I try to have the nest fastened very securely so that the little ones cannot get out, for they will get out of the nest and get chilled. Sometimes they hatch a day ahead of time. I look in the nest the night of the twenty-seventh day and if there are any poults I take out the shells and if there are only three or four poults I leave them in the nest; if there are six or eight I take them out and keep them in a flannel cloth in a basket in the house, as so many left in the nest will cause the hen to sit off the eggs in a hovering position. If you take out only a very few they may get chilled. In the morning I go again and remove the dry poults and egg shells. By night she will be done hatching, but as some of the poults are weak I just put a few of them in the nest with her so she will not refuse to take them in the morning. In the morning I have a quiet place ready for her and I give them to her.

I think I have at last gotten the ideal turkey coop. I found that the large coops with divisions in them were all right when the poults were very small, but when from five weeks old to the time of going on roosts, they were too crowded in the division coops. I now have coops four feet square, with height of back four feet and height of front five feet. The sides are of screen wire, the back and front of plank, with a tight board roof. These are set in the orchard and are moved to a fresh grass plot every week when the poults are very small, and every two or three days as they grow older. I have board roosts put in them as the poults want to go on roosts, and let them roost in these coops until all danger of drowning from heavy rains is past. Turkeys must have plenty of air. They cannot stand confinement in close coops. These I now have are, so far as air is concerned, as good as if they sat out, and they are safe from "varmints."

FEED FOR POULTS

I have tried almost every plan I ever heard of and have finally settled down into one way of feeding. I believe the nearer we imitate nature the more successful we will be in poultry culture. I feed very little of anything to poults, especially very little bread.

I never feed my poults until they are from twenty-four to thirty-six hours old. Then I put them out in a grass pasture in a large, roomy coop, with grass runs attached. The first feed I give is milk curd with onion tops and tongue or pepper grass cut very fine, seasoned with black pepper. I give this morning, noon and night. As they grow older I add other things to the food. Table scraps are splendid for them. If I have infertile incubator eggs later, experience teaches me the raw egg broken in the food from the first is good food, better than hard boiled eggs. I never use a fresh egg, simply because I do not consider it at all necessary. I give milk instead of drinking water when it is plentiful. Milk has all the elements of food for the human or poultry race, hence I feed all I can spare to my poultry. Heat the milk, but do not boil.

I keep grit constantly before them. Wheat is one of the finest of foods for young turkeys, but it must be pure wheat, not cheat. Cracked corn is splendid when they are older. My rule has been to mix grains of wheat in the food from the first, so that when they are old enough to change from curd to grain it will not be hard to change foods.

I have used corn chops and ship stuff, equal parts, put in the stove and made very hot, then pour cold water over it and have found it very good. Still I believe I must have some wheat mixed in. Lime should be kept where they can get it at will, but it should be lime that has been slaked a long time. I believe fresh lime will kill old and young turkeys.

As soon as they are old enough to eat whole corn give it to them, for nothing makes them grow faster and gets them ready for the show room quicker.

It is very hard to get a young turkey to change its habits of eating. If you commence feeding them in a plate it is hard to change to a pan or on the ground. The same holds true of the diet. Whatever they learn to eat at first is what they want until they are grown. If the food could be scattered and the turkeys allowed to hunt for it, it would be much better for them.

The great trouble is not so much what to feed as what not to feed. Turkeys should not be overfed; this is the mistake made by so many amateurs. They think the more they feed the faster the little ones will grow. If it were possible to raise the turkeys and keep them from the clutches of "varmints" (there is nothing more expensive), the very best way to raise them would be to give them to the hen and let her take care of them during the day and feed them just a little in the evening to keep them gentle and make them come home.

Do not allow your poults to become wild. If when you go to feed them you will call them and talk to them, they will learn to come to you anywhere. My turkeys and my Leghorns are gentle, and will come to me whenever they hear my voice. If possible, let none but a gentle hen carry young turkeys. A mild mother makes mild turkeys. "Like mother, like daughter" is certainly true of turkeys.

I find that cracked wheat put into the stove and browned as we used to brown our coffee, with just enough cold water or sweet milk poured over it when taken out of the oven to dampen it thoroughly, makes a very fine food for poults. I grind the wheat in a coffee mill. This I mix with milk curd and fine chopped onions.

Until I have fully tested it I will not give my opinion in favor of doubtful foods, and I confess I was afraid to give the corn chops used as chicken food, though I believed it would be good if fed judiciously. One season I began when the poults were four weeks old giving corn chops at night. I just dampened with cold water and I never saw turkeys thrive better in my life. Be sure you do not get that ground with the cob. It is not fit to feed either to chickens or poults.

I used blood meal one season and liked it very much. I think in order to give it I shall feed soft food at least once per week during the year. I am sure that for growing poults and chicks it is very fine. It seems to be of great benefit to them while feathering.

After turkeys are ten weeks old all that is necessary on a large grain farm is to see that they are protected at night. They will glean their own living from the fields, and while the "gude man" may complain, yet if he will only watch them closely he will be convinced they are a benefit to his crop instead of an injury. Last year the turkeys saved the corn, but the chinch-bug killed the turkeys in many localities. Turn a flock of young turkeys when from two or three months old or even five or six weeks old in your potatoes and cabbage; they will not hurt them, but will keep them free from bugs. Yet there is one kind of potato bug they seldom pick; if they do it kills them. But the cabbage worm does them no harm and they do not when young hurt the cabbage. They clean the corn of grasshoppers and glean after harvest in the wheat fields what everything else has overlooked.

Poults will not bear handling. Mine are very gentle and eat out of my hands, still I never handle them in my hands if I can avoid it. It will not do to try to raise young turkeys in the same yard with other fowls. They are so tender that chickens run over them. One snap from the bill of a domestic hen will kill a very young turkey.

What do you do with your little turkeys during a cold or wet spell?

We shut them up in the house they roost in and let them stay there if it is very wet or cold, but if not very cold we let them out on our front lawn. The grass is never very high, and as a rule the hen will hover them and keep them better than in a crowded spot. Keep little turkeys dry and warm, for if they once get wet or chilled they seldom recover. Some hens are more restless than others. If possible to avoid it never let a restless hen foster turkeys; however, one good feature about them is that they are generally of that spiteful class that will protect their little ones.

It does not hurt them to turn them out soon after a hard rain if the sun comes out warm and bright, but if it is cold and cloudy they will die from exposure and being chilled.

But if at any time they should be caught out and some seem dead when found, make a fire and warm and rub them well. Often I have brought both chicks and poults to life that seemed perfectly dead. Keep them near the fire, but do not let them get too hot, until they are entirely dry. Give each of them a cracked grain of black, or a seed of red pepper. This warms them and stimulates them.

Do not put the young turkeys out near ant holes, as the ants if swallowed sting the crop and kill the fowl, and often the ants sting the poults on the body and kill them.

Poults are greatly benefitted by having their wings and tails cut. I find they get about so much better, and if a rain comes up they do not seem to get as wet, or if they do they dry so much faster. It takes so much strength to support the long wing and tail feathers that if they are kept short until the turkeys are two months old they will be much stronger than if the wings and tail are left to grow without cutting. I cut the flight feathers about half, and the tail about the same.

There is very little expense attached to rearing turkeys, but as a rule there is a great deal of work until they are ten weeks old.

Summing up the requisites for success in raising poults may be done in the following simple words:

First, have vigorous parent stock, not over fat. Take care that the poults are not chilled the first two or three weeks of their lives. Be careful not to overfeed the poults. They require very little food for three weeks; after that time feed all they will eat three times a day until they are ready for market. If, however, you have grain fields for range they will eat very little of your food after they are six weeks old until late in the season. Be sure to keep them free from vermin. It is almost impossible to cure a droopy poult. If one is droopy, try to find the cause and remove it before the entire flock becomes afflicted. Young turkeys will do better with no human attention than with too much.

FIGHTING LICE ON POULTS AND ADULTS

I find that whitewashing the house in which my fowls are kept and keeping it thoroughly clean has been a sure preventative of vermin on my young turkeys.

Use tobacco stems and tobacco dust as follows: Smoke the roosting places with the stems and sprinkle the floors with the dust. If the coop in which the hen is put with the poults is whitewashed inside and outside before she is put in, she will not become lousy.

I swept the roosting coop every day and dusted it once a week with air-slaked lime. Lime must be dusted sparingly, for if too much is used it will make the feet sore.

When the nest has been well prepared and dusted there are seldom any lice on the little ones when hatched. But I dust the hen with Persian insect powder when I take her from the nest, being very careful to shake the dust well out so that it will not get into the eyes of the little ones, as it may make them blind.

The turkey louse is about the color of the poult and is very hard to find by one not experienced in the art of hunting them. They are between the quill (flight) feathers and are often in solid knots, and at first glance will not be discovered, as they do not move until disturbed. A little clear lard oil will kill them, but it must be very carefully used. I prefer using it at night. Dust the hen well with insect powder when you turn her out in the morning. I know most persons say at night, but I have found the powder gets into the eyes of the poults.

One thing is certain and that is that poults must be kept free from lice and mites. Then it is equally certain that if not careful in the use of remedies for these the poults may be killed. A little pure lard on the head, around vent, and on the wings, where the flight feathers come out, may be used to advantage, but too much is absolutely fatal. I would not advise the use of sulphur in lard to grease the heads. The lard is sufficient and the sulphur takes away proper use of legs; it is also liable to cause blindness. Use clear lard or thick cream. Liquid lice killer is equally dangerous if not carefully used. It may be put on the outside of the coops or a little on inside after they are a few weeks old, provided it is done in the morning and the coops are aired well during the day. Never put it on the floors, for if the hen sits over it, it will suffocate the poults. This is equally true of little chicks. I have tried it and know from experience. Yet there are no better insecticides than these liquid lice killers if properly used. They will kill mites and chiggers and everything in that line, even bedbugs, which infest hen houses in some localities.

Southern turkey breeders complain that many poults

are killed by chiggers, which do more damage than any other one thing.

We presume this is the little grass chigger which buries itself in the flesh—at least it does on people—and is very hard to exterminate and very painful to endure. We had never thought of this. The only remedy known to us is grease, and too much of that is fatal to the poults.

In the late fall and winter lice are hard on turkeys—they cannot find good dust baths as they can in summer, hence it is necessary to use our best efforts to kill

is scattered than when it is given to them in pans. I have long since discarded feeding troughs in my poultry yards. They were a disadvantage to both old and young. In my opinion much of the so-called cholera is traceable to the feeding trough. Turkeys especially are naturally inclined to take a small quantity of food at a time and when fed in troughs they will fill their crops and do not take enough exercise to cause good digestion.

For fattening I prefer corn to anything else, unless it be crushed corn. Feed whole corn on the ear or scatter it in straw so they must work to get it.

A Group of Hungarian Turkeys

the vermin on them, for they cannot thrive with vermin sapping their strength.

PREPARING TURKEYS FOR MARKET

Many persons wish to know when to begin to prepare turkeys for market. The best time to begin is when they are hatched and keep up the preparation until they are put on the market. If you live on a grain or stock farm let your turkeys have free access to the feeding stalls and grain shocks and they will take care of themselves. If you, like myself, are limited to a small place, the feeding must be kept up all the year. It will not do to increase the food too rapidly at first. During the summer feed adult turkeys only once a day, but about September I begin feeding them twice a day, morning and evening, all that they will eat, or rather, as I keep the parent stock in the pens, my plan has been to scatter the food in the morning so that they shall be kept busy all day hunting for it. At night I give a full feed where they can get it without any trouble, and gradually increase the quantity of food as the cold weather approaches. I find that both old and young turkeys thrive better and eat more when the food

If you have never noticed the necessity of lime for turkeys watch them pick whitewash off the sides of houses. Make this difference in the treatment of those intended for market and those kept to breed from: Put all the food before the market fowl it will eat; make it as fat as possible—but if you get your breeding stock too fat, infertile eggs will be the result.

Be sure you do not wait until the day before Thanksgiving to try to sell your stock. The highest prices are usually obtainable the week before the holiday feasts. As a rule there is a great rush to market with turkeys two days before Thanksgiving. The rush often causes the price to drop just when the most was expected. I have known the highest prices to be obtained between Thanksgiving and Christmas and in February. Of course the locality has something to do with the price, and there may, in the same locality, be different influences at different seasons. We have to do as our husbands do with their stock, watch and sell at the most propitious time. If I had only a few I would sell all at once, but if I raised from seventy-five to a hundred I should sell at different times. One can sell the oldest first, thus giving the younger ones a chance. Market birds can not be too fat, but they may be too heavy for the highest prices. A few farmers in our county understand this, and do not buy the largest toms to breed from; others run to the other extreme, inbreeding and buying culls until their turkeys are too small to be profitable. I should prefer large breeding stock to small, even if I sold on the market, for if I get a lower price the difference in pounds would more than make the difference in price.

How much ought young toms to weigh at Thanksgiving, is a question often asked me. That depends on when they were hatched. An early hatched, say one hatched in May, will weigh from twenty to twenty-four pounds, and some few will go higher. One market poultryman says that an average of eighteen and twenty pounds is the rule, while those going above that are the exception.

I have been asked if I think it better to dress turkeys or sell them on foot; "which is the most profitable?" The answer to this (as most answers are) is dependent. I have a friend who dresses her turkeys about the middle of February for the St. Louis market. She says she makes money by so doing. I know others who say it does not pay them at all.

The cause of the difference of opinion lies in the difference of surroundings. The lady who says it pays her to dress her turkeys for market does the work herself and says she makes fair wages at the difference in the price between dressed turkeys and turkeys on foot. My opinion is that the average farmer's wife had better sell her turkeys on foot, but this is a question upon which there is a difference of opinion and one which each one must decide for herself.

I never sold a dressed turkey, yet I know how farmers' wives dress them for our market, and I dress them for my own table the same way. We cut the heads off and let them bleed well and then dry pick them and remove their entrails, washing them thoroughly with cold or luke warm water. Plump the carcass by pouring boiling water over it, then salt and let it freeze before cooking, if possible. Very few salt them to put them on the market.

Talk about turkeys eating their heads off! If a man sells hogs at five cents a pound he thinks he is doing a fine business, says he is getting fifty cents a bushel for his corn, but when a woman sells her turkeys even at eight cents a pound she is doing far better and is doing her husband a double favor; it is a favor to him for her to pay her own and part of his bills; besides she gets eight cents a pound for grasshoppers, which but for her turkeys would destroy the corn fodder and injure the hay as well as ruin the cabbage.

PREPARING TURKEYS FOR EXHIBITION

This one thing I never lose sight of or forget—the show room. Not alone for the scores I wish to receive on my birds, but on account of the remembrance of what I gain at the shows in point of knowledge and the pleasure I derive from association with the many noble men and women to be met there.

Many timid ones are deterred from entering the show room because they dread coming in competition with the moguls of the poultry business. To such I say, come! You have nothing to lose by the comparison and you may be a winner of the prizes. At any rate you will know what the judges think of your birds, and will learn how to improve your stock. The show room is an educator and we need all the education we can get if we intend to stay in the business. Nor does it follow that because they fail to win a prize your stock is poor. You

will learn what it takes to make a prize bird and what constitutes a good breeding bird. Attend a poultry show or two each year if it is possible for you to do so.

On large farms it is not necessary to begin heavy feeding until the weather begins to get cool. But where one has limited room they must be fed the year round. Do not select show birds until they are through molting, if old birds are exhibited. A breeder of thoroughbred turkeys, for sale as fancy stock, must feed his entire flock with an aim to getting them in condition for winter shows either in his own hands or in the hands of his customers.

Generally cocks may be depended on molting true to the marking of the cockerel, but hens often are not as good in markings as they were as pullets. Still, I think turkeys are more regular in their markings after molting than chickens.

If a turkey is in a healthy condition the feathers will be glossy, if not, they will not be.

I think that to keep turkeys healthy and gentle and well fed is about all the preparation turkeys need. It will not do to put them in confinement longer than ten days, and then it will not do to have them in a strange place, as they will not eat. Give them all the corn, grit and lime they will eat, with plenty of grass and water, and they will fatten.

How do I manage to feed my turkeys to get them in weight for the shows and not get the entire flock too fat? I keep only a few turkeys on my home place at one time, not more than fifty to seventy-five in winter and only my breeding stock in summer. As I am continually shipping them I select the best in size and that leaves the smaller ones a better chance to grow. I cannot separate those intended for the show room from the others, so I feed all alike and take the heaviest to the show, no matter if they are not so well marked as the others, for it is the heavy turkey which wins in the show room. In fact, I have only a few times taken my best marked turkeys to a show.

I have had very few persons come to my yards who knew how to catch a turkey or chicken. I can pick my turkeys or chickens up anywhere in the yard with the assistance of one whom I have trained. In the first place I am very gentle with my fowls. I talk to them when I feed them. You may wonder what I say. Well, I find they are like the human race, susceptible to flattery, if flattery it may be called; I do not intend it as such, for I mean every word of it. I call them pretty things—tell them they are the prettiest turkeys anywhere around—talk to them about going to the shows, and tell them how they must behave to appear well; in fact, I am never at a loss for something to say to my fowls. When I want to catch one I prefer to go out in the yard, look the flock over while they are out, select the one I want, call my assistant, and point out the turkey. Then I begin to feed and usually I can catch the one I desire while they are eating. Never rush into the flock or shoo a turkey. Very quietly step up behind it and catch it by the legs. Be sure to take hold of both legs as you catch one, then you can easily pick the bird up and it will not flap its wings and hurt itself. If there are several to catch and you do not wish to put them in different coops it is better to catch all you need before cooping any. A child can hold a forty pound tom if he knows how. Just lay him flat on his side or breast and hold his legs close to the thighs and he will not attempt to get away. I have often released one after holding it in this manner, and it would lie still for one or two minutes before getting up.

PACKING EGGS FOR SHIPPING

It may sound egotistical, but I believe I can pack eggs that will go around the globe without breaking, that is, with reasonable handling; yet last year the only chick eggs reported broken did not go two hundred miles, and had they not been sent to a relative as a present I presume I should have heard about them with no

Standard Bred Bronze Turkey wing as bred by Mrs. U. R. Fishel.

uncertain sound. They evidently had been pitched off the car as baggage and crushed under some heavy body.

First line the basket with paper, then put in an inch of hay chaff in bottom if it is a large basket and many eggs are to go in; if it is only a peck basket, three-fourths or a half of an inch will be sufficient, but it must have a soft padding at bottom. Re-line with a good heavy paper. Wrap each egg with paper, but do not wrap too tight; use plenty of paper and do it nicely. I always pack with the small end down, because the white is in the small end and the yolk will not break if allowed to float upon it, while if the large end is down there is nothing to prevent the yolk breaking from the jar of the travel. Of course if the yolk is broken the egg cannot hatch.

Diseases of Turkeys

CANKER

I receive a great many questions as to what to do for sick poults. I am a poor doctor for little turkeys. I really believe that where the parent stock is not related or inbred that it is poor management where there are sick poults.

Canker is more prevalent than many persons suppose, and while often a fowl may die before it is discovered, the rule is it becomes droopy and refuses to eat. The discharges become yellowish green, sometimes looking like the yellow of an egg. The canker extends often to the throat and frequently forms on the tongue at the opening of the wind pipe and stops the air passages.

To cure canker I have found Mustang Liniment better than anything else I have ever used. If this cannot be obtained, wash in a strong copperas water and grease with carbolated vaseline, in which put a few drops of tincture of iodine. This is an effectual cure, but it takes longer treatment and is more trouble. But the fowl, turkey or chicken will need a tonic to correct the

digestion and tone the system. I give a liver pill, any that I would use for a person. Give this at night and a two-grain quinine capsule in the morning. A little copperas and extract of logwood in the drinking water usually cure the trouble. Use whatever poultry tonic or cholera cure you may deem best mixed in food. Make into long rolls and put down the throat, then give the water from a bottle. I also put grit in food. Feed only once a day while the food must be given, but when the turkey can pick food, give twice a day and separate from other fowls. If I use Mustang Liniment I put a few drops down the throat, for I think often the canker extends through the system.

If I am sure there is no canker I omit the treatment for that and give the other treatment. Do not let the fowl have anything to eat or drink which is not medicated until you know it is well. The quinine capsule may be given every morning for a week, the liver pill every other day until three are given.

I have never lost a turkey under the foregoing treatment when I have been able to give it regularly. And several customers have reported that under my directions they have saved their turkeys.

GAPES

To prevent the disease I use a little turpentine in the drinking water. A dash of flowers of sulphur in the food once a week will be beneficial until they are well feathered. Copperas in the drinking water and onions in the food will generally prevent gapes. Turkeys having vermin are more likely to be affected. I have been advised to use sour cream instead of lard to grease young turkeys.

If I find the poults have gapes I put Dalmation or Persian insect powder in the food and have no further trouble. I sprinkle the powder into the food just as I would pepper. I have cured several chicks of the gapes by first puffing the powder in the wind pipe. This kills the worms, and I extract them with a gape extractor made of a piece of soft grass. If the worms are taken out the chicken will recover unless it is injured by the operation. They are easier to take out dead than alive and I find the powder good, but one has to be careful not to get too much in the wind pipe or the poult or chick will not be able to breathe.

AIR PUFF

One night I noticed that the neck of one of my young turkeys was so badly swollen it could not get its mouth to the ground to eat. I picked it up and found its whole body in the same condition. The skin only seemed puffed. I took a pair of sharp scissors and clipped the skin in several places. The air escaped and the turkey began to chirp. I put it with the others and it ate heartily. I put a teaspoonful of coal oil in the drinking water with a few drops of carbolic acid.

The next morning I noticed its wings drooping down and it was as badly puffed as before. I repeated the clipping and this time I clipped around the neck; I went deeper than I intended and the neck began to bleed freely. I felt that this would kill it, but I knew it would die anyway if not relieved, so I did not grieve. I took a feather and dipped it in tar and covered the bleeding wound, then I greased it with pure lard. My husband said: "You have killed that turkey." I replied: "Yes, I think I have, but I was trying to save it." To my astonishment it came up that night as lively as any of the others. I cut both wings and in the morning I showed it to my husband. We were both surprised. Ten days after it was as strong to all appearances as any of the others and it never puffed afterward. I concluded the bleeding was good for it, yet I would not know just how to advise it to be done, as I did that by accident.

BUMBLEFOOT

Bumblefoot is a hard place on the bottom of the foot which often becomes very sore and contains pus. It is claimed that it is usually caused by the fowls roosting high and coming down on the ground with such force as to bruise the foot. I am inclined to favor this theory, though some high in authority deny it. At any rate, turkeys and chickens are often found with feet in this condition. I wait until the sore becomes soft, open it with a sharp knife and squeeze it until all the pus and the core, if I can get it, run out. If the core does not come out it will run out in a few days if the foot is bound up with a good salve.

I find one of the best salves I ever used to be vaseline, turpentine, a few drops of crude carbolic acid and tincture of iodine. I cannot give the proportions because I do not measure or drop by count. I generally make about a teacup full in the fall or early winter and it lasts me all season. A friend told me that resin would add to its merits. I put the ingredients all on the stove and mix them together and the next time I make this salve I think I shall add the resin.

Salve is also good for sore head, but it is better to wash the head with copperas water before using the salve. If you can afford to buy Mexican Mustang Liniment it is even better than salve, but one often does not have the liniment at hand and can make the salve.

BOWEL TROUBLE

The coops in which the poults roost must have plenty of fresh air as well as be rat proof. If the weather is cold and damp they must be kept in pens, so they can be hovered by the hen If she is at liberty she is liable to walk around in the weeds or grass and the poults will chill and become loose in the bowels. And they generally die when this disease is caused by the above treatment. However, if they are not too much chilled, pen them up, make a very weak pepper tea and give this for drinking water. Sweet milk is a good remedy for bowel trouble with poults.

If you do not overfeed your young birds nor give them too much water while young, and do not let them get wet and chilled, thereby contracting cold, they will not have bowel trouble. They are not so apt to drink too much where they can run at large as they are when kept in confinement. When running at large I keep water where they can have access to it, but when penned up I give them a drink only three times a day.

Do not let the poults get wet. I am trying to plan a way to have them roost on a dirt floor, yet not on damp earth. I think the dampness of the ground gives them rheumatism, or makes them delicate, but the hen mashes the poults on a plank floor. I think if the dirt can be thrown up around the coop, so as to keep the ground dry, it will be better.

Where milk curd, seasoned with black pepper and salt, is fed for the first ten days, there will be no danger of loose bowels, provided other health precautions are observed. Lice will cause bowel trouble, as will too much heat. When caused by heat give a teaspoonful of carbolic acid in a gallon of water.

Keep the drinking fountains clean and fresh. This can be done by washing them out with carbolized water.

Logwood is excellent for loose bowels. I have used and recommended it for years. There is no danger of using too much and there is nothing better for ordinary bowel trouble either in chicks, poults or grown fowls. It comes by the pound in boxes and sells here at ten cents per pound. I put a lump of it in a glass fruit jar, using as large a lump as I can get into the jar and pour warm (not hot) water over it. Every morning I put just enough of this into the drinking water to color it and it keeps the bowels in a healthy condition. If fowls are sick I use it stronger.

Overfeeding produces indigestion and indigestion causes bowel trouble. Vermin and overfeeding kill more poults than all other causes. Lice will produce all the symptoms of disease. When a poult dies from overfeeding a post mortem will usually disclose the liver swollen and probably splotched. When it is in this condition there is no chance for the poult. If taken in time a radical change of diet will effect a cure.

HOT MASHES

A lady in Maryland writes: "I can't agree with you that hot mashes cause roup, for in my native home (Canada) I fed my turkeys hot mashes from the time they were a few weeks old until they were grown, and so did my neighbors, and we raised large flocks and were never troubled with roup. Here I have not fed the mash and have the roup." Roosting in trees may be the cause of roup in her flocks now, as she says they never had it when roosting under shelter. I agree with her that in extreme climates a shelter is better. She also gives me a preventative for fighting which I certainly shall use. I

A Fine Mammoth Bronze Turkey Tom from the Yards of Mrs. U. R. Fishel.

give it to the readers of this book: Tie a small bell around the neck of toms showing a disposition to fight. The noise attracts their attention so they forget to fight.

CROP BOUND

In the early spring the trouble most to be dreaded with turkeys is crop bound, caused from eating dry grass. No one can prevent this unless they have green fields or grain for them to run in, rye or wheat fields. Even then sometimes they will fill their crops with the dry grass, which forms a hard ball in the crop and unless it can be made to pass, it will kill the fowl. Sometimes it will pass out after awhile without any treatment. Some recommend cutting the crop, taking the substance out and sewing up the crop, and they say it never fails to cure. This may be true with experts at the business, but with me it is a total failure. I tried it and thought it was a success, but several weeks afterward I discovered that the crops had never grown together where they were cut open and the thread rotted out, so they died. I have lost some of the finest turkeys I ever owned from this trouble and have cured others seemingly as bad off.

I have not found an infallible cure and the most effectual cure I have found is very tedious. I give the turkey a dose of castor oil or Epsom salts as soon as I find it has the trouble. I hold it and pour all the water into the crop I think it safe to give and I also put a tablespoonful of mica crystal grit in some soft food, make it in long rolls and put down the throat. Turkeys are easily choked and unless the food is made in long, slender rolls they are liable to choke. The reason I put the grit in the food is that it is liable to go down the wind pipe if poured into the mouth alone. Then I very gently get hold of the ball in the crop from the outside and work it with both hands, having someone else hold the turkey. I can generally soften the ball very perceptibly the first time I treat the turkey. The grit in the food gets into the softened parts and helps divide the ball, the oil takes all that it is possible to get out of the crop, out of the system so that it does not clog in the gizzard, as it is liable to do if not worked off immediately. The working must be very gently done, as it bruises the crop. I repeat this process every morning at first and give plenty of soft food and grit during the day.

If I discover, as is often the case, that the turkey is getting weak, I give a two-grain capsule of quinine every morning. This increases the appetite and gives strength to the bird. I give plenty of onions in the food. The treatment must be kept up until all the ball has entirely passed out of the system. I do not give the oil more than once a week after the first few days.

One of the best toms I ever owned, a full brother to "Champ Clark," who scored from 97 to 98 by every judge who saw him, was crop bound, and as I had sold "Champ Clark" I was anxious to save the brother, which I considered just as good. I thought he was entirely cured, and he was to all appearances well. He had gained flesh and was as hearty as any bird on the place. I fed him at night and noticed how well he looked. The next morning I found him dead under the roost. He weighed forty pounds and of course looked finer after death than I had considered him in life. My only consolation was that he had waited until after the breeding season was almost over before he died.

On examination I found that a ball (not a very large one, either) of dried grass had lodged in the vent, which prevented anything from passing, and this caused his death. He had been from under treatment about two months and I believed if I had continued the oil once a week he would have lived.

Once I noticed a turkey with the same symptoms, but all my treatment availed nothing and he died. I examined him and found the gizzard packed with dry grass and so nothing could have saved him.

"My turkeys are affected with what I call pendant crop. The crop hangs down like a bag, sometimes low enough to interfere with walking and is filled with dark liquid. The turkeys eat, but are pale about the head. What shall I do for them?"

Give them a teaspoonful of baking powder: soda will not do. This is a dose for one old turkey. I do not find the baking powder an infallible cure, but it is the best thing I have tried. Two doses usually cure. Keep the turkey inclosed and do not feed until the powder has been in the crop an hour or two; then give soft food, wheat bread made into long rolls, and put down the throat. The roll must not be very large. Do not give any water until the liquid has passed out of the crop. A little salt mixed in the food will assist in carrying the impurities out of the system. Epsom salts are better than oil for crop-bound fowls. You will have to be very careful to keep water from them until they have entirely recovered, or the crop will refill and the second attack is always worse or more stubborn than the first. It is very unusual for this trouble to arise in summer. It is prevalent during the latter part of winter and early spring.

CHOLERA

The cry of cholera among turkeys comes to me from many persons, and these are not confined to a given locality or state. From Mississippi, Wisconsin, Pennsylvania, Iowa and many other states I have received letters reporting cholera among turkeys and often they say there are no symptoms of the trouble among the chickens. The fact that the turkeys linger for days and sometimes even weeks is one reason for believing it is not cholera. Another is that in many instances the chickens and turkeys are in the same yard and the chickens are not affected; then, again, about the only symptom common to all inquiries is that the droppings are a yellowish green. Some describe the heads as black, saying they mope around and will not eat. Others say the head is red to the last and they eat up to a few minutes before they are seized with an attack like convulsions, and still others say they have puffs under the eyes, while another flock has a white substance floating over the eye.

It is a fact that almost any disease of a turkey will cause the droppings to become yellowish green, showing that disease in turkeys, like disease in the human family, sooner or later affects the digestive organs.

Often indigestion is the cause of the trouble. I am not quite positively certain that I ever had a genuine case of cholera in my yards, though I well remember when I thought every chicken or turkey that died had it.

I have been informed by one of the R. P. J. correspondents that there is a much larger per cent of deaths from what is known as black head than from cholera, and that it is infectious. He says that what has often been pronounced cholera is black head. He also informs me there is absolutely no remedy for it which can be relied upon to be even comparatively a cure, and that the cause is unknown. This he wrote me some time since. He said that Lee's Germozone is the best remedy known to him. I had some experience with the trouble in the flock of a neighbor, and I decided it was caused from overfeeding while young, and then turning them out without any food; at least I found when I examined after death that the liver was perfectly soft and the gizzard twice the size it should have been.

I find many persons use a great deal of red or cayenne pepper and soda in turkey food. Because I had been taught to do this I did like my neighbors when I commenced raising turkeys, but I soon began to use my common sense and I wondered how on earth anything could live, especially a wee bit of a turkey with the crop filled with pepper, soda, sulphur, copperas, also custard, milk curd and many other things I was told I would have to feed to be successful. I said: "I shall try a way of my own," and whenever I have had the sense to do my own way I have succeeded in keeping my flock healthy.

Red pepper is a good tonic for chickens in cold weather if given in minute quantities.

I find carbolic acid in drinking water, a teaspoonful to a gallon of water, is one of the best things to keep their bowels in good condition I have ever tried. Epsom salts and salt, a teaspoonful of each to a gallon of water, is also good. Too much salt will throw a turkey into fits, so will too much tobacco, but they will recover from the tobacco dust as soon as they get the fresh air, while from salt taken into the system they do not recover.

Whenever the droppings look yellowish I use my Cholera Cure—not that I believe they have cholera, but the droppings indicate indigestion.

RHEUMATISM

Several letters have come in, asking what to do for lameness in little turkeys, describing the poults as being affected with swollen joints. I think this trouble arises from dampness. Either the poults roost in damp places or exceedingly wet weather has been conducive to the disease. The trouble is doubtless rheumatism and the best remedy I know is elder bark prepared as follows: Get the bark and scrape off the outside skin, cut in small pieces and put in apple vinegar. It does not matter how much bark you put in, but the stronger it is the better. Put in a half gallon fruit jar and add a piece of alum as large as a walnut and the same amount of copperas. Put all the bark in the jar you can get in, pouring the vinegar over it. Put enough of this liquid in the drinking water to make it taste of acid, but not enough to be unpleasant to the taste. I am sure this will prevent the trouble if it does not cure it, and I think it will cure it, provided the poults are kept free from dampness. I should use Mustang also or any good liniment that I would use for myself. A little tincture of iodine in the drinking water is good as a tonic.

I should feed either a little black or red pepper in the food for several days. In that time if I found I could not cure the fowl I would kill it, but if it were getting better I should continue the treatment.

Once I noticed one of my poults could not walk, one leg seemed to be perfectly straight and the poult held it so that it appeared to be behind it. I tried to bend it and it seemed stiff in the joints. But I bent it several times a day for four days when it was able to walk on both feet.

ROUP CANKER—SWELLED EYES AND HEAD

I have cured several cases of so-called roup in the following manner. I made a strong salt water just as hot as I could bear my hand in comfortably and dipped the turkey's head in it, completely immersing the head. I use an old tin can for this purpose. I let the head stay in the water as long as I thought it safe for the turkey. I then take it out and give it fresh air, press the nostrils between my thumb and forefinger. If there is any secretion, this will start a running at the nose. I open the mouth and insert a mop made by wrapping a soft cloth on a small stick, into the opening in the roof of the mouth, dipping it first into salt water; then I dip in coal oil. I make a salve of carbolic acid, a few drops of lard, spirits of camphor, a teaspoonful, a teaspoonful of tincture of iodine and anoint the eyes, head and fill the nostrils and opening in roof of mouth. With a clean cloth I wiped the head as dry as possible, (I tried not wiping

the head and found it made the turkey too cold) then I rubbed it hard until it was dry. Put a little salt and Epsom salts in the drinking water. This will almost invariably cure the roup in its first stages. If a turkey has arrived at an advanced stage of roup before it is noticed I would kill it as the only sure cure.

For rattling in the throat I find nothing better than coal oil with a little molasses in it.

Sometimes canker is caused by fighting. I had a tom, for which I had paid $10, that got to fighting and had canker on the side of his mouth, caused by the bite of the other tom. All I did for him was to paint his mouth with iodine. He was a vigorous, healthy bird and produced strong poults. I also advise the use of Mexican Mustang Liniment, used according to directions.

Sometimes turkeys have a soft, swelled place under the eyes. The first thing is to put them by themselves. With the finger press the soft swelling, letting the pressure go towards the bill. The phlegm will go out at the nose in most cases. Take a sewing machine oil can and fill with warm water, into which a few drops of tincture of iodine have been dropped; if the water is almost hot it will be all the better. After washing the head in strong salt water as hot as can be borne, inject the water from the can into the nostrils and the opening in the roof of the mouth. Make a salve of lard, turpentine, crude carbolic acid, copperas melted in the lard and flowers of sulphur. Anoint with this. If this is done once a day for a week the turkey will be well unless it is incurable. If there is pus, an incision made with a sharp knife to let the pus out will be necessary. But the bird will need something to cleanse the system, and Cushman's Roup Cure will be very fine.

However, the trouble is likely to return if you turn the turkey out in the cold. If it is worth the trouble it is better to keep it in the house until cold weather is over. Feed onions, soft food, corn and plenty of grit. I find Littell's liquid sulphur will do for flowers of sulphur in almost every case where flowers of sulphur is needed. I think simple remedies will cure almost any trouble if taken in time. Do not fail to give onions once a week during the fall and throughout the winter. They are a safeguard against roup and any diseases caused by cold.

For canker sores try putting a little alum in the drinking water one day and copperas the next.

WORMS

"My turkeys are dying fast and I found worms in the droppings. What must I do for them?"

If the entire flock is sick, give turpentine in drinking water and in the food—a tablespoonful of turpentine to a gallon of water and a teaspoonful to a quart of food; also add a tablespoonful of Epsom salts to a gallon of water. Give both the turpentine and salts at the same time. If only one turkey is thus affected I would catch it and give it a teaspoonful of castor oil, into which put five or six drops of turpentine; then feed as a tonic cholera cure.

MISCELLANEOUS

I quote from an old number of the R. P. J. from an article on "Turkeys as Hatchers":

"When I first read in an English poultry book of the French method of using turkeys to hatch and care for chickens, I had no incubator and concluded to try the plan. Late in the fall I sent out in the country and bought a late hatched hen turkey for very little money. In February we prepared a box (with plenty of chaff over a layer of horse manure) that could be shut up to exclude the light. Did not give either wine or whiskey, but in two or three weeks she was sitting quietly on the china eggs and when taken off the nest to be fed would voluntarily return. I then filled the nest with hens' eggs, removing them as soon as they began to pip to keep the turkey from wanting to leave the nest and putting in other eggs. After sitting three months she was put in a yard with chickens for the rest of the summer. We put chickens of different ages with her and she received them all with equal kindness.

"This year we have two turkeys besides an incubator, and after hatching three sittings of eggs we thought best to take them off the nest, but one watched her chance and went back on the nest till I filled it with eggs again, so I let her stay. The other is laying and will be ready for work later if needed.

"They make careful, patient mothers, are equal in that respect to any hen, and it is a wonder that farmers do not make more use of them than they do.

C. H. A."

FARMING OUT TURKEYS

I am often asked if I find it satisfactory to farm out my turkeys. It is perfectly satisfactory, because I have no one to raise turkeys for me who is not in all respects reliable; besides they hatch them earlier than I can, as the twenty-five or thirty hens kept at home do not lay eggs any faster than I have calls for them from the time they begin laying until the first of June. I have young turkeys now out on the farms that one has to look at the second time to be sure whether they are hens or young turkeys. Farm-bred turkeys do not get very fat, consequently do not weigh as heavy when I take them as I would make them weigh to please those who demand the pounds of flesh, but the frame is there. Be sure you know with whom you are placing your stock and you will have no difficulty.

Each season teaches us some lesson that is profitable to us for the next. I have learned to take only one flock of hens and pullets and another of toms on the place at one time. When two or more flocks are brought in at the same time they fight so they will not eat and do not fatten. I find it better to pay board for a few flocks on the farms than to bring them together on the home place. I could not raise all my stock at home and furnish pairs and trios not related, nor could I ship as I now do to the same customers every year and insure a change of blood.

To those persons who have written me, asking if I think it will pay to raise turkeys, I can only say that I have never heard any one who has given it a fair trial say that it does not pay. Still I would not advise one to undertake to raise turkeys who is not willing or physically able to expose himself to all sorts of weather, both hot and cold. Turkeys must be kept dry while young and gotten home early in the afternoon.

How shall you succeed with turkeys? The best way to succeed is to keep on trying. If you fail this year, get more in earnest and try again next year.

Across the Atlantic   *Photo by F. L. Sewell*

A flock of Black Turkeys and Faverolles in a quaint old French Barnyard.
Many who have supposed the turkey strictly an American Fowl will study with interest the above illustration and the one on page 54.

THE METHOD OF A SUCCESSFUL BREEDER

Introduce New Blood Each Year—Keep Poults Dry And Free From Lice—Feed Carefully—Do Not Crowd

MRS. H. R. SCHLOTZHAUER

THE first lesson that should be learned by every turkey breeder is that it does not pay to inbreed. New blood must be infused every year, otherwise the flock will lose strength, size and vigor and be more subject to disease. We generally get our new blood by buying eggs from the breeder of the best stock we are able to locate. We have to pay one dollar per egg or ten dollars per dozen. In this manner we do not inbreed and we find that the vigor and size of our flock is maintained without trouble. We have had young toms that weighed forty pounds when nine months old and pullets that weighed twenty-five pounds when the same age.

BREEDERS

We have fenced in our orchard and in this is kept our best breeding pen, which consists of a fine fifty pound, one year old tom and five nice, large, one year old hens. By keeping them confined in this manner we are able to find every egg that they lay.

Do not try to fatten turkeys during hot weather. If they are on free range or in a good orchard where they can find plenty of nature's food, just feed them at night and let them forage during the day. In this manner they can be kept in good breeding condition.

HATCHING AND FEEDING THE POULTS

It is much better to keep the turkeys away from the other poultry.

Just as soon as we get fifty eggs, we set them under one turkey hen and three chicken hens and as soon as we get forty more, we do as before.

At this writing, June first, we have eighty nice, strong, little poults doing fine. The first hatch of forty-five we gave to one turkey hen which is confined in the orchard and through which she takes her brood from one end to the other. The second hatch is with another turkey hen and is kept in the front yard.

We have a rat proof house, 8x10, with a window for each brood. We keep them shut in until the dew is off the grass in the morning and on rainy days they are kept shut in all day. I dust them every week with a good insect powder.

The little poults get their first feed when they are about thirty-six hours old. This feed consists of stale light bread, that has been soaked in sweet milk and mixed with a little lettuce or onion tops chopped fine and seasoned with a little pepper.

After a week or so, they get some cottage cheese mixed with rolled oats. When they are about two weeks old, we mix in some clean wheat, gradually changing until they are getting all wheat.

We put them on free range when they are about one month old, but see that they come up to the orchard

MAMMOTH BRONZE TURKEYS ON THE FARM

A flock of Mrs. U. R. Fishel's Mammoth Bronze Turkey gobblers on the farm in Indiana. These big fellows weigh on an average thirty-five pounds each. As small as they are here the fine wing barring can be seen.

every night to roost.

Good grit, oyster shell, charcoal and fresh water should not be forgotten as an important part of their ration.

It is a pleasure to see them grow, and when Thanksgiving comes, we cannot help but feel proud of our turkeys.

We raise from fifty to one hundred each year and sell a good many for breeding purposes. We also sell quite a lot at market prices and consider that there is a good profit in raising turkeys for market.

We send some of our best ones to the poultry shows and State fair each year. If one sends turkeys to a fair or show, they should be sent in cages or coops, about 4x4, as the coops furnished by the show associations are not large enough, as a rule.

When cold weather comes on it is safe to feed them a little heavier and if possible get them to standard weight and a little above. First get the frame and then you can put on the meat.

We trust that our methods may be of benefit to some amateur and help him to success.

THE POPULAR BRONZE TURKEY

Improvement—Avoid Extremely Large Ones As Breeders—Selection of Breeders—Feeding—Varmints—Lice—
Feeding Poults—Selling and Shipping

EMMET F. PULLIN, Secretary-Treasurer, National Bronze Turkey Club

THE date of our first connection with the Bronze Turkey is lost in the haze of early recollection. We first began breeding pure strains of this breed in 1895.

WONDERFUL IMPROVEMENT

There has been considerable improvement in fancy points since then. Toms with bronze on their backs then, were remarkable, now we occasionally see pullets almost as rich in that section. We see better tails and wings, less green and brass, and more bronze in tail coverts. The white tips have also been considerably improved. In our opinion, the practical points have not

**Standard-Bred Bronze Turkey
Wing**

This cut was made from a photograph of one of Mrs. U. R. Fishel's Bronze Turkeys, the wing being spread to show the remarkable barring.

been improved. As a market fowl the bronze turkey leaves nothing to be desired either in appearance or merit.

GETTING THEM TOO LARGE

The one thing that has threatened to rob the breed of its universal popularity has been the craze to increase its weight, which is already in excess of any other breed. Extra large toms often wound and sometimes kill outright, females in the breeding season. Extra large hens produce a small percentage of eggs that will hatch. Ill-shaped, thin or soft shelled eggs are invariably the product of large, generally very large hens. Thus you see, nature would eliminate the overgrown. They are not in favor in market circles, the final testing of the great majority. The young that survive from the extra large stock, require

more time to mature than the medium sized ones. The former are seldom ready for the Thanksgiving market, the most profitable time to sell, because thus far they have required very little grain. From then on to Christmas market they must be fed liberally. Much more could be written under this heading, but we think the present will suffice to show the folly of going to extremes.

SELECTING THE BREEDERS

As the future usefulness of the breed depends largely upon the specimens selected to reproduce their kind, the selection of breeders is of vast importance. The first essential in a cockerel to head the flock, is vitality. This is indicated by a full breast, wide back at butts of wings and a good depth from back to point of breast bone. A willingness to display his bronze and vocal ability at a slight provocation are further evidence; avoid sluggards. Choose those with snap. Years of experience convinces the writer that the weight demanded by the present Standard is sufficient. Avoid extremes.

The same general principles hold good in selecting pullets as in cockerels. Choose those that are well developed, having plump, well-rounded bodies. If the aim of your selection is to produce prize winners as well as market fowls, the complication of your undertaking is increased many times. Success in this direction requires long experience, a study of the Standard, and some acquaintance with the laws of inheritance. If the theory that like produces like, were infallible, plain sailing would be assured, but it is not. There is a constant variation, otherwise there could be no improvement. The breeder with ability to properly value the importance of every section, has accomplished a fine art, but he who can take those that are of a high class and mate them so they will produce a large percentage of show birds, is several rounds higher up the ladder of turkey fame. They will stand a limited amount of inbreeding with good results. Those that prove themselves remarkable breeders and are not too large, are profitable to six or eight years old.

FEEDING

The tendency in the corn belt is to get breeders too fat. We think better results would follow if no corn at all were allowed. Wheat, oats, buckwheat, peas and the like, make good feed, which should be given rather sparingly. They must have gravel and oyster shell in the laying season.

REMEDIES FOR TURKEY PESTS

In some localities crows are a great nuisance and their elusive smartness is hard to match. Our remedy is to take a few hen eggs, break a hole in one end, take out part of the contents, put in a small quantity of strychnine or arsenic and stir well. Place where the turkeys are not liable to find them, or the wrong birds may get the dose.

A small handful of some good lice or insect powder should be put in the nest, or better yet, on the hen if that can be done without too much danger of breaking the eggs. For lice on the young we think the following by far the best. Take a bottle and fill one-fourth full with fish berries, finish with alcohol and let stand twenty-four hours; apply with a small brush. A small quantity is sufficient and sure death to lice.

CARING FOR THE POULTS

Provide a pen or some grassy spot about 8x10 feet, 2 feet high, covered with wire netting for the brood. The first feed may be hard boiled eggs with onions chopped fine. Another splendid feed is dried bread moistened in whole milk, squeezed almost dry; to either feed, some powdered charcoal should be added, which serves as grit and prevents sourness of the crop, the cause of many deaths. Later, cracked wheat and other small grains such as chickens thrive on may be used. Little care will be required through the summer season. It will not be out of place to offer them some grain in the evenings when they return from their foraging expedition. They

rid the fields of large quantities of weed seed and injurious insects. When the supply of these becomes short in autumn, nothing is better than corn.

SELLING AND SHIPPING

Our method is to sell on the market all stock which we think unworthy to be used as breeders. In shipping breeders, we prefer to use narrow boxes without cracks, except on top; the sides may be lined with paper to prevent undue mussing of the wings.

On long journeys, a feed box and water vessel should be placed in the front end. In such crates, we have shipped to the Pacific coast, where turkeys arrived in splendid shape. We do not take any special pains to prepare specimens for shows. A long pole supplied with a leg hook is used in catching them. We have probably produced some of the largest toms of the breed, one weighing fifty-two and one-half pounds, another weighing fifty-one and taking first in one of the large shows, where we refused a high price for him. However, we have learned a good many things about extra large turkeys since then.

Other delicacies may have their day, but a Christmas without a Christmas tree or a Fourth of July without ice cream would be no more lacking than a Thanksgiving without turkey, when from the newsboy in the street to the President in the White House this is the most popular bird in the United States.

TURKEYS FOR PROFIT

Turkeys in Demand—Varieties—Enclose the Breeders—Fencing—Mating and Housing—Overfeeding—Late Hatched Turkeys—Green Food for Growth—Freeing From Lice—Results of Line Breeding—Supply Grit Observation and Care Necessary to Success

MRS. CHARLES JONES

TURKEYS have been raised longer than the memory of those now living can trace and still the business is in its infancy. People are realizing each year that it is one of the most profitable crops of poultry that can be raised on a farm from a market standpoint. From the fanciers' outlook they are making such great strides in size, weight and plumage, and command such high prices that they are doubly profitable.

If the exhibits of Bronze turkeys at the Chicago show are any criterion, the business of raising Bronze turkeys has reached a point that nearly eclipses all other departments of poultry raising. When one yearling tom will bring $50 and a pair of young turkeys $75 it proves the value of the goods, and these were the prices asked and paid for some fine specimens at Chicago not long ago. Immediately breeders put up prices on eggs from 50 cents to one dollar apiece. From these facts one can safely conclude that the Bronze turkey business is booming, especially when the last year has seen more turkeys shipped to foreign countries than were ever sent before. The turkey has been basely slandered and has been considered to be about as stupid as a mule. I have never had any experience in trying to teach a mule to keep his hind feet on the ground when his best friend stood behind him, but I have taught turkeys to respect my wishes and stay on one plantation.

Seeing a four-horse load of turkeys going to market gathered from four farms, I said, "Surely I must go and

wake up Rip Van Winkle, so that he may see what the despised 'Old Woman's hen business' is now." When he went to sleep about twelve hens and one rooster was the poultry equipment of a farm, and turkeys were wild in the forest. If perchance a hunter brought one down for Christmas or Thanksgiving that was all the people of those days expected.

The newsboys of Chicago were presented with over two thousand turkeys for one Thanksgiving feast, and I really do not know which to pity most, the turkeys or the newsboys. The poultry business at Swift's poultry packing houses in Chicago promises to equal, if not exceed, the hog packing industry.

As our population increases the great tract of land used for grazing will be taken up into farms and the great droves of cattle now raised on them will be a thing of the past. Pork is not good for a steady diet, and the people will demand an immense number of turkeys, chickens, ducks and geese to meet the deficit caused by the lack of cattle.

WHITES, BLACKS, BUFFS AND REDS

I am frequently asked how many varieties of turkeys we have bred. I have only bred the old-fashioned scrub and the Bronze. I prefer the Bronze to any other variety I have ever seen, as it grows so very much larger, is so hardy and it is such a pleasure to have a flock of these brilliant beauties around. I think it is easy to get a good Bronze near to standard requirements in markings, brilliant plumage and weight, although there has been added pound after pound to the weight clause, and one has got to get them almost as large as a calf to answer the requirements in weight. I think the weight is too high, as a turkey will shrink from one to two pounds while en route to the show. I have had them weighed in the show room where they have shown a shrinkage of over three pounds. It is a settled fact that the Bronze turkey matures slower than other varieties, as they grow until four years old. I think the Black turkey comes next as a desirable turkey; they nearly equal the Bronze in size and beauty. I breed the Bronze now for size and beauty as well as for their popularity. There is a great demand for them. The White Holland comes next in popularity. They are liked by people who have small range, as they are what one may call a domestic turkey, not given to extensive wandering, and possess very little of the wild spirit. I am quite partial to white fowls, but on account of hardiness and great weight, as well as beautiful plumage, I prefer the Bronze.

I once owned a trio of Black turkeys for a short time. In one of my orders for turkeys to go to Europe I had a call for a trio of Black turkeys and a trio of Buffs, and as I did not breed them I had to find some good enough to ship across the pond. I sent to a well known Ohio judge and he sent me a Black tom that had never been beaten in the show room, a pullet that took first premium at the Ohio State Fair, and another equally as good. Well, that trio was so dazzlingly beautiful that it almost shook my allegiance to the Bronze. If ever I should change my breed of turkeys it would be to take up the Black turkey. I also got a very fine trio of Buffs from a reliable breeder in our own state and those with the trio of the best of my Bronze birds made a shipment that any turkey breeder might be proud of. The honor did not all belong to me, however.

MATING AND HOUSING

I am in receipt of a very interesting letter from a lady in Ohio in regard to the Bourbon Red turkey. She has bred them only one year. Her tom and hen were both young and to that she attributes the weakness of the poults, but as only one died a natural death it goes to show that they are quite hardy. They were very large when first hatched and very pretty. They are about as hardy as the Bronze when raised under similar conditions, and make beautiful birds when grown. They are marked something like a peafowl, are very quiet and not much inclined to wander and want to be left entirely alone to attend strictly to their own business. My correspondent thinks that for a market fowl a cross of the Bronze and the Bourbon Red would give good results.

I am often asked which is the best way to mate turkeys—young toms with hens or old toms with pullets. I like an old tom, but sometimes one suffers a serious loss among the hens, resulting from injury caused by a vigorous male. I always make cots for the spurs the same as a finger cot, and wire them on the legs with a fine copper wire. If the spur is very sharp we saw the sharp point off and cut the toe nails very blunt. I find this an indispensable treatment if one expects to escape loss.

A correspondent asks how many turkeys she ought to keep, and how many hens and toms she should buy to begin breeding on forty acres of land. She is building a house for them. I wrote and told her not to build a house for turkeys, an open shed is all they ever need. A high shed covered with prairie hay or anything that will keep out rain and sun. I think when the Ever Ruling Hand made turkeys He make the sky their covering. I really do like an open shed for rainy or stormy days and

when the terrible blizzards sweep over the country, but you might as well try to chain the lightning or hold a cyclone in the hollow of your hand as to attempt to make turkeys break the laws of nature that made a roost on the topmost branch of the tree an ideal place for them to spend a cold night. While we cuddle down in a warm bed, they are taking a constitutional on the tree top, swaying in the blast and they come down full of vigor and with an appetite that almost equals the ostrich. I never try to control them as to their quarters for the night unless we have a severe ice storm, or one of our terrible blizzards. The rest of the time they are left to "paddle their own canoe" at night. When the Creator put into turkeys the instinct to sleep in the open air He knew more about raising turkeys than I do.

As to the number of birds my correspondent should begin with, I would under no circumstances get more than ten hens and one tom. I started with three thoroughbred hens and a tom, even though I had raised turkeys for some years before this. I always advise inquirers to begin upon a small scale in any branch of poultry raising. One may work into the business and will not then lose the money invested, nor think the business is unprofitable. One turkey hen will lay two litters of eggs in a season, and this is all it is profitable to have her lay, for if she laid a third litter it would be too late to bother with them. She usually lays about thirty eggs in two litters, sometimes more, sometimes less. If this lady raises one hundred and fifty turkeys from ten hens she will be doing well, as the eggs will not all hatch and the poults will not all live. There are always some that are weak when first hatched. One hundred and fifty turkeys will be as many as should be kept on forty acres, for they are not like chickens, they must have range and must hunt for the larger portion of their food if it is desired to raise them to perfection in size, vigor and plumage, and of course it is.

Turkeys raised on a large range are best to use as breeders, as they develop on nature's plan—bone, muscle and frame, and that is what we want instead of heavy weights and small frames. Some people think weight is the criterion of excellence in turkeys. I wish I could take them out with me in my morning rambles and show them the points of excellence my birds are developing by roving around and picking up the food that nature contributes so lavishly for their benefit. The large, long legs and well proportioned bodies with the morning sun glancing from their brilliant plumage make a sight worth seeing. Exercise and the right kind of diet go a long way towards making a perfect turkey.

The Bronze turkey does not develop until four years old, and it stands to reason that a bird which develops slowly and healthily will make a better breeder and produce healthier and larger stock than those which are pushed to maturity, and which attain great weights simply by over-feeding and lack of exercise. First secure good health and a large frame, then let nature put on weight at maturity. If this course were followed we would not hear so much about diseases and non-success in raising turkeys. They were created for a special purpose and intended to be healthy and when we undertake to run against nature there is war at once and we have to pay the penalty.

YARDING AND TRAINING TURKEYS

I raise turkeys and like the business and attribute much of my success to keeping my turkeys yarded through the breeding season. People generally think it a great expense to build a fence that will keep turkeys in, though I do not find it so. A three-foot woven wire fence with barbed wire above to make the fence four or five feet high will keep them confined if the flight feathers of one wing are cut. I keep the young turkeys yarded in the same yard until they are six weeks or two months old, which makes it convenient to protect the young poults from the wet and I can look them over once a week for lice, and never have to be hunting up my turkeys.

People ask me if they are not hard to raise. I raise a larger per cent of those hatched than I do of chickens.

is generally enough. I have had them caught that way and hang until dead. I use the breeding yards for the young turkeys until they are large enough to drive out on the range, putting fifty in each yard. At six weeks or two months they are driven onto their summer range, driving them home at night until they have learned the trick of coming home to roost. There is considerable work getting them started to run out on the range and come home at night. If you allow them to run at large and stay out at night they will wander away to neighbors and sometimes go miles from home, but if they are

A Pair of Mrs. Chas. Jones' Prize Winning Bronze Turkeys

For the last two years I have raised over 95 per cent of all turkeys hatched.

I have found that fifty turkeys in a yard or field are enough to do well. If you keep more than that together they are apt to pile in together and smother after they are about a month old. When I get a flock of fifty I start another drove in another field. I set four or five turkey hens and at the same time give to domestic hens as many turkey eggs as I think the turkeys can take care of. If possible I set an incubator with chicken eggs. When they all hatch I give the turkeys all the poults and the domestic hens all the incubator chicks, and that makes business lively all around, and keeps me very busy.

I raise from three different flocks of turkeys, ten hens and one tom, in each flock. We have from one acre to three acres fenced in with a three-foot wire netting, three-inch mesh, with barbed wire at the top, making the fence five feet high. Turkeys will never try to fly over a barbed wire fence. They will crawl under if the wires are not close together, but they will never try to fly over it. If they ever attempt it they are almost sure to run a barb through their foot and one experience of that kind

driven home nightly for a week or two they will soon come home of their own accord, and then your work in the turkey yard is nearly over, as they can take care of themselves, only you must watch that they do not forget to come home.

Turkeys like a large range as they grow older, but while young, one to three acres makes plenty of range. You will soon find out when they get dissatisfied with their quarters, as they will crawl out or fly into your garden or yard, showing that they are anxious to start on their foraging expeditions. If the hay and oats are cut so that they can get around without trampling things down, or finding too much to hide in, we turn them out.

Turkeys can be made to go almost anywhere their owner wants them to by driving them to the farthest fields when they are first started out, but they must be brought home nights until they learn to come home. I bought a telescope to save steps and I find it a very great help, especially as I have to watch my turkeys on account of the railroad track. In the early dry part of the season I had a great deal of trouble with my turkeys wandering so far that they could not get back at night. We discovered that they invariably went where they found water last year, and we concluded it was water they were after, so we took large dishes and put out where we wanted them to run, and then they only went about one-half mile away and stayed on our own place. Their going where they found water last year shows that turkeys have memories. I believe animals have much more intelligence that we give them credit for. Only their language and way of giving expression to their wants is all Greek to us.

To show how turkeys measure time our turkeys invariably start for the house in time to reach the west edge of the pasture at four o'clock, and it takes them until about sundown to reach the house near where they roost. Now, how can they tell the time of day, which they seem to do as well as we do?

I did not learn in a day nor in a year the art of raising nearly all the turkeys hatched, nor until I had lost hundreds each year, I acting as pall bearer and chief mourner, and I assure you I filled the position of mourner admirably, weeping copiously over buried hopes (and those hopes were of a well filled purse).

I hope I shall not have to meet those turkeys in the next world and be held accountable for my unpardonable ignorance, but perhaps, by sincerely repenting my past mistakes the sin of ignorance will be forgiven me. If I can be of any help to those who raise $50 and $75 turkeys it may help condone the past. May our great American Thanksgiving bird soar still higher and grow bigger and reach the thousand-dollar mark. He is sure to have his praises sung in foreign tongues, and the fun of it all is, how is he ever with his stupid brain going to learn those foreign languages, when they call him to breakfast, dinner and supper? How will he know what it all means?

INDIGESTION

A turkey grows very fast and has an appetite like an ostrich, but without an ostrich's digestive ability. As the natural way for a turkey to eat is to pick up a grain here and there in such a manner as to give the digestive organs a grain at a time to digest, then the digestive mill grinds slowly without being clogged. This method of feeding keeps up a steady circulation and the turkey keeps growing larger and stronger, the digestive organs being developed as the turkey grows, and they are therefore better able to do their work when more food is required to be digested to build up a large frame. On the other hand, when the poults are overfed, the machinery is clogged and there is a general smash-up, the effect being similar to that caused by throwing a bushel of corn into a corn sheller. The machine will do its work all right if fed slowly, so will a turkey's digestive organs. A turkey is a voracious eater and will eat as often as you feed it.

There are other causes that will bring death with very nearly the same symptoms. One is lice and one is lack of sharp grit. A turkey cannot grind its food without grit any more than a miller can grind wheat without millstones; we might as well try to chew our food without teeth.

A neighbor told me that her turkeys were dying and I sent her word to come and get some Mica Crystal Grit and give them, as I knew she was not giving them any grit. I advised her to put a little in the food every morning. She did so and her turkeys are no longer dying. It was the absence of sharp grit that caused them to die.

I have adopted a treatment for turkeys and chicks that has proved a great success. If I see them act as though they were not feeling well I give a calomel pill.

These I buy from the druggist, each pill to contain a tenth of a grain of calomel. I give the pills one a day for three days, then follow with quinine pills twice a day until the birds are well. If noticed and treated when first they show symptoms of not being well I have never failed to effect a cure. The calomel stirs up the liver and gets it to work, as most cases of sickness among poultry commence with a disordered liver. After the system has had a thorough cleansing the quinine acts as tonic to build the birds up and gives them appetites, then nature does the rest. By this course of treatment you ward off what might terminate in serious sickness and death. I have used similar treatment in the human family and saved a great many doctor's bills, to say nothing of long spells of sickness and suffering.

OVERFEEDING CAUSES DEATH

Overfeeding is a common cause of loss in young turkeys. I feed only three times a day for the good reason that I could not possibly find time to feed oftener with the large number I raise. I find it sufficient. They take more exercise if fed less, then when they are fed they are hungry. The time between feeding, too, allows the food to digest and gives the digestive organs a little rest.

I feed more green food than most people do, as I find it has the same effect on turkeys that it has on ducks. It produces a large frame. I chop dandelion leaves for them in the morning and at night chop up onions, tops and all. I notice there is never a scrap of the green food left when they are through eating. They make rapid growth when fed this way, besides it is a cheap way to feed them.

I give a little sharp grit in their food every morning. I use grit and oyster shell, the larger part grit, as turkeys to be healthy must have it. I have lost hundreds of turkeys I know by not having plenty of grit with which to grind their food. If they get a little sharp grit in their food every morning it keeps their grinding apparatus in perfect order. Very young birds do not find the grit of their own accord, and as they grow older they are liable to gorge themselves with the grit as soon as they discover it, thereby clogging their digestive organs, while a small quantity in their food each morning keeps them in excellent condition.

I have my little poults so they will fly over a board a foot high when but one week old. There are more turkeys killed by over feeding and lice and want of grit than all other things combined. If you do not keep them near the house so that you can run them under cover when a heavy storm comes up you are liable to lose a large per cent. I find a large shed with a board floor is fine to run them in in case of sudden storms. Of course you must stay close at home to meet all these emergencies. It is not more confining than other occupations. The merchant, lawyer, doctor, mechanic and farmer have to confine themselves closely to business, and the poultry raiser, whether for the fancy or market, must make it a business and work on business principles.

EVILS FROM LACK OF EXERCISE

I learned something about exercise for very young turkeys this year. I hatched some under hens quite early; it was wet and cold and of the two evils I decided I would not turn them out to run through the day, so I kept them cooped a week or more. When I went to feed them I found one that did not seem to have the use of its left side. I thought it had got hurt in some way and would soon be all right. It got no better and I still kept them cooped, as it was so cold and wet; then another got that way. They would push themselves around with their right foot as they lay on their left side. When the third one was taken sick I decided it was paralysis of the left side, brought on by lack of exercise, and so I turned them out. Those that had been affected died. It was still cold and wet when my other turkeys began to hatch, and I kept the first lot of chicks cooped perhaps five days, when one of them acted in the same way as the early hatched birds. I turned them out to run through the day and that was the last of it. This convinced me that it was paralysis brought on by lack of exercise. The peculiar part of it was that it was always the left side affected. My turkeys are making rapid growth out on the range. I feed them a little grain when they come up at night, and we have such quantities of apples that I put the small ones in a box and chop them up with the spade and feed them to all the poultry, and they do enjoy the cool juice these hot, dry days, and the apples keep them in such good health and are so much better for them than green food or even grass-hoppers exclusively.

The only road to success with turkeys is to keep them healthy. Give them plenty of exercise, commencing to let them run through the middle of the day at three or four days old; keep the lice off and give a little grit in their food every morning, with good, clean water to drink and they will have very few diseases. Exercise they must have, but very young turkeys can have sufficient exercise on an acre or two, and a great many young turkeys can be saved by enjoying this exercise under your control. Coop at night until they begin to want to roost.

PUNCHING THE POULTS

I always mark my young poults when I put them out on the range, as otherwise they would be forgotten or neglected. With care there will be found web enough to allow a good mark and it will not grow together if, as sometimes is the case, you cut into the edge of the web, it will do no harm and will always show the mark. It is different with ducks, the mark will grow together if made in the edge of the web, but if several punch marks are made you can always see the scars, as the webs of their feet are very transparent. Sometimes I make so large a hole in a duck's foot that it does not grow together and I often find them with a weed run through the hole. In their efforts to release themselves they get twisted and hang there until they die if not released.

PULLING WING FEATHERS

I am asked if I pull the wing feathers of sick poults to improve their health, and I reply—No, not to improve their health, but to prevent too much strength being taken from their systems by the extreme growth of flight feathers. I usually pull the first flight feathers on the wing when the turkeys are from three to six days old, as at that time they come out so easily that it almost seems as if nature intended those feathers to be pulled. Sometimes I cannot get the time to attend to it, and I notice the quill feathers are making such rapid growth that they hang down, almost drag, and the turkeys appear much weaker than those that have had their feathers pulled; after this period, too, they are much harder to pull and the poults have lost all the strength that it took to grow them. They should be pulled almost as soon as they start to grow, then your turkeys will put

growth into the body and the other feathers. This greatly increases our chance of success.

A thought was suggested at one of the Chicago shows. Does the second growth of flight feathers make as finely marked a wing as the first, or is the reverse the case? I had never thought of it in that light before and shall experiment this summer and let the readers know. This much I do know after years of experience, the little turkeys certainly are stronger and stand a better chance of living if the first flight feathers are pulled when they are from three to four days old, and they come out so easily at this time that it has no evil effect.

LICE AND MITE DESTROYERS

Another correspondent asked about carbolineum,

A Group of Mrs. Chas. Jones Breeding Turkeys

wishing to know if it is the same as carbolineum avenarius. It is the same article. It was originally manufactured in Germany and sent over to this country in barrels. Some claim it is still made there, but I am of the opinion that what we use is an American product. Its original use was as a wood preservative for painting fence posts where they are set in the ground. It is claimed that if posts for corn cribs are painted with it, it will keep rats out of the crib, although I have heard this contradicted. She asks if it is dangerous to use. The only danger is, it will cause the face and hands to swell if it is used in strong sunlight. She also asks if it is lasting in its effects on mites and lice. It is a wood preservative and penetrates right through an inch board in a very few minutes, and it is there to stay so long as the board lasts. For this reason it has been found to be one of the best preventatives of lice and mites that is known. I gave it enough of a trial to know it will do all that is claimed for it. I painted all my turkey and chicken coops with it and never had healthier birds. I painted my coops only once. It costs ninety cents a gallon. I painted all perches and intend to spray my houses with it, as it is not expensive when used with a fine sprayer, such as can be bought for $1.

However, I do not trust entirely to any one thing. I paint a box, which I keep for the purpose, with some good lice killer, and put turkeys and chicks in it for an hour or two, leaving sufficient provision for fresh air. I also use good insect powder on the little chicks and turkeys. Whether or not carbolineum avenarius or lice killer is dangerous to use on old fowls in the way recommended I cannot say, but there is one thing certain, it will not poison them. Any strong insecticide will kill little turkeys or chickens if they are shut in a box which is painted with it and allowed no fresh air. This I know by sad experience. For spraying houses and painting perches I prefer the carbolineum, but I like the lice killer best for painting a box in which to place the birds. I use lice powder for the very young birds.

SOME DISEASES OF TURKEYS

A lady wrote that she hatched sixty-six little turkeys and had only ten left. Her turkeys had a diarrhoea, a thin yellowish discharge. This might be from lack of grit.

As the cold rains and cool nights come, colds that take the form of roup often attack turkeys, though I have very little if any trouble of this kind since I learned more about turkeys and their ways and since I feed them just clear, dry grain. When I used to feed mashes often hot or very warm, both chickens and turkeys had roup, but now it is almost an unknown disease on our place.

I saw a remedy recommended which I think worth trying. It was to bathe the swollen head, mouth and throat with turpentine. It is said to work a speedy cure.

A lady telephoned me recently that one of her hens was suffering from a peculiar trouble. Although it had a good appetite it could not get its head to the ground to eat. The trouble appeared to be in her neck. I advised rubbing her neck with turpentine and putting her food up high where she could reach it, and thought she would get over it as she appeared to be very hungry, which proved that her digestion was all right. A few days later the lady reported that the hen was all right.

Several cases have been reported to me in this vicinity, of sick turkeys whose droppings are yellow. I have recommended linseed oil, or what has proved much better, olive oil. A lemon extract bottle of the smaller size holds about three doses. It should be given about twelve hours apart, and about six hours after the last dose of the olive oil give a capsule of quinine. Give quinine twice a day until the turkey has regained its strength. Quinine is a very strong tonic for turkeys, and I am never without it. But never doctor poultry if it can be avoided, as poultry, like people, are better kept well than doped to make them well. They, like ourselves, are machines. If they have the kind of food nature intended them to have and they have exercise to grind that food, it goes to build up the system and to repair the waste that is constantly taking place. We must all exercise the muscles that do the grinding.

The Bible says that man must earn his bread by the sweat of his brow. Working until the sweat shows on the brow means hard physical labor and that promotes health. Of course we have thousands of men today who have the get-rich-quick idea in their heads, who are determined to avoid earning their bread by the sweat of their brows. The result is that our prisons are full and thousands of men are broken in health. Let us learn a lesson from our birds and be wise. Animals of all kinds eat and exercise to digest their food, but man alone covets ease and luxury without physical labor. We always have among us men broken down in health and in mind who fill early graves because they are not willing to submit to nature's ways and so retain their vigor and health.

TINCTURE OF IODINE FOR LICE

I have been in the habit of using tincture of iodine for lice. I take a feather (but intend getting a small brush) and brush the top of the head and across the quills of the wing feathers, under the wings, and the fluff below the vent with the tincture of iodine. It is a fact that I have proved time and again that those treated with iodine for lice outgrew those treated with other remedies, the only objection being the expense,

but if one will send and get a large bottle at wholesale price it will not be expensive.

When turkeys are making very rapid growth, I find the lice are making rapid growth also. When I take the old turkey off the nest I paint a box with lice killer, put her in and leave her for two hours. I do not shut her in an air tight compartment, only close enough for the lice killer to thoroughly fumigate her feathers. This kills all the lice and nits. I grease the heads of the little turkeys to destroy the large head lice; I also dust them thoroughly with a good lice powder and paint their coops with carbolineum, but with all the precautions I find I must look over them once a week for lice. One of the most essential things during July is to keep the turkeys free from lice.

The first of July generally ends the turkey egg business. Occasionally turkeys lay a third clutch of eggs after that time, but I never consider them of much value, as they do not hatch well and the young turkeys never grow very large. I remember one exception to that rule. I had a brood of young turkeys come off about the first of August, and a pullet from that flock weighed sixteen pounds on the 10th of December. I took first premium with her at Dixon, Ill., before the weight was raised in the Standard. That was one pound above standard weight on a pullet ten days over four months old.

The work for August in the turkey yard is very light as the turkeys are, or should be, out on the range on farms. I only feed them a little in the morning so that they may be induced to run out in search of food, and a little at night to get them to come home. After they have started out, all I have to do is to bring them home at night and keep on the watch for lice. They go through a corn field and I have noticed the old turkey and young ones stop and wallow in the loose dirt to dust themselves, so I hardly ever have much trouble with lice when they are out on the range.

In November I have watched them with a great deal of interest to see how they make up their bill of fare for breakfast. They work lively, for they have voracious appetites and have nearly cleared the place of grasshoppers. Now they make their breakfast of weeds or grass seeds with occasionally oats that have been left lying on the ground. I notice as the fall advances they spend a lot of time in the corn field, picking corn from ears that have been blown down.

The following is a good story, although I do not vouch for its truthfulness: A farmer in Kansas has started a novel plan, based upon the prevalence of grasshoppers. He has about one thousand turkeys. After his neighbors saw the way his fields were cleared of grasshoppers they proposed hiring one hundred turkeys by the day to eat their grasshoppers, so he divided them into flocks of one hundred and hired them out at $2.50 per one hundred for a day's work, which made $25 income a day for the use of one thousand turkeys, and what turkeys those turkeys will be this fall. This of course settles the grasshopper question in Kansas and Nebraska. If they can settle the rainfall question as easily, the two states will never hold the emigration that will rush there.

INBREEDING AND NEED OF RANGE

Turkeys deteriorate quicker by inbreeding than any other animal. Inbreeding indiscriminately for a long time weakens their constitutions. Turkeys, like horses, in their wild state, elected their leaders, or rather the leaders elected themselves by their prowess. When an old leader began to show signs of feebleness a young turkey tom challenged him to mortal combat. If the old chief was equal to the combat the young aspirant was compelled to fall back to the rear or remain where he fell. When the old chief showed renewed signs of feebleness another young aspirant for royal honors stepped out of the ranks and the old tom rarely came off conqueror. One of our hunters who goes west every year to hunt has often told me of seeing the footprints of an enormous wild turkey that he had tracked and had occasionally got a glimpse of. He described him as being as large as a calf. That old tom had evidently ruled supreme for many years and had grown too smart to be

A Winner from the Yards of Mrs. Chas. Jones

caught napping, so the hunter could never get a shot at him. Turkeys in their wild state range in large flocks, but when they are domesticated it is necessary to keep them in small flocks. I think eighty acres little enough range for 150 turkeys. They could be bred in and left to run in flocks of three hundred if they had a range of three hundred acres. The reason large flocks cannot be kept on small range is that they do not find sufficient insects and the thousand other things that they pick up to make their bill of fare. Fifty can be kept on from one to three acres until they are six weeks or two months old, then one just simply cannot keep them in a small enclosure, as they will crawl under or through or get out some other way, for they are growing fast and must have what nature demands. I always make a virtue of necessity and turn them out on the range.

I change males every year. I do not go out of the strain I am breeding, but take another branch of the same line of blood, and have found that I do not impair their vigor in the least, but am building up strong, healthy birds with plumage that for years has kept my whole flock above a score of 93, and that in a flock of one hundred and fifty birds. Last year 94 was the lowest. While I have improved them in shape and plumage I do not find one sick turkey in twenty-five throughout the season.

LINE BREEDING

At one of the great Chicago shows two things were very strongly impressed on my mind; one was strain or line-breeding of turkeys. The two leading strains exhibited there have been line bred to my certain knowledge; one at least ten or twelve years (perhaps longer, but I am speaking of what I know), the other from information gained in different ways I am led to believe has been line bred the same length of time. They have formed two distinct types; both strains very large birds

and beautifully bronzed, but with this difference in color of plumage—in one strain the bronze or gold band across tail coverts, and in fact throughout the whole plumage was a greenish golden color; in the other it was just the color of gold without the greenish hue. From what I know these two strains have won most of the premiums in our leading shows from Madison Square to Chicago. Upon comparing the plumage after the premiums were awarded the exhibitors were convinced that the birds represented two distinct species of the same bird. The strain that had the pure gold color had the gold band the entire length of the back. This was absent in the other strain.

The prevailing idea in looking over this Chicago show was that the old avoirdupois way of mixing blood was out of date, and if we expect to get to the front, the blood must be weighed by apothecary weight, or better still, on the alchemist's scales, although the alchemist, I believe, has never been able to brew in his caldron ingredients that turned out gold. One breeder proved beyond a doubt that he could put a clear, even gold band on Bronze turkeys, and the inference is that he has been for years using the alchemist scales to reach this much to be desired point of excellence.

If the exhibits of Bronze turkeys continue to grow I am afraid there will have to be erected a new Coliseum for the turkey exhibit alone.

If we all bred Plymouth Rocks and there was only one breed and one club, the poultry business would be tame and we would lose our incentive to strive for our ideal in the variety that met our fancy. Now if the admirers and breeders of each variety of turkeys were to organize a club to push the interest of their particular breed, to look up their origin and write up the good qualities that commend them to breeders the turkey business would be pushed to the front in a way that could not be accomplished by an indiscriminate pushing of all varieties combined.

TURKEYS VS. GRASSHOPPERS

In looking over a Chicago paper some time ago, I saw an account of a Kansas farmer who was starting turkey raising on a large scale. His idea was a good one as they are raising large fields of alfalfa and the grasshoppers are proving a great detriment to that crop. Alfalfa has been a great boon to the drought-stricken parts of our country. Irrigation, the raising of trees and then the great crops of alfalfa have made the desert blossom like the rose. But the grasshopper lays its eggs, and the young when hatched feed on this alfalfa, the best paying crop of these districts. They eat off the blossoms and so make the raising of seed very difficult as the second crop is the seed crop that is saved, and that is the very crop that is ready when the grasshopper season is at its height. The seed is valuable. We paid nine dollars a bushel for enough to sow three acres.

I have always thought that if Kansas farmers would go into turkey raising on a large scale, they would do away with the grasshopper plague to a great extent. I have watched fields where grasshoppers were thickest and I found that as a rule they are not migratory in their habits. I know that in the early days of the settlement of Kansas and Nebraska they were said to go in swarms, but here when they are thick in one field one year they are usually thick in the same field the following year. Along the railroad they are thick every year, because nothing is allowed to go on the track for fear of it being killed. And so they lay their eggs there and they hatch and the young thrive, and this is repeated year after year while in adjoining fields there are comparatively few grasshoppers.

If each Kansas and Nebraska farmer would raise from one to two hundred turkeys each year he would find his farms cleared of grasshoppers, and the weed seeds that are so great a detriment to farming would go into the crops of the turkeys and what had been an injury to farmers would be turned into many dollars for their use.

I have been told that the alfalfa in western Nebraska was full of grasshoppers when cut, and that they smothered. During the winter the chickens scratch preserved grasshoppers out of the hay. Turkeys would find there their natural food all cut and dried for them, except the exercise of scratching to get it. It is a good story and it has an advantage over some told of that country, for this one might be true.

No one need be afraid of overproduction of turkeys as the demand will always exceed the supply. In the states where both alfalfa and grasshoppers grow, farmers will raise three crops in one—the hay for the stock and the grasshoppers for the turkeys. And so the states that have had so hard a struggle to produce paying crops year after year, may yet become the greatest money making states in the union as they are also in the great corn belt. Look back across the years when the first Thanksgiving turkeys were killed to feed the starving Pilgrims and note the marvelous changes that have taken place. The greatest nation on earth was born and kept from starvation by wild turkeys and wild game with the meagre supplies sent across the ocean by slow sailing vessels that took months to reach our shores. If ever in the future our supply of turkeys should exceed the demand, our fast going steamships will take them to foreign markets in six to eight days where there will be an unlimited demand for anything so delicious to the taste as a properly grown turkey.

Down-To-Date Bronze Turkeys—By Sewell

THE WATCHWORD OF SUCCESS

Experience, Watchfulness and Common-Sense are Necessary to Raise Prize-Winning Bronze Turkeys—Something About Coops for the
Mother and Her Poults—Do Not Overfeed

MRS. NELLIE BULLOCK

ERE I to begin the breeding of fancy turkeys and could have the benefit of my present knowledge, I think I should buy stock, the very best my purse would allow, even if I had to limit my flock to a pair. We bought eggs at different times from three noted fanciers, but something went wrong each time, either the eggs were infertile, or not strong enough to hatch, or the poults would manage to die. So I think the quicker way to secure a good flock would be to purchase birds. Turkeys are hardy after they are half grown, and most persons would sell cheaper then than after they are grown. It would not be a bad idea to invest in half-grown birds.

I should advise any one who has not raised turkeys to get the cheaper grade of some thoroughbred variety you fancy, and learn with them. Then if you have losses it will not bankrupt you, and when you have mastered the details necessary to raising these successfully you can invest in birds of fine plumage and other fine points possessed by fancy fowls, to the extent of your much enlarged purse—never forgetting, however, that there is always something to be learned.

For those who have had success in raising common turkeys and who wish to start with some special variety of thoroughbred turkeys, I should advise them to get a pair, trio or pen of the best your purse will afford and apply to them your knowledge of care and feeding gained while raising the common birds.

CARE OF POULTS

Raising the poults is the hard task for most beginners, and some of the more experienced ones have their hands full when they try to raise a large per cent. Practical experience, watchfulness and plenty of common sense applied to the varying circumstances, are necessary to success. Our plan is somewhat as follows: First, we require a roomy coop with a dry floor, covered with timothy or clover chaff. Confine the mother, either a chicken or a turkey hen, on rainy days. On dry, sunshiny days, tether her to an apple tree limb, having the coop near. Clean the floor twice a week at least. If the earth is dry, it will serve very well as a floor, otherwise, a raised board floor would be better. Dust both the mother and the poults thoroughly twice a week with Persian insect powder. For dusting the poults, I keep a two gallon, flaring earthenware crock. We put a handful of powder in the crock, then hold the poult by the feet over the crock and dust it until it looks yellow all over. I do not have so much trouble with lice as I did when I put the powder on in spots. Keep the water dishes clean and full.

We try not to overfeed, and neither do we starve them, for one is as bad as the other. We console ourselves if occasionally a poult dies, or several of them die at one time, with the thought that our neighbors, too, lose poults and that very few, no matter how much knowledge they have on this subject, can raise all that hatch.

TURKEYS AS HATCHERS

There was an interesting item in the Reliable Poultry Journal some years ago over the initials C. H. A., which we reproduce:

"A great deal is being said lately about using turkeys for hatching hen eggs, so I will give my experience. It has been really comical to see the look of doubt on the faces of people when told that we had turkeys which had never laid any eggs, sitting. Too polite to dispute the statement, their looks plainly said, 'Does he expect me to believe that story?'

"When I first read in an English poultry book of the French method of using turkeys to hatch and care for chickens, I had no incubator and concluded to try the plan. Late in the fall I sent out in the country and bought a late hatched hen turkey for very little money. In February we prepared a box (with plenty of chaff over a layer or horse manure) that could be shut up to exclude the light. Did not give either wine or whisky, but in two or three weeks she was sitting quietly on the china eggs and when taken off the nest to be fed, would voluntarily return. I then filled the nest with hens' eggs, removing them as soon as they began to pip to keep the turkey from wanting to leave the nest and putting in other eggs. After sitting three months she was put in a yard with chickens for the rest of the summer. We put chickens of different ages with her and she received them all with equal kindness.

"This year we have two turkeys, besides an incubator, and after hatching three sittings of eggs we thought best to take them off the nest, but one watched her chance and went back on the nest till I filled it with eggs again, so I let her stay. The other is laying and will be ready for work later if needed.

Ideal Turkey Coop for Hen and Poults

"They make careful, patient mothers, are equal in that respect to any hen, and it is a wonder that farmers do not make more use of them than they do."

DESCRIPTION OF IDEAL COOP

We have a coop for turkeys and poults which we find almost ideal. It is two feet high in the back and three feet in front; six feet long and three feet wide. The door is large enough to allow a turkey hen to walk in and out without inconvenience and the coop is large enough to allow a turkey hen and twenty poults to walk around when they are confined during a rainy day. We use two doors, one made of lumber for stormy times, the other of inch mesh wire netting for warm nights. Thus plenty of fresh air is admitted and small rats or larger animals are kept out.

Down-To-Date White Holland Turkeys—By Sewell

WHITE HOLLAND TURKEYS

Beautiful in Shape and Chaste in Color, They Form an Excellent Foil for the Brilliant Hues of the Bronze Variety, While Their Many Excellent Qualities Make Them Worthy Rivals

JOHN R. GARBEE

EARS ago we raised only the common turkeys and we counted ourselves among the lucky ones if we, or rather I should say the old turkey hens, raised sixteen or twenty a year. If the young turkeys weighed when dressed in November eight or ten pounds they had done well. Along about 1890 I developed a severe case of "poultry fever." I have been a reader of the Reliable Poultry Journal ever since it came into existence. I have a complete file of it down to date, which fact is explained when I say that I consider it the leader among poultry papers.

I also read other poultry and farm papers, and soon I was convinced that better poultry and turkeys ought to be raised on farms and that turkeys could be managed so that there should be a good profit in them. Hunters were killing our common turkeys for wild ones because they wandered so far from home, thereby causing us considerable vexation and loss.

We had never seen a pure white turkey, but we read about their gentleness and that they did not roam like the other varieties. So we sold all our common ones and purchased a trio of White Holland turkeys from an R.

A flock of White Hollands
The Property of Mr. John R. Garbee

P. J. advertiser, paying $7.50 for them and $2 expressage —which seemed a big price then. Since then we have paid more than that for a single bird. These first birds were rather small, though pretty. Up to this time I never had seen a Standard, but I soon bought one and learned that my birds were under weight, and feed them how I would, I could not get that trio up to Standard weight.

I soon learned where I could get large White Holland turkeys, and I bought some more, still keeping the little, plump hens. The next season the young poults were larger than their mothers—the result of using a large tom. The results have been about the same whether I used a large young tom or an older bird, provided the young males were big boned, blocky fellows mated to good blocky hens or pullets. Still, I prefer a tom from two to five years old. I wish to state here that when I began breeding this variety of turkeys the toms at their best weighed only sixteen pounds and the pullets and hens eight to ten pounds, but during the past three or four years, by following my own rules of mating as given here, my turkeys have doubled these weights, so that now my young toms and pullets weigh from fifteen to twenty-four pounds.

I use both pullets and hens as breeders, though I am careful to select the best shaped ones—those that are blocky and in first class health. The first eggs that are

hen) or are put in an incubator. We get successful hatches either way, but we never have had success when we put the poults in a brooder. It may be the fault of this particular make of brooder, as I never have thought well of it, though it is a high priced one. So we give the poults to hens. Now, it is easy enough to hatch the poults, the main trouble is to raise them. I am free to confess I do not know it all, but some things I have learned from experience. I know I have lost more poults from lice, over feeding and chilling than from all other causes combined. Lice are the poults' worst enemies, and next they suffer from overfeeding. Our rule for feeding chicks is "any sound, wholesome food, fed a little at a time." This rule applied to poults works equally well.

We are most successful when the weather is fair and the food is given to them three times a day, and not faster than it could be digested. We find cottage cheese is good for them and they like it, but judgment must be used in feeding it. I repeat that any clean, wholesome food fed in moderation is good for them. We find a varied diet—corn bread, cracked corn, wheat, chopped vegetables, table scraps, even corn dough occasionally—works all right, while some breeders claim success on one straight diet.

After the second and third clutches of eggs are laid we set the turkey hens. We always prefer to move them to a suitable coop or barrel nest in the yard or near a poultry house, so they can be protected and cared for better. They can be moved with but little trouble when broody. They are confined to the nest for a few days by a slat coop, after that they get off and on at will, food and fresh water being kept near them. Remember always that lice are the great drawback to successful turkey raising, and try to have your sitting hen absolutely free from lice, mites or jiggers when the eggs hatch, and then keep her free. Watch the poults, too, and do not let them suffer from lice. A clean coop and pure water are essential to success.

Do not overfeed nor underfeed either. Provide a comfortable place for the hen and poults, so that the latter may not get unduly chilled, and give the hen all the food she will eat, so she will not be restless, but put her food out of reach of the poults. Note how the latter will grow with this care. By the time they are feathered and large enough to roam they will be but little care and they will get a large share of their food from the fields, but if you follow the method I have outlined they will always come home for supper and will

ADVOCATES WHITE HOLLAND TURKEYS

Their Beauty and Market Qualifications Make it Both Pleasant and Profitable to Raise Them—Preferred Weight of Turkeys—Inbreeding—Black Ticking on Feathers

J. A. LELAND

AFTER several years of experience with White Holland Turkeys I have come to the conclusion that there is no better variety for beauty and utility. The standard weight for adult toms is twenty-eight pounds, for adult hens eighteen pounds, for young toms twenty pounds, and young hens fourteen pounds. These weights are often exceeded, but not as a rule to the advantage of the breed, although the majority of fanciers try to produce the heaviest birds possible for show purposes. In our experience young stock must reach these weights when about six to eight months old if they ever attain standard weight when mature. Very heavy specimens are not prolific breeders and stock weighing standard in breeding condition is generally to be preferred.

White Hollands, as bred by Mr. J. A. Leland

Inbreeding is a thing that turkeys cannot stand, therefore, it is imperative that new blood be obtained each year if we wish to raise a large number of hardy, heavy boned fowls that will top either the market or show room. As to color I have never seen a White Holland turkey that did not show some black ticking in its plumage during some period of its life. However, there is a great difference in specimens in this respect and we should breed from stock as free from this fault as possible, if we ever expect to correct it. We believe an ideal White Holland should have a very full, round body (an egg with large end forward gives a good idea), neck of good length, rather long tail and pure white plumage. They should have stout legs, the shanks should be bright pink or flesh color, the former much to be preferred from a beauty standpoint, and rather large feet. My turkeys are never housed, nor should they be, except for convenience in handling, but we consider it best to have them roost some place sheltered from severe winds and storms.

I would clip the flight feathers of one wing so that an ordinary five-foot fence that they could not get through nor under, would confine them.

We would not consider it profitable to raise large numbers of turkeys in small enclosures as they require a large range, where they obtain the greater part of their food at no cost. If all food were bought the cost of production would be too great and turkeys do not thrive in close confinement.

About the middle of March we place boxes and barrels for nests in out of the way places about the farm buildings. The hens find them and soon begin to lay. If turkeys are not furnished suitable nests they are apt to choose them in places exposed to crows and vermin. A crow will watch a hen half a day to get an egg and generally finds the nest, while I have found hens dead on their nests, killed by minks or skunks. If their first clutch is taken away they will lay another and sometimes a third. The broody hens should be confiled a few days if their eggs are taken, as they sometimes will sit on their nests all the rest of the summer and may die while molting in the fall. It is often a good plan to set the first clutch under domestic hens, as the conditions in early spring are frequently unfavorable to outdoor incubation, and these hens are more easily handled in confinement. It is best to let the turkey hatch her second laying, as the third comes too late, if at all, and early hatched turkeys are most desirable.

BREEDERS AND POULTS

Ordinarily I mate six to twelve hens with a tom and find the eggs are very fertile, but I think that as many as twenty might safely be mated to one male. Only one tom should run with the flock during the breeding season, but it is well to keep an extra one to use in case of accident.

My breeders have the run of the farm and get only what they pick up about the buildings, which amounts to considerable in winter, but to almost none when good weather comes and then they glean the bulk of their food in the fields. Turkey eggs are very fertile and hatch in twenty-eight days. At hatching time the hen should be closely watched and, if necessary, the poults taken away when dry until all are hatched, in order that she shall not leave the nest with them and so chill the other eggs.

During incubation and at hatching time the hen should be frequently dusted with some good insect powder, so you may be sure she is free from lice, which, with filth and dampness, are the worst enemies of young fowls. Should this be neglected and the poults become infested, a mixture of kerosene and lard—just a few drops of the former, as it is so strong, will usually rid them of the nuisance. Apply it around the head, under the wings and about the vent.

After the poults are hatched place a coop with a good roof and slatted end over the hen. This will allow the poults to range about, but keeps the mother from tiring them out or leading them through the wet grass. When the dew has dried the hen may be given her liberty, but should be carefully watched and driven to her coop in the evening, or in case of showers. These coops should be moved each day, so that the young will roost on clean ground. The first feed may consist of infertile eggs boiled hard and chopped fine, or a little cracked grain—oats or wheat preferred. A mixture of coarsely chopped or ground grains with a little millet should be fed until they are from four to six weeks old, when they will be able to eat whole grain. From now on, in good weather, they will need only a little grain in the evening, which will serve to bring them home at night and keep them tame. They will get their food in the fields until frost comes, after that they should be fed all the corn they will eat to prepare them for market.

MARKETING TURKEYS

Young turkeys command good prices by the first of November or even earlier in our large cities, and all the heaviest, old and young turkeys, should be marketed between a few days before Thanksgiving and Christmas, because after that time heavy stock is at a discount. Through January the demand is usually only fair, but it is a good time to dispose of any heavy turkeys that were not in condition to market earlier. Let us add right here that marketing thin poultry is throwing money away, as we might almost say that the difference between thin and

White Hollands at Woodside Farm, Mr. J. A. Leland Proprietor

The two at the left are old birds, winners of 1st prize as pair at the Illinois State Show. The others are young stock.

prime stock is the profit. From March on the only demand is for medium to small turkeys, and that is when spring hens can be marketed best, for they are then scarce and consequently bring a good price. It will pay well to dress them if the work is properly done.

As with other poultry, good, healthy stock must be used, it must have good care, be fed regularly and constant attention must be given to every detail of the business. Given good stock and suitable surroundings success depends largely on the owner or caretaker. Common sense must be relied on to carry us over the hard places.

In closing I will say that I believe there is no more hardy and profitable turkey than the White Holland. They meet all market requirements and their dressing qualities, flesh and beauty are unexcelled.

Standard Bred White Holland Turkeys, by Sewell

WHITE HOLLAND TURKEYS

Can be Grown to Weights that Rival those of the Bronze Variety—May be Raised on a Small Place—A Clever Plan of Hatching—
Feeding the Poults

A. E. BLAKER

WE HAVE handled White Holland Turkeys for many years and the longer we keep them the better we like them. They are the stay-at-home turkey and a large flock can be raised on a few acres of land. Those now bred by the leading breeders are very closely approaching the weights of the Bronze. One of our head breeders for this season weighs over forty pounds, so I am inclined to think that those who have small birds only, have an inferior strain. Forty pounds is fourteen pounds above standard weight, but it shows what can be accomplished by selection and breeding.

The White Hollands are the best layers of all the turkeys. They will lay all summer long if not allowed to sit. We have had them lay four clutches of eggs in a single season. Our breeding flocks are yarded and boxes and barrels are placed about in out-of-the-way places for nests and when a hen wants to sit we set her in those places. The fronts of these boxes and barrels are generally covered with brush and hay or straw put inside. We use about an acre of ground for the breeding flock, but one can yard them in a very small place if necessary. We yarded a small flock one year, before we built our present yards, in a yard about five rods square and we never had eggs hatch better nor turkeys do better than that spring. Out of 108 hatched we had eight accidentally killed and raised 96 to maturity.

HATCHING AND FEEDING

We raise our turkeys altogether with turkey hens, yet we have them to lay out their second clutch before we let them have the young ones. We started here in Kansas six years ago with only two hens and a tom and the way we managed them is illustrative of what can be done with them. We saved up the eggs until the hens became broody. Then the eggs were set under chicken hens and we "broke up" the turkey hens. They began to lay again in about five days and were ready to sit by the time the eggs hatched. Although they had been sitting but a few days they were ready to take the poults and mother them just as if they had gone the full time.

The poults hatch out very strong. Give us a few days of sunshine after they are hatched and we will bring nearly all of them through all right. We never feed the little ones corn chop, for we think it is too heavy a food. The first feed is good sharp grit and we keep it before them all the time. The first few days we feed stale bread soaked in sweet milk and squeezed dry with the hands and plenty of green food such as dandelion, lettuce, onion tops or whatever we have handy. Boiled rice is an excellent food, so are boiled eggs, but I think one can feed too many boiled eggs and so cause liver trouble.

The poults are yarded for the first few weeks, but after we think they are old enough we turn them out and let them roam over the farm, being always careful that they come home every night. They require very little food and when grasshopper time comes they do not require any at all, but we always feed a little when they come in at night as an inducement to have them come home. They roam over the fields at their own sweet will in the day time, but they are made to understand from the start that they must come home and go in their yard every evening.

BREEDING WHITE HOLLAND TURKEYS

Methods Used by a Successful Breeder—Selecting Breeding Stock—Preparation for Shows—Exhibiting—Diseases

C. C. HERRON

T PRESENT we are breeding White Holland Turkeys as we think they are the best turkey raised today. We have bred the Bronze, the Slate and the Bourbon Reds and have found the White Hollands to beat them all in many respects.

In our opinion, there is nothing as stylish as a well developed White Holland, with its pure white plumage, pink shanks and feet and bright, red head. They are of a very gentle disposition, make excellent mothers, will stand confinement better than any other variety we have tried and will mature quicker and lay more eggs.

They are the most thoroughly domesticated of any turkey raised today and by careful breeding the size has been improved until they today get to be as large as any turkey on the market. I have raised young toms that would weigh 24 pounds at Thanksgiving and never saw those weights beaten by any other breed or variety.

They can be successfully raised in confinement, the same as chickens, until they are able to take care of themselves and they will come home at night to roost, the same as a flock of chickens.

BREEDING STOCK

I am very careful in selecting my breeding stock. I select four to six yearling hens with long backs; broad, deep breasts, good plumage and all around shape. These I place with a large, heavy-boned, vigorous, young tom, and I find this is the best mating I can get. I can get a larger per cent of fertile eggs and hatch out large boned, vigorous, young poults and can raise almost every one. I think a large per cent of the loss is due to the parent stock.

I keep from five to six breeding yards each year and raise from two to three hundred. In the fall I cull out all the bad ones and place on the market about Thanksgiving time, and save none but the best to ship and breed from the coming season.

I aim to keep breeders that are show birds and at the same time are excellent breeders. When I find a good breeder, I keep it as long as it lives, for I think they never get too old.

I select my breeders and place them in a lot about one acre in size, for each pen. I have a nest for each hen (a sugar barrel makes a good nest). Place the nest in a quiet place where they will not be bothered; it is best to conceal it a little and let the turkey think she is stealing her nest. I gather the eggs every evening and place them in a cool, dark place; turn each day after the first day, as they will keep longer when handled in this manner.

The first hens that want to sit, get the eggs. I place from fifteen to seventeen eggs under each hen and aim to set her on the ground, if possible. Be sure and keep her free from lice. When the little poults are hatched, I place them in a large roomy coop and let the poults have free range, after the dew is all gone in the morning. When they are three or four days old I give them a good dusting with lice powder and turn them and their mother loose upon free range.

THE FARMER'S FRIEND

There is no fowl that is as profitable for the farmer as a flock of turkeys. They will destroy more insects than any other fowl and eat but very little grain until cold weather comes. Turkeys bring from 12c to 15c per pound in this section and will bring from $2 to $3.00 each, so there is a large profit to be made in breeding turkeys

FANCY END IS NEGLECTED

I think that the greatest trouble in the turkey industry is that they are neglected in the show room. They are not given near the attention that other poultry is, and for that reason they are not bred by more fanciers. I exhibit at some of the leading shows and as a rule the turkeys are placed in some back corner where they will not be seen by any one but the judge.

CONDITIONING FOR THE SHOWS

In July I start my old birds to moulting, then I put them up for about thirty days before they are ready to start. It is at this time that I handle them and get them tame and in condition. When they get so tame that I can handle them, I turn them out for a day or so and then place them back in confinement. This makes them very gentle and so I can handle them with ease, without their losing flesh, which they will do if kept shut up all the time. A turkey needs lots of exercise and will not stand steady confinement without losing in flesh.

I have my birds fully feathered and in good condition and as they have their new coat of feathers they are clean and ready for the show, except a few stains which can be easily removed with a damp cloth or sponge.

SHIPPING TO THE SHOW

I place them in a good tight crate with plenty of straw. This keeps them clean while on the road. Be careful not to leave any cracks in the crate; it is one of the worst things you can have to muss up the feathers, as the birds will be restless and move around more or less.

DISEASES AND PREVENTATIVES

Turkeys are an easy fowl to raise, yet are subject to several diseases such as cholera, roup and black-head. While I am never bothered much with any of the above diseases, I think they can be prevented by keeping your birds healthy, with roosting places in the open air, also by using clean food and fresh water.

Jove I.
A forty-five pound White Holland Tom from the yards of the Royal Farms

I think the most common disease in turkeys is cholera and the greater part of that is brought on by the way they are fed. In the first place never allow the turkeys to drink stagnant water, such as they get in the fall when streams are low, or around the stable, etc.

Do not over feed. During the seasons when bugs and insects are plentiful, feed very little grain, just a little in the morning and night. Too much animal food will get their bowels too lose and this is the first stage of cholera. Cholera is an easy disease for me to cure as I use my own remedy and it has never failed yet.

There is not as much disease as there used to be and there would be still less if the farmers and breeders would use a little more judgment and caution in their feeding and breeding. Inbreeding is almost a sure sign of failure in the turkey business.

GET THEM LARGER

There is one thing we all want to work for and that is to get more size and that is what you will not get if you inbreed; so, let us work together and build up our turkeys until they will be true to the name—Mammoth White Hollands.

RAISE MORE TURKEYS

A Western Breeder of Turkeys Thinks the Farmer Who Does Not Raise a Flock of Turkeys Makes a Mistake—She Finds Them Easy to Raise—It is Essential to Have Good Parent Stock

MRS. W. N. JEWETT

WHEN one decides to raise turkeys the first thing to do is to invest in good, sound parent stock. I do not believe much in buying turkey eggs to set, as so many persons are not careful enough about the breeding stock. A turkey that has been cured of roup or any other disease will not make a good breeder and the young will not be as sound nor do so well as you expect them to do. I would advise beginners to buy good stock.

In selecting my own birds I always pick the largest boned birds that I have. If both the hen and the gobbler have large extended breasts the young will be strong and healthy.

I feed my breeding turkeys just the same as I do my breeding chickens and they lay around the barn or hen house and do not wander far away.

Ten or twelve hens may be kept with one gobbler and almost every egg will hatch if the gobbler is vigorous. He should be a year or a little older. I prefer that the hens be one or two years old as they are stronger and know better how to care for their young.

I always set the first laying of eggs under good, old Plymouth Rock hens and then break up the turkey hens. In a few days they will be laying again. This second laying the turkeys are allowed to hatch and they will rear them so that they will make fine birds by Thanksgiving if they have any show at all.

As we live on a farm we give the turkeys free range. As the grain ripens, the alfalfa is green and the grasshoppers are plentiful, so with plenty of fresh water at hand, the turkeys do not need my care—except at nightfall—after they are old enough to allow them to roam.

FEED AND CARE OF YOUNG TURKEYS

The young poults are kept in a large coop until they are two weeks old, at which time they are strong and ready to follow the old turkey. She knows when they have roamed far enough and she will hover them when they need it.

Great care should be taken not to feed the young poults too much at one time. This is the rock, if I may be permitted to use this figure of speech, on which the frail barks of thousands of poults have struck and gone down, together with the plans and hopes of their zealous but misguided owners. The natural habit of turkeys is to hunt for their food and they do it slowly and deliberately all the long day. Thus the process of eating and

digesting are simultaneous; but when they are fed with a lavish hand they gorge themselves and in a few weeks fall victims of their own greed.

I prefer the White Holland because they do not roam nearly so far as the Bronze. If you mate them well they will grow very large. The first feed the poults have is hard-boiled eggs. They are boiled a long time so that they will be crumbly when mashed with a fork. Eggs so cooked are easily digested, and they should be sprinkled with black pepper. This is all I feed for two days, giving them fresh water to drink. Then they are fed Dutch cheese, peppered well, and prepared chick feed with green onions chopped fine.

There are no floors in my turkey coops, but the coops are removed every day to new ground. A large shingle is kept on which the little turks are fed. It must be kept clean, for when it gets dirty they will not eat their food from it. They are fed four times a day while they are cooped, but only twice while they roam, that is in the morning and at night. Some feed small turks too often. Their digestive apparatus seems to be very delicate at first. Overfeeding causes the death of a very great many little turks. If one fed them every time they come running they would be eating all the time and they cannot stand it.

BENEFIT TO GROWING CROPS

Turkeys by nature are prone to wander over the fields for a great share of their living, thereby gaining a healthy, robust constitution and at the same time ridding the fields and meadows of grass and weed seeds, grasshoppers and other insects that are harmful to growing crops. This certainly is converting evil into good. They will do this in the fall of the year when the corn is ripe and never disturb the ears of corn. Mine do, but I always feed my turkeys at home some.

Put the turkey coops near the alfalfa field if you can and all the day they will roam through the alfalfa hunting bugs. It is interesting to watch them and hear them chatter away while at work.

The turkeys that are not fit for breeders are dry-picked with the head and feet off and sent to market. Out here I received twenty cents a pound and furnished the hotels with them. I sell as high as one hundred and fifty pounds to a hotel at a time, so it is easy to get rid of all the surplus. I think that the farmer who does not raise a flock of turkeys is making a great mistake.

Seven Hardy and Vigorous Wild Cockerels

WILD TURKEYS

The Hardy Nature of the Turkey has Suffered from In-Breeding and Too Intimate Association with Domestic Fowls—Relief Found in Return to More Normal Conditions and the Infusion of Wild Blood

ROBERT LEE BLANTON

THE turkey raising industry has recently suffered greatly from a multiplicity of diseases that have infested these fowls. The losses have been chiefly among the poults. For many of these diseases, no sure remedy has been discovered, and many persons who hith-erto found this branch of poultry culture quite lucrative, have given up the business in despair.

It is almost certain that the originally hardy nature of the turkey in the wild state has suffered most from too much inbreeding and from too intimate association with barnyard fowls. Those familiar with the nature and habits of wild turkeys are well aware that these birds are the hardiest and most virile of the gallinaceous species. They have for several centuries struggled with man, beast, birds of prey and the elements so that their existence has depended upon the survival of the fittest. Thus it is that only the fittest survive.

For years I have made a careful study of wild turkeys in their native haunts. I know where they feed, what they eat, how and where they seek their nesting places, how they rear their young and how they escape the hunter.

I have never seen one that seemed to have died from any disease, and it is a mistake to believe that the young turkey cannot be raised upon damp ground. I have observed that they prefer the creek and river bottoms, and I have repeatedly seen flocks of young wild turkeys retreat from the rising waters of creeks and rivers after prolonged rains, and noticed that they returned to the swamps as the water receded. The young feed almost entirely upon insects, and swamps with nearby fields and woodlands abound in this kind of food.

Not only is the wild turkey the hardiest of our na-tive gallinaceous birds, but it is also the largest and most handsome. No one who has ever seen a magnificent gobbler strutting in the sunlight, his rich bronze feathers reflecting colors of gold, green, red, purple and blue, will forget the sight. I have seen males that appeared to be eight or ten years old, judging from the length of their beards and their spurs. The older they are the richer their plumage becomes. I recall shooting one some years ago that had a beard fifteen inches long and spurs an inch and a quarter in length and almost as sharp as those of a game cock. I suspect that I have killed as many of these splendid game birds as anyone of my age.

Some years ago I concluded to try an experiment in domesticating them. I succeeded in capturing five young ones only a few days old. These I raised with a domestic turkey that had just hatched her own brood. Fortunately, one of these I captured was a male. When they were three months old and began to show indications of longing for their kindred in the woods, I enticed them into an enclosure that I had constructed for their future home. This enclosure was made with six-foot poultry wire and was covered with the same material. I made the pen thirty feet wide and a hundred and fifty feet long, constructing a roost at one end of the enclosure twenty feet high. The following year the hens laid and I set the eggs under domestic turkeys and raised quite a flock successfully. I then began to enlarge my enclosure, and to construct others similar to the original one. This I have done from time to time until now I have three acres thus enclosed. The pens are well set in grass and clover and are furnished with abundant shade by vines and shrubbery. I have now sheds to protect them in bad weather. The first birds captured had no protection from the weather.

I have added to my stock from year to year by capturing other birds and finding eggs until I have all the varieties except that found in Central America. Our Virginia variety is the largest of all the varieties. I have one gobbler that weighs thirty-eight pounds, and my friend, Mr. N. R. Wood, the taxidermist for the Smithsonian Institute, agrees with me in believing that this bird is likely the finest specimen in existence. Only one other of which I have read approximates this one in size or markings, and that one is described by Audubon. That one weighed thirty-six pounds.

By judicious mating, I have increased the size of my birds each year. And as I have my pens divided in sections, I can mate the birds as I please.

I keep the feed bins well supplied at all times with corn, oats, kaffir corn, grit and charcoal. They never lack food, drink or shelter. By kind treatment I can now turn out on free range all my birds except those most recently captured.

I do not allow my wild hens to hatch the young, as I have learned that environment is worth more than heredity in dealing with both the young of man and other animals. I always select the gentlest domestic turkeys to do the incubating, and I raise the young on free range. I feed them just the same as I would the domestic turkeys, and I have learned that it is best to feed young turkeys very sparingly; in fact they seem to get along very well making their own living. The bug or

grasshopper that can escape the keen eye of a young wild turkey is indeed fortunate.

By careful experiments I have found that the wild turkeys are not subject to many of the diseases that infest their domestic cousins. But I am careful to avoid

Section of Enclosure Showing Portion of Flock

inbreeding. Every year since I began breeding them, new blood has been added.

On the fifth of April I set twenty-one eggs, and twenty-eight days after this, twenty healthy poults were hatched. They are now giving every indication of surviving the long rainy season we usually have in May. I have two hundred eggs that are due to hatch the last of this month (May).

The demands for my stock and eggs are so great that I can not fill all the orders. I am shipping birds to foreign countries. On the eleventh of this month I shall send a pair to Italy.

The wild turkey can be crossed with any domestic turkey and the infusion of wild blood is sure to add vigor to the stock. I would, however, advise all those who intend purchasing wild birds or eggs to be sure that they get genuine wild and not some that have either lost their virility by long inbreeding or by continued crossing with the same domestic turkeys.

It is my firm belief that the hope of the turkey industry depends upon the breeding of wild turkeys or upon crossing them with the domestic turkey.

A Wild Tom

THE GREAT MARKET TURKEY

The Claims of the Narragansetts to this Distinction—Inbreeding—Care of Poults—Nine-Year-old Breeders—How to Begin

S. T. JONES

I BREED all varieties of turkeys, the Bronze, Narragansett, Buff, Slate, White and Black. The Whites are the easiest to breed to standard requirements on account of their color and the Narragansetts are a close second, because they breed so true to color. I find the Bronze are the hardest to breed up to the standard, as it is very difficult to get a good color throughout and when the birds are under a year old they are not matured. They are tall, leggy, and look light in the breast. If you breed what the public demands, and you must do that, you have to breed the leggy kind, because four out of five letters inquiring for young Bronze turkeys demand size. That is the cry—size—size—size. "We want them good in wing and tail color and great, big heavy weight fellows." If you breed the plump, early maturing kind you cannot make forty or forty-five toms out of them. You must breed the big, tall, leggy kind, and when the toms are two and three three years of age you wil find that they will weigh forty, forty-five and even forty-eight pounds, and then, truly, you have the most magnificent bird in America. But the Narragansett, Buff, White and Slate varieties are the best market turkeys, for they mature early. The Narragansett heads the list and is usually ready for market at five or six months of age. The Buffs and Whites are next in order. The standard weights for Narragansett males (thirty, twenty-five and twenty pounds) are too high. The cocks and cockerels should weigh the same as the Buff and Slate turkeys, viz.: Twenty-seven and eighteen pounds, for they are short legged, plump and mature early.

An excellent illustration of the Narragansett turkey appears on page nine of this book.

INBREEDING—RANGE

I introduce new blood into my flock every two or three years. I do not think it necessary to do so oftener, as I keep from two to six flocks of each variety, but I never inbreed turkeys, as I find it will not do. I breed all the varieties for exhibition, and when getting new blood I aim to improve in all sections, both in shape and color. The breast, body and back are the most important sections in shape and the wings and tail the most important in color. We do not raise turkeys in confinement. They must have a large range if we are to attain best results. I never house my turkeys, as I think they do better when raised in the open. The nearer we come to raising them in the natural way the better it is for them. I do not try to fence against them, but give them unlimited range. We keep only one variety on a farm and give that variety the run of the

A Young Mexican

entire farm. Turkeys that are hatched in the spring will lay the following spring and different turkeys will lay a varying number of eggs. The Narragansetts lay more than any other variety and the Buffs are next. I have had turkeys that laid the entire season and did not offer to sit, while others will lay from ten to fifteen eggs and become broody. We keep from five to eight hens with one male, as we think that we get better results as a rule than we do if we have a greater number of females, though we have had from twelve to fourteen hens with one male and the eggs were all fertile. Probably 90 per cent of all turkey eggs are fertile unless the turkeys are overfed, and consequently are too fat. Let them get their own food by roaming over the pasture and stubble lands.

CARE OF POULTS

It takes from twenty-seven to twenty-nine days to hatch turkey eggs. We have not tried hatching them under hens. For the first twenty-four to thirty-six hours after they are hatched we feed very small grit or gravel, and then we feed clabber cheese dry and some corn meal, a little millet seed or small cracked wheat. We keep the hen and poults in a small pen for eight or ten days and then put them out on pasture land. They need very little food from this on, and should not be fed more than once or twice a day for the best results. Turkeys get nearly all their food from the fields in summer and fall.

Pasture and stubble land are the best places for them to run. In the fall begin feeding corn, or, if you are feeding cattle or hogs, the turkeys will get all the food they need, for they always manage to find the feed lots. The main secret in successfully feeding turkeys is to give them their food regularly, but be careful not to give too much. More turkeys are fed to death when they are young than die from any other cause. Nine out of ten breeders feed their poults until they kill them. I have had persons tell me what they feed young turkeys and then say: "My turkeys do not seem to grow well, and I know I feed them well." I do not see how they manage to raise any at all. I am sure I could not if I fed as they do. Remember to feed lightly, always using the best of food and never feeding any damaged grain at all. A bushel of corn will feed a turkey from sixty to seventy days if it has the range of the farm. The dealers want turkeys weighing from ten to sixteen pounds and not over twenty pounds.

A PREMIUM ON NARRAGANSETTS

There is a difference in the quality of turkeys and I claim that the Narragansett is king. There are turkeys that can beat them on weight, but when it comes to quality, no other breed can be compared to them. I sell most of my market turkeys here at home, and sell them alive if I can. One firm here buys most of my turkeys and they always engage all the Narragansetts I have to spare and ask me why I do not breed them exclusively. I get a premium of 2 to 2½ cents per pound on Narragansetts. The Buffs are my next choice.

Any turkeys that are off in color or the least bit out of shape and all of the late hatched and under weight turkeys are classed with our market turkeys. Before marketing I feed all that they will eat in order to have them fat, and market all that are ready at Thanksgiving time and the balance of them at Christmas. As a rule, yearlings make the best breeders, but I have kept some breeders until they were eight or nine years old.

A turkey is most delicate from the time it is hatched until it is six or seven months old. If I were to name the two principal causes of the mortality among turkeys I should say overfeeding and lice. They should never be allowed to live on low, swampy ground. It is not fit for turkeys or any other kind of poultry. We raise from three hundred to a thousand.

If I were to embark in the business of raising turkeys and had the benefit of my present experience, I should buy from some reliable breeder a tom and four to six hens and should insist upon getting good ones. I should not begin by buying eggs. I should also insist that the tom and hens be not related, and I should never inbreed.

Writing for the Reliable Poultry Journal on the subject of turkeys, a prominent eastern poultryman said the following about our favorites:

"We have always had a particular liking for the Narragansett turkey. It is nearly as large as the Bronze and equally as good for the table. Its plumage is very striking, giving one the effect of a black and white barred plumage; and as a resident of Rhode Island, the writer feels that the state which has the beautiful Narragansett Bay ought also to breed quite largely the beautiful Narragansett turkey. But it does not. Patriotic as Rhode Island is in other respects it does not let its patriotism extend to any great extent to its selection of turkeys.

"The Narragansett took its name from the Indians who once dwelt here, and was at one time more extensively bred in Rhode Island than now. We are reactionary to the extent of wishing for a return of the good old times in turkey raising when the Narragansett turkey was the favorite breed, although, gentle reader, we will confess that any Rhode Island turkey, once bred and fattened here, if stuffed with Providence River oysters and nicely roasted, has a very satisfactory effect upon our palate. It may not equal a genuine Rhode Island clam-bake, but it comes when clam-bakes cannot be had, and it is so good that one can say, after eating of such a dish:

"Let the world do its worst,
 I have dined today.' "

A Wild Tom

This bird is believed to be the largest wild turkey in existence. weighs thirty-eight pounds and was two years old at the time the photograph was taken, Note the perfect wing. See page 80.

MONEY IN TURKEYS FOR THE HOLIDAYS

Great Magnitude of the Business—How the Commission Men Obtain the Birds—The Care of Turkeys on the Farm—Methods of Fattening—Steady Rise of Prices in Recent Years—The Methods of Killing and Dressing

FRED HAXTON

HE turkey is king. In November the "Great American bird" holds undisputed sway in every butcher shop from Maine to Oregon and from Canada to Mexico. Not until a week after New Year's day does his rule expire.

There is money in raising turkeys for the holiday trade—lots of it. Going into South Water street, Chicago, on an afternoon as early as November 1 and seeing drayload after drayload of turkeys unloaded, with seemingly no end in sight, the spectator departs with the impression that enough turkeys are grown in the middle west alone to supply every man, woman and child with one for every meal and leave a few thousand for the Fiji Islanders and other benighted heathen.

MAGNITUDE OF THE BUSINESS

During the holiday rush or preceding it 678,000 turkeys, valued at $1,356,000, are received in Chicago, according to estimates made by a number of prominent poultry dealers. The bulk of the business is so great that exact figures are impossible, but an idea of its magnitude may be secured when it is stated, in the words of the largest buyer, "The cars required to contain the turkeys shipped to Chicago for Thanksgiving, Christmas and New Year's dealers, etc., would make a train seven miles long."

"It will surprise some people to learn that on hundreds of farms in Iowa, Illinois and Missouri turkeys constitute almost the principal 'crop,'" said a large dealer. "Trips of buyers through the turkey country show that it is common for one farmer to have 300 turkeys, and flocks of 700 or 800 are not extraordinary. As high as $1,000 has been paid for a single consignment of turkeys. Nearly 25,000 have been disposed of in Chicago in a single day."

While warm weather lasts a large part of the shipments of turkeys received in Chicago are live birds, but when the temperature becomes low enough to insure the safe keeping of the meat, the fowls come dressed and packed in barrels. The production in the middle west is about equal in all the states near Chicago, but Missouri is the greatest producer in the world. During recent years Texas has made remarkable advances in turkey raising, the climate during the spring season being especially favorable. Marketmen are depending on this source of supply for a large increase during the next few years.

Chicago is a strategic point in the turkey trade, for a large proportion of the birds sold in New York and other eastern cities as "Vermont" and "Rhode Island" fowls are shipped from the west. Desperate campetition rules among the fourteen firms which ship stock east, as each is trying to "corner" the market. One of them almost succeeded a few years ago by a novel plan. To each dealer or farmer who shipped to him he allowed a guess on the highest price which turkeys would bring at any time before New Year's and to the winner he awarded a $70 wagon. Many of the commission men offered prizes for the same sort of contest later, one of them putting up as stakes checks for $100, $75 and $25.

HOW TURKEYS REACH THE MARKET

"How do we get the turkeys?" repeated the proprietor of a store in front of which were stacked coops containing nearly 500 birds. "I'll tell you: We have a couple hundred regular shippers, some dealers and some farmers, in country towns. Each spring we write them letters pointing out to them that the raising of turkeys is the most profitable business a farmer can engage in, and urging them to be sure to hatch more turkeys than ever before. Then late in the summer we write to the men, asking them how many turkeys they can provide for the holiday trade, and to be sure we will have our fair share of the birds we send our buyers out on trips, some of them 800 miles long.

"The buyers visit certain towns where the turkey production is enormous, contract wherever possible for the purchase of all the fowls, and then drive to the farms and see the farmers themselves—or rather the farmers' wives, for we have found that the women are the ones who really have the 'say' as to when and where the stock will be sold. My head buyer the other day handed a Missouri woman $563 for her flock, and she said she was saving the money to buy another farm to raise more grain to fatten more turkeys with, so as to buy another farm, etc. She finds there is more money and less trouble in turkeys than in hogs."

METHODS OF REARING

Letters received by commission men from some of their largest growers of turkeys tell the story of their success. Some of the hints gleaned from them are:

Do not try to raise the fowls in small quarters. Wherever possible turkeys should have free range. An excellent place for the fowls is an orchard, with a high fence. They will keep the trees almost clear of insect pests and secure a good deal of their food in this way. An orchard is an excellent place to keep them when the grain is ripening and they would do damage. Be sure the breeding stock is large and healthy. To avoid close breeding exchange toms with a grower who has different stock, or buy fine males. Have one tom for every dozen fowls or less.

Turkeys should be allowed free range the year around, if possible, except when the grain is ripening, or even then if they can be kept out of the fields. Turkeys like to hide their nests, and if they do this there is a strong chance that a sudden rain will catch the poults and kill them. For this reason the hens should be set where they can be kept shut in after the poults are hatched. Many breeders let the fowl select the place for her own nest and then, to protect the turkey from rains and the young birds from storms, place a V-shaped roof over the nest. In early spring the eggs should be removed daily while the bird is laying, to prevent chilling, but a nest egg should be left.

After the eggs are hatched care should be taken to prevent the chicks from being wet or going out in the wet grass, until they have grown considerably. Many make runways about eight feet long and four feet wide, with the top and sides covered with wire netting. With these a coop four feet long and two feet wide is used, having a wooden bottom to prevent the poults from being flooded out in case of sudden storms. As the runway keeps the mother from wandering it also protects the young chicks. This device is in general use in the "turkey country."

Most of the growers permit the turkeys to roost the year around, principally because the birds never were taught to roost in sheds or houses, but the most successful erect lean-tos against the sides of barns and place roosts under them. These are shelters without fronts, attached to the buildings at an angle a little greater than the middle line of the letter Z.

When turkeys are allowed free range they do not require a great deal of grain or other food in summer, as they eat thousands of grasshoppers and other insects. The process of finishing them for market generally is begun along in August, when some grain is fed. The grain feed gradually is increased, until in September the birds are given all the corn they will clean up twice a day.

"The finest turkeys we get," said a dealer who makes a specialty of fancy birds, "come from farms in Missouri where they are penned up about the first of October and just stuffed with corn, skim milk and any other feed

Fig. 1.—Method of twisting the wings of a turkey on the back.

when they are dressed. The yard is about a quarter of an acre in size and from 300 to 500 turkeys are fattened in it annually. The owner tells me that the corn he puts into the turkeys brings him about three times what it would fetch in the market; this is in added weight alone, not counting the extra price per pound paid him because of the fine condition of his stock."

Comparatively little of the turkey crop is killed and dressed by the farmers. Most of them actually drive their stock to market, taking a flock of a couple hundred or more turkeys and conducting them to the wholesale purchaser in the nearest village or to a point where crates are waiting to take them to the nearest large city. When the grower is ready to market his stock he generally notifies his dealer in Chicago or elsewhere, and the latter immediately sends by express enough coops to contain the shipment. These are taken any distance by the express companies for only 10 cents apiece, which is much cheaper than the making of new coops for each shipment would be.

HOW PREPARED FOR MARKET

In late November and December most of the turkeys are dressed in the country. Each of the dealers demands that the fowls be prepared to suit him; if they are not, he sometimes refuses to purchase them at all. Following is the "letter of instruction" sent to each large turkey grower by Geo. McCutcheon & Co.:

"Keep from food twenty-four hours. Kill by bleeding in the roof of the mouth or by cutting a vein in the neck; never take off the head. Hang by feet until through bleeding, and leave the feet on. Never scald a turkey. Dry-pick while the fowl is still bleeding. Do not wait until the body gets cold. Be careful not to break the skin; do not draw entrails or crop; remove all the feathers from the wings. Remove pin feathers thoroughly. Hang in a cool place until the animal heat is entirely out. This is very essential.

"Wrap head of turkeys with clean light brown paper. Pack snugly (to prevent moving about) in boxes or barrels lined with clean paper. Boxes holding 100 to 200 pounds are best for all fowls.

Turkeys show up best if the body and legs are straightened out. Mark weight plainly on cover, and secure box carefully to avoid breaking open in transit. It should be noted that dry picked turkeys or other poultry is best for shipping in warm or doubtful weather. Poultry frozen will not command as good prices as that which is not. Old and heavy tom turkeys should be marketed before the holidays, as later the demand is for round, fat hen turkeys only."

Another dealer gives this advice:

"Turkey feathers should be pulled out with a twist. A straight pull will 'set' them. Dressed turkeys, when dry-picked, always sell better and command a higher price, as the appearance is brighter and more attractive. Broken ice should be placed all through the barrels—that is, a layer of turkeys and a layer of ice broken to the size of a fist. Fill the barrels in this manner and then on top of the turkeys place a large cake of ice. If turkeys are shipped alive, strong coops should be used, as they get especially rough handling during the holiday rush, and they should be high enough to allow the tur-

FEATHERS HAVE A VALUE

"Save the feathers. They are valuable. We offer the following prices per pound:

Turkey body, dry and choice 6
Green and little damp .... 1@
White turkey body, dry prime 50
Tail, choice and clear 40
Tail mixed with skirt feathers ....20@25
Wing, from first two joints 20
Wing, tail and pointers 17
Wing and tail, clear 27
Wing and pointers 13
Pointers 7

"Despite the fact that all dealers agree more turkeys have been raised this year than ever before, the prices are unusually high. The ten pound Thanksgiving dinner that $1.25 would buy a few years ago at a shilling a pound was retailed at $2.25 to $2.75 this year. The high prices are explained by a turkey expert as follows:

"For some time before the Thanksgiving demand came the retail butchers catering to select trade were placing their orders for turkeys at 23 cents a pound, dressed. This means the wholesale price, and as the retailers figure out a profit for themselves of 2 or 3 cents a pound, the consumer had to pay 23 cents a pound for turkeys delivered on these orders. Only the finest birds were pre-empted at this high figure, but the average range of prices was around 21 or 22 cents.

"There is an obvious reason for the 'kiting' of the price of turkey meat. The current explanation in South Water street is that the big stockyards packers and other large purchasers go into the country early and succeed to a large extent in 'cornering' the turkey market by the expedient of buying up the entire visible supply through agents in the choicest turkey raising districts. This is declared to have happened in many states, especially Kentucky, Missouri and southern Illinois. It is common gossip among the South Water street commission merchants that the leading packer in the so-called Chicago 'big-four' combination sent his agents into Kentucky a few years ago and purchased virtually all the 'turkey futures'—the Thanksgiving crop—in the great turkey-producing district known as 'the territory north and south of the Ohio river.'"

The great Thanksgiving rush begins the Monday before Thanksgiving, but preparations for it are made for weeks, the birds being killed as fast as received, the surplus after the daily sales going into coolers. One hundred and sixty men were engaged last year in dressing turkeys alone, several large establishments being in the business of killing and dressing poultry for other dealers. These are known as poultry slaughter houses. More than 500 turkeys a day are dressed during the rush season for each of the large commission houses.

The grower of turkeys is sharing in the prosperity brought by high prices, but investigation shows the wholesale dealer and the retail butcher get a large share of the profits, together sometimes making almost 10 cents a pound, although their profit generally is around 6 cents. One of these dealers, talking of the high price of poultry, said:

EXPORT TRADE INCREASING

"The export trade has grown to immense proportions in the last few years, turkeys leading in the foreign demand. The home trade has grown by leaps and bounds at the same time with the foreign business.

"All the finest American poultry goes to Europe. The big packers are the great exporters of American turkeys."

The immense business done in poultry by the "beef trust"—amounting to millions of dollars a year—has a great effect on the turkey market. Swift & Co. filled a contract for 55,000 pounds of turkey for the United States army.

The price of turkeys varies more than any other kind of poultry. In summer the birds sometimes sell as low as 13 cents a pound, live weight, and in winter they occasionally reach eighteen cents, alive. Immediately after the New Year's demand is supplied there is a slump in prices, and it is then that the speculators buy their stock of thousands of birds to be placed in cold storage and sold the next summer. The "good prices" for turkeys, as the dealers call them, begin to come around November 1, when the birds bring about 16 cents a pound, live weight. The prices will keep up well this year, probably equalling those of last winter. Even last August, when turkeys generally are at about their lowest point, live birds brought 15 cents a pound.

During November and December there is a great demand for young turkeys, which dress about three to five pounds. These bring fancy prices, and the demand is not filled. Few are seen in the wholesale markets because the growers generally contract directly with butchers to take off their hands all they can raise. Such stock has sold for 22 cents a pound, dressed. The smaller of the baby turkeys, as they are called, were used as "fryers," and those that weighed four pounds or more were roasted. The bulk of the old turkeys that come to the market weigh about 12 to 15 pounds apiece, but several that tipped the scales at more than thirty-five pounds were seen in the stores last fall. The extremely large turkeys, however, are not in great demand, as they are too heavy for family dinners and difficult to roast when bought by hotels.

A FAMOUS GROWER

The most famous grower of turkeys in the United States is Horace Vose, of Westerly, Rhode Island. Mr. Vose last year followed his annual custom of sending a Thanksgiving turkey to the president of the United States, a custom which he began in Gen. Grant's first term. He has autograph letters of thanks from all the presidents since then. Mr. Vose goes to a great deal of trouble to get the president's Thanksgiving dinner. Besides growing turkeys he deals in them, and after the chicks have been hatched a month or two he makes a tour of the farms for miles around. If he sees a particularly fine chick he secures an option on it, and directs that it be given special care. He makes other visits later in the season and bids for every fine turkey that he sees. When Thanksgiving approaches the Rhode Islander has control of practically all the finest birds for miles around. He is the largest shipper of turkeys for the New York market. This is Mr. Vose's philosophy:

"The object of fattening a turkey is to produce firm, finely flavored, luscious flesh. Therefore it should be fattened on whole corn—not meal—as the corn gives a firmer consistency to the flesh. It should never be stuffed artificially or confined in close quarters. If sweet apples are available they may be fed, as nothing will give a nicer flavor to the flesh."

"In July and August growers near fashionable resorts sometimes sell turkey 'broilers,' weighing from 1½ to 4 pounds each, for $3.50 to $4 a pair," writes Helen W. Atwater, government food expert.

The last government report shows there are 6,599,-

367 turkeys in the United States, of which only 529,993 are in the North Atlantic states—Rhode Island, Maine, Vermont, etc. The bulk of the turkeys in the country are in the north central states, which have 3,072,456, while the far western states have only 304,950.

MACHINE FATTENING TURKEYS

The London Board of Agriculture reports great success in fattening turkeys with a cramming machine. A mash of equal parts of ground barley, corn and oats, with a small amount of melted fat and linseed meal was used, enough skim milk being added to make it the consistency of cream. At first there was difficulty in feeding the turkeys, owing to their size and strength, but the operator finally overcame this by placing the fowls on a low stand so that their heads were on a level with the nozzle of the cramming machine. It is stated that "after a day or two the turkeys became accustomed to this manner of feeding, and when meal times came they showed much eagerness to mount the stand and receive their share of the food." The feeding period covered three weeks; the birds were hatched in the spring and weighed an average of seventeen pounds apiece, and made an average gain of four pounds four ounces. This was done at a cost of 41 cents per head.

Proof that turkeys fatten much better when kept in pens has been secured by the Manitoba experiment station. It took two lots of birds, exactly alike and gave them the same rations for six weeks, two parts of wheat, one of oats, and one of barley. At the end of the test it was found the turkeys in the pens had gained an average of a trifle over four pounds each, while those allowed their liberty added only a little more than 1¾ pounds each to their weight. Most of the gain was made in the first three weeks. The penned turkeys when dressed shrank 5 per cent less than the others and were more attractive in every way.

TURKEYS SENT TO ENGLAND

Canada does an immense amount of business in exporting turkeys to England. The Canadian commissioner of agriculture gives the following description of the proper way to prepare the birds for the British market, which is extremely exacting in its requirements:

"The bird is hung up by the legs, the wings being crossed to prevent struggling. Next it is given a sharp blow on the back of the head with a stout piece of wood, which renders it insensible. The knife is then inserted into the roof of the mouth, so as to pierce the brain, cutting it along the entire length. The bird is left hanging by the legs for a few minutes to allow the blood to drain out. Pluck at once, while still warm. Feathers should be left on the neck for about 3 inches from the head; also a few feathers on the tail and tips of wings. Do not tear the skin in plucking, and do not under any circumstances dip the bird into water. Remove the intestines from the rear. Care must be taken not to break the gall bag. All the rest may be left inside. Twist the wings on the back of the bird (Ill.1). A string, which, however, should not encircle the body, may be used to keep them in place. As soon as the feathers are off, hang the bird up by the feet to cool. Do not lay it down or hang it by the head. The blood should drain toward the head and become coagulated there. One dealer says to lay the birds on their breasts on a setting board, pressing the rumps square, letting the heads hang down until the body is set, when the birds will always retain their plump shape. Cleanliness is necessary. The feet and legs of the birds should be clean also. The legs of the dressed birds are often tied up as in illustrations 2 and 3. If the birds are to be displayed in a shop the head should be pushed up under the wing. The birds should be thoroughly cooled (not frozen), and they should be cold through and through before being packed in cases.

Fig. 2.—Breast view showing method of tying legs and pushing head under wing.

"Pack in any one case only birds of nearly the same weight, graded to within two pounds. In no case should any bird be lighter than the lightest weight or heavier than the heaviest weight marked on the package. Pack the cocks and hens in separate cases. Mark the cases at both ends plainly. Wrap every bird neatly in paper. The head of each bird should be wrapped with a quantity of thick paper, to absorb any blood. Spread a small quantity of wood pulp or dry, clean straw in the bottom of the case. Put paper on the bottom and top of the birds to keep them clean. A small quantity of wood pulp or dry, clean straw may be put on top, directly under the cover. Pack the birds with backs down, with heads at one side. Put from twelve to twenty-four birds in a case. Every case should be packed quite full and close to prevent damage during transit. Do not export any old, tough birds. Every bird should show a good, plump, white, broad breast."

Fig. 3.—Side view showing method of tying legs and pushing head under wing.

TURKEY GROWING PROFITABLE

There is more money in raising turkeys now than there ever was before and there will be more next year, for the trend of prices is irresistibly upward, market experts declare. The figures for several years, furnished the Reliable Poultry Journal by Howard, Bartels & Co., official statisticians for the Chicago poultry dealers, point out clearly the great advance in the wholesale market prices of turkeys in the last ten years. In the table below the prices from April to October, inclusive, are for live birds, as hardly any dressed turkeys are shipped in summer owing to the danger of spoiling. Where there is a wide variation in prices during the month the bulk of the birds were sold nearer the higher figure than the lower. Prices quoted for January, February, March, November and December are for dressed turkeys:

The quotations in the accompanying table are for the common run of stock, fancy turkeys being disposed of at special prices. The following table will show the gradual rise in prices for a ten year period. The figures for 1907-8 were unobtainable:

nearly all of the 4,000,000 pounds went to the New England markets and to the smaller eastern cities.

As a rule the birds grown in Kentucky are not of large average size, W. T. Seibels of the Packer says, and for this reason they are most desirable for buyers of large lots for holiday distribution by commercial concerns and large factories, to their employees. The average size of the hen turkeys is about 8 pounds, and toms run from 10 to 12 pounds. Ten thousand pounds are put in a refrigerator car, and whole trainloads are shipped at once.

The Kentucky association each year meets to fix the price which it will demand from the wholesale buyers,

Month	1906	1905	1904	1903	1902	1901	1900	1899	1898	1897	1896
January	17 to18	17 to19	16 to17½	17 to18	8½ to12	7½ to 9	9 to10	8 to11	10 to11½	8 to12½	8 to12
February	18 to19	19 to20	16 to17½	18	9½ to14½	7½ to 9½	8½ to10	8 to11	9½ to12	8 to12½	9 to13½
March	16 to17	19	16 to17	15 to18	10 to15	7 to12	8 to12	8 to13	9½ to12½	8 to13	13
April	12½	14 to15	11 to12	12 to13	9 to12½	6½ to 8	7½ to10	8 to10	8 to12	9	8 to12
May	11 to12½	14 to15	11 to12	10 to12	9½ to12½	6 to 8½	6 to 9	7 to10	6 to 9	6 to 9	7 to10
June	10 to12½	13½ to15	10 to12	10 to12	10 to12	5½ to 7½	5 to 7	6 to 9	5 to 8	5 to 7	6 to 9
July	11 to12½	14 to15	10 to11½	10 to11	11½ to12	6 to 7½	5½ to 7	7 to 8½	6 to 8	6 to10	7 to10
August	12 to18	15	12 to17	11	12 to12½	6 to 8	6 to 7½	7½ to10	6 to10	7 to10	8 to11
September	13 to16	15 to16	12 to14	10 to11	18	7 to 9	7 to 8	8 to12	7 to11	7½ to10	8 to11
October	13 to16	18 to17	12	11 to14	11 to13	7 to 8½	6 to 9	8½ to10	7 to11	8 to10	7½ to 9½
November	16½ to21	16 to18	15 to18	15 to18	10 to16	7 to10	6 to10½	9 to11	8 to11½	8 to10½	9 to11½
December		16 to17½	14 to17	15 to17½	13 to18	9 to11½	8 to 9½	9 to10½	8 to11	8 to13	10½ to11½

Think of live turkeys selling in the Chicago market at 5½ cents a pound, after express had been paid on them for hundreds of miles, and figure out what would be left to the grower! This was done in June, 1901. Think of dressed turkeys bringing only 7 cents a pound, which occurred in November, 1900, and figure how much less would be left to the shipper! In fact, 1901 was a "black year" for turkey men, the highest price on dressed stock being only 11½ cents, and the average for the year not more than a dime a pound. The prices given in the table are those paid to shippers, and not those at which the wholesalers sold the stock to dressers and meat markets.

The change from 6-cents-a-pound dressed turkeys was especially marked two years ago, when on November 13—before the Thanksgiving demand was hardly more than started, dressed turkeys were bringing the country shippers 16 to 18 cents a pound when even in fair condition, while choice stock commanded its own price. A 20-cent market was expected by many, and this means that the butchers would have to pay 23 cents upward for their turkeys and the city consumers from 26 to 29 cents a pound.

"Baby" turkeys were in especial demand that fall, and not one-tenth of the call for them could be met. These weighed around 5 pounds, some even reaching nine pounds, and found a ready market at 20 cents up, at wholesale.

KENTUCKY TURKEY ASSOCIATION

One thing that is increasing the price of turkeys was the formation of the Kentucky Turkey Association, in 1906, with headquarters at Lexington. This is composed of about fifty of the largest dealers in turkeys in the southern "turkey country," a single one of whom handles more than 250,000 each Thanksgiving season and the smallest one of whom handles 65,000 pounds each fall. From meagre proportions the turkey industry has grown to such size in the country around Lexington that 4,000,000 pounds of the birds were contracted for to supply the holiday trade in 1906. Dressing in Kentucky for the Thanksgiving demand was begun November 10, and

and during the year of 1906 disposed of the entire lot to Armour & Co., of Chicago. The association also tries to fix the price to be given the farmers, a frank admission of this fact being made in this statement after the meeting:

"The association met also to set the price that the buyers should pay for the turkeys. Nothing definite was given out, but the principal line of talk was that the farmers would be paid 10 cents a pound, live weight. With a stronger demand this might be increased to 11 cents in the country, which would mean about 12 or 13 cents at the pens (the points where the turkeys are confined until they are shipped alive or are dressed.)"

The farmer gets it in the neck every time, even from the "turkey trust." Oklahoma is coming to the front as a turkey raising state, the crop of 1907 amounting to 5,000 head, for most of which the farmers got 12 to 13 cents a pound, live weight.

"Poor stock is what keeps the market down on all kinds of poultry, but especially on turkeys," said Mr. Seibels. "If a shipper sends a lot of poor birds in with a large shipment of extra fine ones, the whole consignment will bring 2 or 3 cents a pound less than it would if he had kept the bad stuff at home. Dealers lay stress on the point that only good stock would be marketed, and agree that it is best to keep the poor, stringy birds in the country and fatten them up until they are fit to appear in the best markets and meet the highest class demand. Most of the regular shippers know this and act accordingly, but some lose their better judgment and send stock that has no business being shipped.

LIVE POULTRY PREFERRED

"The whole poultry business is being revolutionized, I believe, by the present cold storage trouble. Within a short time, present indications are, the bulk of the poultry sent to market will be shipped alive and will be bought alive by the butchers, who will kill the birds to order thus proving to the customer that they have not been in cold storage. Owing to fear that the city health commissioner, Dr. Charles J. Whalen, would cause trouble for them, few of the dealers put turkeys in storage this year, and as a result nearly all the stock sold for the Thanksgiving market came directly from the farms."

A commission of 5 cents on the dollar is charged by dealers in almost every city for selling stock for country shippers, and if the birds are sent alive a charge of 10 cents a crate is made for hauling them from the train to

is nailed round both ends and the middle of the coop to keep the other strips from loosening.

For packing turkeys to go into cold storage or for the eastern market the style of box which is most in favor is 24 by 26 by 15 inches. This will hold twelve young toms, or six young toms and eight hens, or 16 hen tur-

Methods of Killing and Plucking Turkeys

2—First stage in the operation of dressing. Operator holds the bird between his legs, pulls neck upward and back, and cuts a vein in the neck with a razor-edged knife. 3—Another way of killing by wringing the neck. This to be done successfully requires a knack that comes only by long practice. The birds wings are drawn together over its breast and the body is held between the knees. A sudden twist and jerk dislocates the neck and the fowl is dropped to the floor. 4—This operation follows that shown in illustration 3. The dresser is dry-plucking the turkey. Great care is required in the operation in order that the appearance of the fowl be not damaged. 5—Dressing a turkey by scalding. The birds are dropped two at a time into a metal vessel holding a barrel of water. This method is quicker than dry-picking but destroys the value of the feathers. 6—The dressing tables to which the turkeys go after being scalded.

the wholesale market. The standard poultry coop, used in all the markets in the country, is four feet long, 30 inches wide and a foot high for chickens and ducks, and 15 to 18 inches high for turkeys and geese. For broilers it is two feet wide and 10 inches high. The crates must be built substantially. Pieces two inches square should be used for the corner posts, and half inch boards should be nailed on the bottom, which is tight. Strips of lath a half inch thick and two inches wide are used for the sides, top and ends, being placed an inch and a half apart. Two laths are left loose on the top for a door, and lath

keys. The boxes should be lined with clean white or parchment paper and the stock should be carefully graded, and classified as No. 1, No. 2, Fancy, Culls, etc. For storing poultry a quarter of a cent a pound is charged for the first sixty days or less and after that time an eighth of a cent a pound for each month. Eighty per cent of the value of the goods put in storage will be advanced to the owner by the warehouse company or by banks.

Baby turkeys, 3 to 6 pounds each, should be marketed from August 1 to Oct. 15.

PLUCKING AND DRESSING

The pluckers of turkeys are paid high wages, some of them earning $20 a week. Many of them are paid regular wages, but most work by the piece, getting generally 5 cents a head. There were only twenty-five women, against two or three hundred men, dressing turkeys in Chicago the season of 1907. The women are all Italian or Bohemian immigrants or negresses. Several years ago, Z. E. Stewart stated, it was customary to employ women altogether, but when the Poultry Pickers' union came into existence it issued a dictum against it and every man refused to work with a woman picker. The union's existence has ceased, but women are not wanted. As the president of the union said:

"Dressing poultry by wholesale is no fit work for any woman. Where scalding is done none of them can endure it. Standing in water all day in a room filled with steam and then going on the street in the cold is not exactly what you would call health promoting. The men all get sick at it, and they're a pretty tough lot of fellows, too. Nobody can stick to it more than two years."

In the room where the turkey plucking was done in one of the largest plants the women wore wooden shoes to protect their feet from the water used in scalding other poultry, and their dresses and hair were covered with feathers. The women were Italians and said they were paid $14 a week each and handle 800 chickens or 200 apiece daily, although they do not do all the work. The men, called tippers, take off all the heavy feathers and pass the fowls to the women for finishing. The latter do the "pinning," as it is called, taking off all the down and small feathers. If they find it impossible to remove a refractory feather without tearing the skin, they cut it off close with a razor-edged knife. For pinning a dry picked turkey the employees get 3 cents each, and often finish 100 in a day. For pinning a chicken, if they are not working by the week, they get 1½ cents each.

KILLING, PLUCKING AND MARKETING TURKEYS

The Money Value of Attractive Appearance in Market—Manner of Killing and Plucking—Saving the Feathers for an Added Profit— Cooling and Cleaning the Carcass—Packing for Shipment to Dealers—Dressing and Packing for the Family Trade— High Prices Obtained from Private Customers—Advantage of Knowing the Market

H. A. NOURSE.

A GREAT deal depends on the manner in which turkeys are killed and prepared for market. Frequently it makes the difference in price between the highest and lowest quotations. Be the live specimen ever so fat and well fleshed, if it is carelessly picked and improperly packed it is often passed by for a bird not quite so well fattened, but presenting a better appearance when it reaches the market stalls. Obviously no producer can afford to send to market any bird that is not in good condition.

It is not difficult to properly flesh and fatten healthy turkeys. If they can be confined in a covered pen of good size, without becoming worried and losing their appetites, they will take on the most flesh, for the grain fed, in the shortest time. But young ones that have been accustomed to a wild life upon a large range do not take kindly to confinement and can seldom be improved if enclosed.

As the supply of bugs and other food gets short in the fields the old hens will lead the young birds to the feeder and a good ration of whole corn each day for two or three weeks will put them in good flesh, with sufficient fat to give the meat and skin a bright, attractive appearance.

There is a flavor belonging to the meat of a range fed and fattened turkey that cannot be found in one raised in confinement or one that has spent its days near the buildings eating with the chickens. The diet of grass, roots and berries not only produces flesh at less cost per pound, but improves the quality.

Before killing, the stock should be kept for eighteen hours in a clean, airy place where no food can be obtained. They may have water up to within eight hours of the time of killing, for water gives a healthy look to the skin and assists in cleansing the digestive organs of matter which would become sour and taint the flesh. A short, stout club, a long, sharp steel blade, a strong arm and a quick hand are required for the operation of killing.

THE MANNER OF KILLING AND PLUCKING

The bird should be suspended head downward with its feet in a noose of strong cord, far enough from the walls of the house and other objects so that it cannot injure its wings when it struggles—as most of them do at some time. After stunning by dealing a sharp blow at the base of the skull with the club, pass the left arm around the body of the fowl under the wings, which usually drop down when the bird is stunned and the muscles relax, holding the side of the breast towards you. Grasp the head in the left hand and forcing the bill open with the thumb and fore fingers, thrust the knife blade in through the mouth to just back of the brain and make a sharp cut directly across the roof of the mouth, severing the arteries. Then holding the bird firmly with the left arm and hand in the same position, begin at once to remove the feathers with the right hand, beginning at the juncture of neck and breast and working up over the breast and body, then giving the bird a turn which presents the back to the operator, begin at the neck or between the wings and pluck towards the tail. The short feathers of wings, tail, shanks and neck are picked next and the long feathers of the wings and tail, if removed at all, are plucked last. As a rule the feathers of the last joint of each wing are left on and are much appreciated by the purchaser of the bird to use about the kitchen in place of brushes. The long feathers of the tail are removed or not as the market for which they are intended requires.

While the skin of a turkey is less likely to be torn when removing the feathers than that of a chicken or duck, it is needful to be careful and none but experienced pickers can safely attempt to hurry the work. The thumb and forefinger do most of the work by firmly grasping a few feathers and removing them by a quick jerk which begins upward toward the tail and terminates outward, which movement is accomplished by a quick twist of the wrist. This motion first loosens the feathers in their sockets by starting them the way they grow and then removes them at an angle which is least likely to tear the skin.

A well grown turkey is very powerful and requires to be held firmly yet with due care, for if the wings are

McKinley

A Superb Bronze Turkey, that was sent to President McKinley by Horace Vose, who for more than thirty-five years has each season presented the President of the United States with a Thanksgiving Turkey.

grasped by their extremities or are held too firmly in any position the bird may struggle and break or wrench them out of joint, making the carcass unfit for sale.

Careful handling after picking is very desirable, for a bruise will cause discoloration which is very detrimental to the appearance of the flesh in market.

SAVING THE FEATHERS

If many birds are killed it pays to save the feathers, especially those of the tail and wings. Those of the tail proper and the two lower joints of the wings are salable at fifteen to thirty cents per pound and can be saved by no more extra labor than is required to toss them into a clean receptacle when picking and later dry them by spreading upon the floor of a loft where there is a good circulation of air. The shorter and body feathers seldom command more than 4 to 6 cents per pound and most turkey men do not care to save them for so little remuneration.

COOLING AND CLEANING THE CARCASS

Marketing is usually done in the cold weather of late fall and during the winter the cooling can be done by hanging the picked turkeys in the open air, out of the sun, long enough to allow the escape of all animal heat, but not long enough to freeze or become stiff if the temperature is low.

Most markets do not require the turkeys to be drawn, while some will pay less per pound for stock so prepared. It is always best to find what your market wants before killing, for if drawn turkeys are shipped where undrawn stock is wanted the loss on a consignment is considerable. Feet and heads should be washed clean and wiped dry and all blood removed from the mouth and throat. If care is used when killing and handling it will not be necessary to wash the body of the bird and the skin will retain its bright, yellow appearance longer than it would if dampened or if cooled in water rather than by the air.

PACKING TO SHIP

Packing is as important an operation as picking, but not so tedious. All consignments should be packed tightly, not jammed, in clean boxes and sufficient packing put in before the cover is nailed on to prevent shifting enroute. Birds of different sizes, but not of different qualities, may be packed in the same box and the contents of the package should be correctly described on the outside of the cover. If the description says "Ten young toms and ten young hens" and the dealer, on opening the box finds one old tom and perhaps some old hens, he of course loses confidence in the shipper and does not dare to recommend his goods. But if the contents of the package never fail to tally with the description the goods are satisfactory to handle and the returns as a rule are better. Large boxes are inconvenient to handle and less desired by small dealers than boxes weighing from one hundred and fifty to two hundred pounds and the smaller packages require to be packed less solidly and the contents show less evidence of hard pressure in the box. If the market catered to favors drawn stock it is easiest done before the bird is hung up to cool. The incision made should be as small as possible. A sharp knife should be used to cut the skin close around the vent and cut away the fat around the intestine, making an opening into the cavity.

Through this the entrails must be drawn carefully, the operator reaching with his fingers into the cavity to free the upper end from its attachment. Nothing else need be removed.

DRESSING AND PACKING FOR PRIVATE TRADE

If the stock is intended for a high price family trade, all the birds should be picked and handled with extreme care, the intestines drawn and the shanks and feet and the head removed. When cutting off the heads considerable blood will frequently be found clotted in the neck and unless removed it will turn black and show through the skin. If it happens that there is any food left in the crop it is wise to remove it before cooling. This is accomplished by pushing back the skin of the neck and working the crop out under it with the thumb and fore finger, taking care not to tear the crop in separating it from the tissues surrounding it. Removing the crop does not leave the breast looking quite so well as when the crop is empty and left in because its absence allows the skin to sink deeper in front of the breast bone; but if the food remains it will show black through the skin and mar the appearance of the bird. The skin should be drawn well over the end of the neck and tied with a clean string. Each carcass when thoroughly cooled should be wrapped in clean wrapping paper and packed in excelsior in a clean, new wooden box to be shipped to the consumer's kitchen door. Paper without much color should be used or at the end of the journey the color will be found to have deserted the paper to cling to the skin of the turkey, which will give it more the appearance of the "tattooed man" in a circus than that of the mainstay of a family feast.

The family trade is usually very profitable, paying well for the extra labor and other expense involved. One establishment, noted for the show room quality of its turkeys, has been furnishing private customers in several states with Thanksgiving and Christmas turkeys of the finest grade for several years. These are prepared and shipped in the manner described above, the weight is taken as soon as the feathers are off and the bills for them call for thirty-five cents a pound. No exceptional ability is needed to figure that there is money earned by properly growing and fattening, and carefully picking, packing and shipping turkeys at that price.

FINISH KILLING AT NEW YEAR'S

It is well to kill all stock unsalable for breeding or exhibition at or before the New Year. Occasionally, however, the poultryman will be caught with a few very

late hatched poults presented by some wily old hen that hid her nest so well and was so cautious in her "comings and goings" that it was not discovered until she brought off a brood contrary to her owner's wishes and intentions. Some breeders kill these late hatched ones on sight, believing that it is nothing but time wasted to look after them. Others allow them to run with the hen until cold weather and then house them with the chickens, giving them the same care. They appear to do better when confined in cold weather than in warm, but

The Thanksgiving Turkey

Illustrated on the opposite page, dressed and ready for shipment to President McKinley. Mr. Vose, the donor, is holding also another choice specimen, which he has just dressed, to assist in balancing the weight of the larger one.

them seem to breed lice faster than chicks and must be continually dusted for body lice and their heads and necks greased frequently to discourage the head lice. If the youngsters take kindly to confinement they will make very good growth and sell readily in the spring to the trade calling for small sized turkeys. These birds should never be kept for breeding, for they seldom make very strong birds and do not molt in the proper season.

Every turkey raiser who markets any considerable number each year can well afford to study his market closely; to find just what it wants and when it will pay most for it, and then bend his energies to furnishing the right stock at the right time.

Marketing often determines the profit.

CATCHING, HANDLING, AND SHIPPING TURKEYS

Building a Trapping Pen for Separation of the Flock—Using the Catching Net—Training for Exhibition—Coops for Local and Foreign Shipments

H. A. NOURSE

IT IS wise to separate from the flock in the fall the birds intended for sale, as constant raiding of the flock for birds to ship not only keeps the breeders wild and suspicious, but makes it extremely difficult to make an intelligent selection.

The best device for "rounding up" that I have seen is a covered yard or trap about thirty feet long and twenty feet wide. Sometimes this may be built between two of the farm buildings, using the buildings for the two sides, thus avoiding the necessity of setting posts and erecting sides of the enclosure. The poultry netting which forms the top and one end of the trap may be stretched between the buildings and fastened to them, supported by several pieces of heavy single wire drawn tightly from one building to the other. The other end, which is the entrance to the trap, is left open and provided with a drop which will be described later. The turkeys will not distrust the farm buildings and will more readily enter a trap between them than one separate from them. A wing should be constructed of poultry netting five feet high to extend from one corner of the entrance to a distance of fifty feet outward or away from the trap, to form an extension of the side, unless one of the buildings happens to be so extended. The turkeys may be driven gently along the side of the building towards the entrance and wing, and an occasional handful of corn may be thrown down to occupy their attention until they are at the entrance to the trap. Here the wing on the far side of the entrance prevents them going beyond and they may be quickly turned into the enclosure.

Constructing a trap in an open lot with no building is quite different. Four strong posts should be set up to form the corners of a space say thirty feet long and twenty feet wide and no other wood should be used. The posts may well be old ones, or those not carefully trimmed, and with the bark left on, so that there will be little about them to attract attention and arouse the turkeys' suspicions. It is not best to use bright wire or to turn up much earth for the same reason. The posts should stand five feet above the ground and have a heavy single wire like stock fence wire, stretched around their tops and also diagonally across the tops from corner to corner to support the wire netting which is stretched over it in forming the top of the trap. More netting is stretched around the sides and one end. This is tightly wired to the top and its lower edge is firmly pegged to the ground. One end is left open to serve as an entrance and is rigged with a drop. A piece of netting large enough to cover the open end is loosely wired to the strand of heavy stock fence at the top of the entrance. At the opposite side of this netting, which reaches to the ground, a heavy cord is attached, put through pulleys at the base of the entrance posts and carried to a distance of sixty or seventy-five feet directly in front of the entrance. By pulling these cords the drop will be hauled from a position on top of the trap down over the front, closing the entrance. Two wings will be required for this trap, for there is no building to assist in guiding the turkeys in. These

wings, or leaders, as fishermen would call them, should extend from each side of the entrance, spreading laterally to form a sort of funnel into the large end of which the turkeys may be toled and then driven into the trap.

The posts supporting the structure must be set deeply in the ground and all the wire stretched very tightly or it will be pressed out of shape by the flock running against it when trying to get out. Sometimes the trap may be built in a grove of trees and the trunks of trees used in place of posts, at the same time securing the benefit of the branches and possible low brush as a screen to partially hide the trap. If it is convenient the turkeys should be given their daily allowance of grain in this pen and when it is necessary to handle them the drop can be closed and the flock confined, thus avoiding the necessity of driving them in; but if they are trapped too often they will not go in, and cannot be driven or coaxed. Three times in a season should be enough to do all the selecting necessary.

CATCHING THE BIRDS

For the actual capture a net of heavy twine eighteen inches deep hung on a stout iron ring eighteen inches in diameter, which is attached to a handle seven or eight feet long, is the best contrivance I know of. This if put suddenly over the head of the bird and quickly drawn back will hold it so securely that it cannot struggle and damage its feathers. Always grasp the turkey by the shanks. If by mistake you take hold of the thigh almost every feather will be stripped off. After obtaining a firm hold, quickly remove the net and swing the bird clear of all objects until it stops struggling; then, retaining the hold on the shanks, take the turkey under one arm in such a way that its wings will be held tightly against its sides. This has no application when the bird is tame enough to be easily handled, which, however, is not often the case with turkeys on wide range.

PREPARING FOR EXHIBITION

The preparation of the turkey for the show room consists principally in taming and training the subject to appear to the best advantage in the coop. If the birds are wild it requires some days to teach them to pose. For this purpose large coops covered with canvas, or in some manner constructed so that the bird cannot cut or bruise its head trying to get out, should be provided in a light, well ventilated room, without drafts, where the temperature ranges but few degrees higher than outside.

Fronts of strong slats or rods having no sharp edges or rough surfaces, with doors of generous size, are better than those of wire because they offer more chance to make friends of the birds confined and less opportunity for the occupants to injure themselves by dashing against it, as they frequently do when introduced. A little patient work with the birds will win their confidence, but the attendant should be careful not to frighten them when feeding or when cleaning the coops or the good work will be undone. If the specimen will allow the handler to turn it around in the coop with the hand or judging stick, without becoming nervous and retreating to the far corner of the cage, it is fairly well trained and will show for what it is worth under the judge. Too long confinement tires the bird and detracts from its appearance, if it does not make it actually sick. The wisdom of this coop training is evident to any one who has studied the turkey exhibit at the large shows. Frequently a bird is so frightened at any person approaching the coop that it will crouch in a corner or dash against the top of the cage, making it practically impossible to fairly estimate its quality. Young toms are more prone to nervousness than females or old toms.

COOPING FOR TRANSPORTATION

Coops for shipping to exhibitions should be large enough to allow the bird to stand upright, without rubbing its head against the top, and either so narrow that the occupant cannot turn around or wide enough so that it can turn without breaking its tail. I believe in the wider coop, for it is less likely to damage the plumage by constant friction. Coops for this purpose can be used season after season and should be solidly constructed of three-eighths inch lumber over frames of inch square stuff; it need not be heavy, but it must be strong. The top may be hinged and provided with hasp and staple to be hooked or locked. Ventilation may be provided in the back of the cover by an open space one inch wide and as long as the coop, and another space of equal size along the front of the coop two or three inches below the top. These will admit plenty of air for birds shipped in cool weather, will not make a draft and the turkey cannot get its head out and get hurt. Handles conveniently placed should be on all large coops of this kind to facilitate handling by the expressmen and in a measure protect the birds from the rough handling to which large coops not so equipped are sometimes subjected.

For shipping breeding stock to points within a few days' journey a wood coop, with solid sides and slat top for cold weather and slat sides and top for warm weather, three feet long, three feet high and fifteen inches wide, is right for toms and large hens, and one six inches less in height and length will suffice for small hens and pullets. Coops of this size allow the birds to stretch to their full height and they arrive in much better condition than when closely hemmed in. Shipment to long distance points and to foreign countries should be in more roomy quarters. Foreign consignments should be forwarded in coops three feet long, three feet high and three feet wide for each bird, with a little extra length added when large toms are to go in them. These coops should be made with solid sides if they are to go on deck when crossing the water, with a space an inch wide left for ventilation near the top of the front, but may have slatted sides if to go below decks. The only door should be at the bottom of the front, just wide enough to admit the turkey turned down on its side, and should extend the length of the side and be hinged at the top to open outward. Cleaning and feeding may be done through this door with but slight chance for the turkey to escape. The water dish should be placed well up in the coop with provision made for filling it through the sides.

Unless special arrangement is made, a bag of grain and a few heads of cabbage should be forwarded, marked the same as the coops. Very good care is accorded consignments on board vessels and if the shipper supplies food and utensils he may rest assured that the caretaker will do his part. These instructions apply only to consignments forwarded in cold or cool weather; it is not safe to attempt long distance shipments in the hot weather of midsummer.

HOW TO DRY-PICK TURKEYS

Good Turkeys Properly Dressed Always Sell Themselves—Badly Butchered Ones Hard to Sell

GEORGE SIXEAS

THIS article deals with the method I use in handling dry-picked and dry-packed turkeys for express shipments to the eastern city markets. I have handled as many turkeys as any one of my age and have a record of never losing one pound of dressed poultry by spoiling in transit. Good turkeys properly dressed always sell themselves—badly butchered turkeys are hard to sell at any price.

I pen the turkeys for twelve hours so that their crops will be empty; if they are killed with full crops they quickly sour and turn black. But I do not starve the turkeys so that they will lose weight or have a gaunt look. When ready to kill, I hang the turkey by the legs in a string attached to the ceiling so that the turkey's head comes within about four feet of the floor. Then I lock the turkey's wings so that one can have better control over it in sticking and picking. To lock the wings bring one over the other and catch the tip of the upper wing under that of the lower. I always aim to bleed the turkeys well so that they will show up bright and yellow and keep long.

To stick the turkey I use a long, keen, sharp-pointed knife. I open the turkey's mouth and quickly plunge the knife down its throat, drawing it twice towards the bill so that I sever the jugular vein on each side of the throat, then quickly push the knife up through the roof of the mouth into the brain, giving the knife a slight twist. In making this thrust I aim to slightly touch the turkey's brain with the point of the knife so as to paralyze the turkey and make it loosen its hold on the feathers. If you cut too much of the brain away it will tighten its grip on the feathers and you cannot pick it without tearing the skin. I had stuck ten thousand turkeys before I learned the art of sticking, and often in the holiday rushes when the picking gang is getting tired and their fingers are sore they have begged me to do the sticking, saying that when I stick they can blow the feathers off.

As soon as the turkey is stuck I begin pulling the feathers off, and the quicker the better. Aim to get the turkey picked before it is dead. The pickers are not allowed to remove a turkey from the string until it is clean, and they are never allowed to scrape the pin feathers out with a knife. As soon as the turkey is picked I plunge it into a barrel of cold water for about an hour. Then take it out of the water, catch the turkey by the feet and hold it so that its head reaches nearly to the ground. Give it a quick jerk so that the blood that has accumulated in its throat will be jerked out. Place a string around its feet and hang it up to dry and cool. It is then ready to pack for shipment as soon as it is thoroughly dry and all the animal heat has left its body

Method of Sticking Turkeys

Ten years ago most turkeys were shipped in boxes of all sizes, shapes and conditions. No attention was paid to uniformity, and second-hand shoe, hat, coffee and canned goods and such other boxes as were available were used, together with barrels of varying sizes and conditions, from the little western apple barrel up to the coffee and sugar barrels. The result of this method of packing was not altogether inviting to the eye of the buyer. Gradually more attention was given to the matter and a steady improvement has been made until at the present time boxes are made especially for the purpose.

Barrels to some extent are also used at the present time, but not nearly so commonly as in years past. The size of the packages has also changed. The rule used to be to get as large a box as possible, cramming in as many turkeys as it would hold without splitting.

In some ways this made business good for the wholesale and jobbing houses, as there were many small dealers who were unable to handle full packages, who had to pay an extra profit for the privilege of selecting such birds as they needed.

It is a question, however, if on the whole there was much gain to the wholesale handlers, as there were generally enough odds and ends left to seriously detract from the profits as a whole. The demand for smaller packages came to be felt by shippers as well as wholesalers and commission men and steps were taken to supply the want. At the present time the boxes rarely weigh more than 150 to 200 pounds each, and great numbers are packed in boxes holding from ten to fifteen selected birds, while a less number hold from eight to twelve. This makes it possible for the small marketmen and provision dealers to buy a full package without any extra cost for breakage or selection, and at the same time does away with a great deal of work and with much of the waste which was prevalent in the old method of packing and shipping.

The common method of packing birds is to make one layer of tom turkeys in the bottom of the boxes, while the upper layer is made up of females. This gives a selection of sizes, and is better for the retailer than where they run pretty nearly one size throughout. The best shippers are known by their private shipping marks and it is understood just how the birds may be expected to turn out. Generally the case is marked so many hens, so many toms, and if any old hens or old cock birds are in the package, they are specified on the outside so that the buyer may know just exactly what he is getting. In the long run honesty in packing makes returns in dollars and cents and there is no other one thing which tells better for a shipper than a reputation for honest methods of boxing.